Internet E-mail Fraud
Encouraging the Stupidity of Some; testing the Intelligence of Others
By
John V. Tieso

Copyright © 2012, 2013, John V. Tieso
All rights reserved. This book may not be copied, reprinted, distributed, or sold, without the express permission of the author. Brief, non-commercial quotes for publication are authorized, provided a copy of the quoted work is furnished to the author.

THE E-MAIL MESSAGES SHOWN IN THIS BOOK ARE ALL SCAMS—NONE OF THEM WILL RESULT IN YOU RECEIVING ANYTHING STATED IN THEM.

This book is based on e-mails received by the author through various e-mail services, and the comments represent only the opinion of the author on these messages.

PLEASE NOTE: I have not attempted to correct the spelling or punctuation, so please do not get frustrated by either the often tortured sentence construction, or the myriad of errors, mostly due to inadequate translation from other languages to English. In a very few cases, where matching the original e-mail to the text here, any changes made by the copying process itself were adjusted back to their original state. Thus, every message in this volume is exactly as it arrived in my e-mail box.

PREFACE

Some months ago, I received the following e-mail. It is reprinted here just as received. I was really amazed, both by its content, and the sheer ridiculousness of its concept. I kept the e-mail, as I have the others in this book, which arrived over the past several years; and present them here for your enjoyment, in their original format, spelling, and sentence construction, as a reminder of the often ridiculous nature of e-mail scams. All the messages were received by me; addressed to one of my e-mail accounts, to 'undisclosed recipient', or in just a few cases, simply to 'recipients.'

International Monetary Fund Compensation Unit, In Affiliation With World Bank.
1900 Pennsylvania
Ave NW, Washington, DC, 20431
Our Ref: IMF/USA/00111

RE: SCAM VICTIMS COMPENSATION OF US$300,000.00

Attention Beneficiary,

Sequel to our series of meetings for the past 6 weeks, which just ended with the Directors and Secretary to the IMF, World Bank and United States representatives respectively in full attendance. The above organizations after her prolonged deliberations on series of complaints received from scam victims has unanimously agreed to compensate all scam victims with a clear verifiable proof with the sum of US$1,250,000.00 each.

This includes victims of purported foreign contracts; Inheritance, Investment, Dating and Lottery scams together with people that allegedly had unfinished transaction or international Lottery payment that failed due to purported Government policies etc. Your email was among the list of victims submitted to our office by the United States Fraud investigation Department and final investigation by our secret agents who has been monitoring your correspondence via special tracking device has shown that you are truly a victim of scam. In respect of the above subject you are therefore strongly advised for your own interest to desist from any further correspondence with any person or group who purportedly claims to have your funds in their custody without due clearance from this office otherwise you have yourself to blame.

You are hereby urgently advised to contact Mrs Edna Mary who has been assigned to handle your compensation payment, contact him immediately for your compensation amount of US$300,000.00. (three hundred thousand Dollars) With your information as stated below

1. FULL NAME:
2. CURENT ADDRESS:
3. DIRECT TELEPHONE NUMBER:
Email: unofficeusa@inmail24.com fxdepartment@inmail24.com
Contact Person:
Mrs Edna Mary
Email: [unofficeusa@inmail24.com]

First, I want to assure my readers, I had not been in correspondence with the writer of this e-mail, nor have I been, to my knowledge, one of her victims. Instead, I am the victim of a scam, at least an attempted scam, since someone with less-than-noble purpose has my e-mail address, but this is, after all, the Age of Information, and hiding almost anything from diligent seekers is becoming much more difficult as time goes on.

It occurred to me, though, that someone else out there just might have taken this e-mail seriously, and may have corresponded with the scam artist, to their detriment. So, like many others, on any number of blogs on the web, I decided to publicize it, with others in the chapters that follow, all of which I have similarly saved, so others will be aware of the extent of e-mail fraud across the Internet.

I do not intent this small volume be an exhaustive review of e-mails scams; that task I will leave to others. I only want to leave a message; if this can happen to me, it can happen to you, and you need to be prepared.

Returning to the e-mail for a moment, two other things amazed me about the message, which like others in this volume, has apparently received wide circulation. This one like many others, was addressed to 'undisclosed recipient', and arrived in my junk mail box, because I take the precaution to make sure such suspicious e-mails go directly to junk, or the 'trash' box.

Luckily, I also have e-mail carriers who are reputable, and try to isolate these types of messages to prevent any damage or inconvenience to their customers. In my case, not only does the e-mail go to the 'junk' folder, but its connections, and e-mail reply addresses are disabled, along with any attachments which might accompany the message. In some cases, I have moved the message to see what is included, but only after shutting down the network to any connectivity, just in case of problems.

In a couple of cases, my virus protection software prevented the opening of a file, and I left it at that, so those messages are not included unless otherwise received. In several other cases, code attached to the e-mail went looking for my network connection, or my contact list, to start harvesting information. In each case, my software prevented those actions. A good firewall and good protective software saves a lot of problems later, if you keep it up-to-date, and make sure it scans your files and messages frequently. As you will also see throughout, there are a number of e-mail providers who make no effort to maintain the same levels of quality controls for their customers.

The most obvious thing to notice about the e-mail above is the spelling and composition. Anyone who received one of these messages, with its bad grammar and obvious errors, but still decided to respond, deserved to be scammed.

You will also see text boxes with alerts throughout the book, each of which describes one or more e-mail service providers; the services they provide, where known; and the level of protection they provide their customers. Most of these services

> **ALERT:** 'Inmail24.com' is a free Internet mail service, and not an official mail site. While the e-mail says it is an unofficial e-mail address, please ask yourself WHY someone who is working fraud issues for the International Monetary Fund, which has an official e-mail address, would need to use an unofficial one. You should be hearing a very loud bell ringing right about now.

are free to the user. As a result, many explicitly disavow any responsibility for the use of the service by anyone. A number of these, particularly in Eastern Europe, and Asia, are notorious for their use by scammers, and messages from any of these services should be avoided. These alert boxes describe the e-mail service provider cited by many of the e-mails throughout the book.

NOTE: These 'ALERTS' throughout the book let you know about some of the more common sites, where this type of scamming and phishing is allowed by the e-mail provider, who takes no responsibility for content, and often refuses to do anything about the e-mails put out by their subscribers, even though they may have an 'official' statement of policy on their site saying otherwise.

The most amazing thing about the e-mail message though, was its content. As you can see, I supposedly received a previous message from this person, indicating a scam occurred. I was now being informed (by a person unnamed), of my eligibility for compensation from the International Monetary Fund, and the World Bank, as some type of atonement for the scam perpetrated against me.

Of course, this is all a big lie. I never, to my knowledge, received a previous message (I checked carefully over the hundreds I have received over the years), and assuredly would not have replied in any case. The message goes on to make a promise to pay me for having received previous scam e-mails; if only I would send additional personal information to yet another person, whose e-mail address contains no indication of their official position with either international organization. Why would I do that?

What you often see as well is an address, which might seem official, like 'unofficeusa.inmail.com', which is apparently supposed to reassure you that you are working with someone from the UN. Please be assured you are NOT. The official website of the UN is 'un.org'. Their offices do not use national or local addresses, and their official representatives all have e-mail addresses coming from the 'un.org' domain. End of story.

In some cases, but not all, the writer will claim they are using another e-mail address because they are really trying to scam their own organization, or so they say, and they want you to help. You will see a lot of that in the pages which follow. The sense of the mysterious adds to the sense of honesty or caring, in their message, or so, at least, they think. In any case, coming up with that kind of a story takes real courage and ingenuity.

Most of us, at one time or another, are confronted with messages such as this. These messages are usually outlandish in their assertions, ridiculous in their content, and usually scams. The most laughable, and, at the same time, the most serious, are those that offer legacies, inheritances, winnings, from everything from lotteries to frankly illegal distributions, and usually involve large amounts of money supposedly ripped off from mostly African countries. This book covers all of those areas and more.

There is seemingly no limit, to either the rewards, or the promises of the large rewards, if only the recipient of the message will send a 'small' amount of information to some third party, often described as a bank officer or solicitor (i.e. lawyer), who will validate the amount and send the reward. The small amount of information needed is to show good faith, and assure that the reward, whatever it is, goes to the right person, at the right address, and bank.

Unfortunately, the 'right' person and bank is decidedly not YOU. These scams are organized solely to make SOMEONE ELSE rich. Even though they read so badly, and are so outlandish to possibly be true, too many people respond and the result is that they often find their own accounts emptied, their credit ruined, and end up significantly embarrassed for their efforts. Far too many are so embarrassed they don't report the scam to the authorities; something else the scammers count on for their efforts.

From my perspective, the messages involving people, those who have all kinds of diseases; families with infirmities, wives whose husbands have been killed by some government or insurgency, or someone who claims to believe so firmly in God that they want to share their blessings with others are the most reprehensible. While these messages truly bring a tear to your eye, as the writer relates his or her issues, it is nearly impossible, for at least a moment not to think the message might be real. Even if you don't believe what you read, it is easy to agree that it took someone with a very fertile mind to create whatever the scenario describes for you.

These types of messages go back to the early days of the Internet. I wish I had saved some of the earliest ones, and the discussions that went on early as well, because much of what you will read in this book is reflective of what many have been saying for years, as warnings to people to avoid these scams. A few of the early scam e-mails are included, where I did save them in my files.

Nonetheless, the sadder fact is that people do respond, and for a variety of reasons. Some think they won something, much the same as those who responded to the early publishing house scams; which really wanted you to buy books, but offered drawings for a million dollars to a 'winner', usually twice a year. The publishers 'forgot' to make it clear to people there was only one winner; instead they sent out millions of flyers that said in bold letters – "YOU HAVE WON A MILLION DOLLARS – or some similar grand statement.

People believed the advertising, and filed for their winnings, only to be told they were only in a drawing. Several sued and won on false advertising claims. For the most part, though, all that came out of it were consent decrees to stop the advertising, or correct it, and a lot of money went to lawyers. Very little went to those who had been scammed.

The scams here are similar; they count on a few people to respond with the requested information. When these people respond, the scam artists go to work using the person's identity, with the information they received, and find ways to clean out accounts, borrow money, and make themselves rich. Unfortunately, there is another side of the coin as well; their actions leave YOU poorer, often with a bad credit rating and almost certainly empty bank accounts.

Conversely, another use of the information provided is the sale of a number of responses, with the attached personal information, and a validated e-mail account, to others, for a fee. You quickly begin to receive other, more-directed e-mails, designed to get you to bite on yet another scam. In short, everybody makes money ON you, EXCEPT you.

By the way, the easiest way for people like this to get your information is as simple as replying to their seemingly innocuous, but important, e-mail, such as those from someone who claims to represent the United Nations, the Federal Bureau of Investigation (FBI), or some other seemingly reputable organization or government agency. A number of the scammers rely on the hope that people who formerly lived in the countries where the scammers are active, such as Nigeria, will respond to someone they might feel is a fellow countryman, and to be trusted.

Many of these messages really sound legitimate, and that is the intent—the message gets you to drop your guard, and respond. To the scammers, every response is a validated e-mail account, which has a value to others on the scam market, even if their original intention is more sinister.

Take a look at the next message, and think for a moment what you would do, if you received in in your inbox.

Attention Fund Beneficiary,

I am theresa MOrgana a seniour investigator working with united nation,Have you received your funds which was suppose to be transferred to you on 28th of febuary,if NOT send the below information immediately

Nmae:
Address:
phone:
age:
sex:

Country:

Await your reply,

Theresa Morgana

    This message is a good example of a poorly constructed and probably translated message, where the originator has selected a large swath of e-possible e-mail accounts from a vendor, and sent out what we call a 'robo-message', a blast message to thousands of recipients. Someone will use a major service, let's say for a moment 'Yahoo.com', and send a message to everyone who has the name 'john' in their e-mail address on Yahoo.

    Thousands of messages go out, and, if even a dozen people respond, the writer of the message knows he/she has some validated e-mail addresses of gullible people, which he/she can now sell on the market to those who want to use them for illegal purposes. Most of these message writers do the same thing with a number of e-mail services, over many weeks, and the lists they sell have thousands of the same gullible names, so they make a profit for their time and effort. The 'free' e-mail services throughout the world, especially those who do not monitor their accounts, facilitate the profusion of these kinds of scams.

    The only way to kill these types of message scams is to refuse to respond. Delete the messages from your e-mail, and don't ever respond to any statement at the bottom of their message, one which tells you that 'if you wish to unsubscribe', simply click on a URL provided. All your response does is validate you have an active e-mail address, and soon your mailbox will be full of messages you don't want.

    I present a broad, but nonetheless limited, range of these scam messages in this book. It is by no means comprehensive, and only documents the breadth and depth of these types of scams. A much larger set of such e-mail messages can readily be found on a myriad of internet sites, collected by others who have similarly experiences such trash in their inboxes. A listing of some of these sites is at Appendix D at the end of the book.

You will often readily recognize some of these scam attempts from a quick reading of the messages you see in your own inbox. Some Internet providers try to screen these type messages out to junk mail, but some still get through. Every one of the messages in this book, coming over my internet e-mail providers, arrived in my 'Junk Mail' box, rather than my general Inbox.

Be careful and you will not be burned. *A good rule of thumb is to look at the e-mail provider—if you have never heard of the service, don't know the person sending the message, or have not signed up for messages from those you know to be a reputable source, the message might well be a scam. Delete it. Then add the service to your list of sites you do not want to receive messages from in the future. With the larger services, that is a difficulty, but with most e-mail applications, such as Outlook©, and a number of others, you can designate individual e-mail accounts to block from your inbox.*

In any case, if the message is legitimate, and they really want to hear from, they will send you another message, call you, or send you a letter.

One important caution: Never open any attachment provided with the message from a person you do not know, or not expecting a file from in your inbox, or you might find unwanted viruses, Trojans, dangerous attachments, or other scurrilous applications on your system. These types of programs steal your information anyway, even without your active assistance.

A final note as well. It has been a very interesting experience collecting this small microcosm of e-mail messages, which are so often found in mail inboxes throughout the world. While hindsight is always better than 100%, it is the initial reaction that often causes trouble. Don't take a chance, hit the delete button, and save yourself financial and emotional harm, and, in some cases, a pressing need to reformat your drive before you can again use your computer.

Be warned and be happy.

John Tieso

March 2014

Table of Contents

Preface 3
Table of Contents 13
Introduction 16
Part One – The World of Fraud 29
    Chapter 1 Scams 101 30
    Chapter 2 Nigeria – Scam Capital of the World 40
        Nigerian National Petroleum Commission 53
        Nigerian Economic Financial Crime Commission
        (EFCC) 56
        United Nation Office of the President in Nigeria 58
Part Two – Personal Appeals 70
    Chapter 3 Business Claims 71
    Chapter 4 Alliances with Dictators 80
    Chapter 5 Military Claims 83
    Chapter 6 Medical Claims 89
    Chapter 7 Partnering Scams 102
    Chapter 8 Other Personal Claims 113
        People Dying 113
        Solicitors 118
        Indirect Claims 126
        Non-Existent Follow-up Claims 128
        Outright Theft 131
        Widows of Dead Executed Patriots 134
Part Three – Using Organizations as
Cover - U. S. Organizations 137
    Chapter 9 U. S. Federal Departments & Agencies 139
        The Federal Bureau of Investigation 139
        FBI Transaction Department 157
        Direct Appeals citing the FBI. 159
        The Department of Homeland Security 162
        US Department of the Treasury 166
    Chapter 10 US Commercial Organizations 169

US Banks... 169
The Better Business Bureau.. 175
Social media – Facebook... 177
US Corporations – The Microsoft Corporation.......... 181
PART FOUR 185
FOREIGN ORGANIZATIONS 185
Chapter 11 Foreign Governmental Organizations 186
Benin Republic... 186
Government of Ghana 188
Great Britain... 190
British High Commission for Nigeria, Benin Republic, Ghana and Burkina Faso 196
Chapter 12 Foreign Banking Organizations 200
The Classic – Central Bank of Nigeria 202
Oceanic Bank International (Nigeria) 210
Intercontinental Bank PLC (Benin)............................. 215
Financial Bank PLC (Benin)... 217
Barclay's Bank (London)... 220
Bank of East Asia (United Kingdom Branch)............. 222
Natwest Bank (London).. 224
Hang Seng Bank (Hong Kong) 225
HFDC Bank (India)... 226
Reserve Bank of India 228
HSBC (Japan) 233
National Bank of Abu Dhabi....................................... 234
Allied Irish Bank (Ireland).. 237
Gulf International Bank (Bahrain) (London Process Unit) 239
Royal Bank of Scotland 240
ECO Bank (Nigeria) 241
ECO Bank (London).. 243
WEMA Bank PLC (Nigeria) 246

United Bank of Africa (Nigeria), Directorate of
International Payments 247
Zenith Bank International (Nigeria) 250
Chapter 13 Foreign Commercial Organizations 257
West African Committee of Commerce (Ghana) 257
Chapter 14 International Organizations 265
United Nations 265
International Monetary Fund (IMF) 287
The World Bank 289

Part Five – Other Ridiculous Opportunities 292
Chapter 15 We want to buy your product 293
Chapter 16 Great Banking and Loan Opportunities 300
Chapter 17 Commercial Appeals 305
Chapter 18 Lotteries 309
The Euro Million Scam 310
RealGems International 315
Yahoo International Lottery Draw 317
Chapter 19 Western Union Scams 320
Chapter 20 A New Generation of Scams 324
Who's Who Directory Scams 326

Epilogue – Saving Yourself from Fraud . 329

Appendices 333
Appendix A – United States Secret Service 333
Appendix B – Internal Revenue Service 338
Appendix C – Disclaimer of the Central Bank of
Nigeria 342
Advance Fees Fraud (419) 342
The CBN Disclaimer 342

Index 344

Introduction

The wonderful world of frauds and scams—very serious issues -- yet, in so many instances they appear ridiculous, even to those who are eventually hurt by them. Before the Internet, there were 'flimflam' men (and women), who lived their lives through the pockets of others. They have existed for many millennia; even early records of the Egyptian empire discuss instances where people were put to death for stealing, for various subterfuges and lies. The description of these crimes is so close to what we see today, it makes one wonder if genetics and inheritance might somehow be involved.

The onset of the Information Age, especially the development of the Internet, and the Worldwide Web (WWW), has taken some forms of thievery to new heights. Increasing numbers of people now rely on cell phones, e-mail, and instant messaging for their routine daily communications; forgoing the government mail systems, or the even older telegraph, both of which seem headed quickly to the dustbin of history.

In this book, I concentrate on internet-based electronic mail, and the proliferation of e-mail scams, exponentially increasing over the last nearly twenty years. These are the personal scams—those which involve a direct person-to-person relationship, usually exposing recipients to an 'opportunity', one which will make them wealthy beyond their dreams, and which, on reflection, should easily be seen as a scam, rather than reality.

Most of the current generation of scams, such as described here, started as mail scams, and go back many years. In fact, in 2002, the U. S. Secret Service became so concerned about these scams; they published an advisory letter, found in part at Appendix A.

The granddaddy of all the modern scams, the so-called 'Nigeria Bank Fraud' Scam, was the first broadly-based e-mail scam. A recent iteration of that scam is below:

MR.SANUSI LAMIDO AMINU
EXECUTIVE GOVERNOR,
CENTRAL BANK OF NIGERIA
REPLY TO AUTHORNATIVE
EMAIL:zainabtradrng@gmail.com CALL ME TO MY MOBILE IMMEDAITELY +234-80-24398933

ATTENTION:SIR/MADAM,

THIS IS TO NOTIFY YOU THAT YOUR OVER DUE INHERITANCE FUNDS HAS BEEN GAZETTED TO BE RELEASED, VIA KEY TELEX TRANSFER (KTT) -DIRECT WIRE TRANSFER TO YOU OR THROUGH ANY OF OUR CORRESPONDENT BANK NOMINATED BY THE SENATE COMMITTEE FOR FOREIGN OVER DUE FUND TRANSFER.
MEANWHILE, A WOMAN CAME TO MY OFFICE FEW DAYS AGO WITH A LETTER, CLAIMING TO BE YOUR TRUE REPRESENTATIVE. HERE ARE HER INFORMATION'S FOR YOU TO CONFIRM TO THIS OFFICE IF THIS WOMAN IS TRULY FROM YOU OR NOT SO THAT THE FEDERAL GOVERNMENT WILL NOT BE HELD RESPONSIBLE FOR PAYING INTO ANY WRONG ACCOUNTS.
CLAIM'S NAME: JANET WHITE BANK NAME: CITI BANK ARIZONA, USA. ACCOUNT NUMBER: 6503809428.ROUTING.314085504. PLEASE, DO RECONFIRM TO THIS OFFICE, AS A MATTER OF URGENCY IF THIS WOMAN IS FROM YOU.

YOU ARE REQUESTED TO FILL AND SEND THIS INFORMATION'S FOR VERIFICATIONS PURPOSES SO THAT YOUR FUND VALID US$7.5M (SEVEN MILLION, FIVE HUNDRED THOUSAND UNITED STATE DOLLARS) WILL BE REMITTED INTO YOUR NOMINATED BANK ACCOUNT ANY WHERE. THIS FUND IS AS A RESULT OF INHERITANCE ON YOUR BEHALF. INFORMATION NEEDED FROM YOU FOR VERIFICATION IS AS FOLLOWS:

1. YOUR NAME:......................................
2. YOUR FULL ADDRESS:......................

3. YOUR TELEPHONE....................
4. FAX...
5. AGE...
6. SEX:..
7. YOUR OCCUPATION:............................
8. YOUR BANKING DETAILS........................

AS SOON AS WE RECEIVE THIS, WE WILL COMMENCE WITH ALL NECESSARY PROCEDURES IN OTHER TO REMIT THIS MONEY INTO YOUR ACCOUNT. THE CENTRAL BANK GOVERNOR, IN CONJUNCTION WITH THE FEDERAL MINISTRY OF FINANCE (FMF) EXECUTIVE BOARD OF DIRECTORS AND THE SENATE COMMITTEE FOR FOREIGN OVER DUE INHERITANCE FUND HAVE APPROVED AND ACCREDITED THIS REPUTABLE BANK WITH THE OFFICE OF THE DIRECTOR, INTERNATIONAL REMITTANCE/FOREIGN OPERATIONS, TO HANDLE AND TRANSFER ALL FOREIGN INHERITANCE FUNDS THIS QUARTER PAYMENT OF THE YEAR 2012.

HOWEVER, WE SHALL PROCEED TO ISSUE ALL PAYMENTS DETAILS TO THE SAID MRS.WHITE, IF WE DO NOT HEAR FROM YOU WITHIN THE NEXT SEVEN WORKING DAYS FROM TODAY. WE ARE SORRY FOR ANY INCONVENIENCE THE DELAY IN TRANSFERRING OF THIS FUND MUST HAVE CAUSED YOU.

CONGRATULATIONS.

MR.SANUSI LAMIDO AMINU
NEW GOVERNOR, CENTRAL BANK OF NIGERIA (CBN).
CC: SENATE PRESIDENT
CC: BOARD OF DIRECTORS [FPD]
CC: ACCOUNTANT GENERAL OF NIGERIA .

As with many similar scams, some type of public institutions, such as a bank, a security company, or even a government office, is usually quoted as the source or holder of funds. A 'representative' is designated to work with the respondent. That person, the message says, will help secure the funds, usually 'guaranteed' to be on deposit. The writer will cite all kinds of boards, laws, regulations, or anything else, which might make the scam seem real and trustworthy.

In many cases, the origination point of the message is one of the countries of the Third World, such as Nigeria, where many people live under conditions of poverty, and where unrest and revolution are more commonplace. Some will speak to war zones, such as Iraq and Afghanistan, and the so-called 'war booty' that was pilfered from those countries.

Still others will cite international organizations, such as the United Nations, the World Bank, or the International Monetary Fund, and claim to be working for the Secretary-general or some other official of the organization, with authority to disburse funds to recipients who have been deprived of their lawful winnings or inheritance.

Most people, with any level of common sense, will realize these international organizations are not generally involved in these types of notifications, but there is always someone out there gullible enough to bite on what seems to be a 'once-in-a-lifetime' opportunity. These are the people scammers love to identify and make contact with from their messages.

EACH OF THESE PLEAS FOR YOUR HELP IN SECURING THE FUNDS IS A SCAM — THERE IS NO MONEY TO BE DISBURSED, AND EVEN IF THERE WERE, YOU ARE DECIDEDLY NOT THE RECIPIENT.

A considerable amount of research and analysis on e-mail scams already exists in the literature, and on the Internet. Those sources seem to indicate several common attributes of the widely spread e-mail scams. These are:

- Crude and obvious sentence construction in messages
- Messages which seem to be created in other languages, and badly translated into an English version
- Very large amounts of money involved

- Naming of high-level political and/or international figures, who are said to 'guarantee' the legitimacy of the message, and the payments
- Tales of hidden, illegal, family, and 'official' riches waiting to be claimed
- A fee, of some type, for processing the transaction
- Return e-mail addresses that are not what you would expect to see (i.e. Not official addresses of people claiming to be official representatives of an international or national organization, or those which might originate in countries far from the country cited)

Let's look quickly at some of these common attributes, and see what others have found, as they researched and analyzed the e-mail scam artists.

Crude and obvious construction of messages An article in 2012, in the Washington Post[1], discussing the crude construction of e-mail messages offered, *"Our analysis suggests that is an advantage to the attacker, not a disadvantage. Since his attack has a low density of victims the Nigerian scammer has an over-riding need to reduce false positives.* **By sending an email that repels all but the most gullible the scammer gets the most promising marks to self-select**, *and tilts the true to false positive ratio in his favor."*

Isn't it interesting that conceptually it is better for the scammer to make the message look really crude, and almost offensive to the educated person, because they want to take in only those most gullible. With Internet messaging being virtually free (since most of the scammers, as you will see, use free internet mail services (usually without restriction or oversight), and create messages that go in large bursts, say to everyone named 'john' at any e-mail service, it is easy to get to just a few to respond; those who may be the most receptive, and the most gullible.

---

1 "Why Nigerian e-mail scams are so crude and obvious". *Washington Post*, June 22, 2012. **Retrieved from:**
http://www.washingtonpost.com/blogs/wonkblog/wp/2012/06/22/why-nigerian-e-mail-scams-are-so-crude-and-obvious/

As the Post blog message continues, *"Scamming people, after all, costs time and money. Herley[2] (the author) notes that everyone who responds to a scamming ploy "requires a large amount of interaction." The 'worst' thing that can happen, from the scammer's point of view, is that savvy people start responding to the messages, and then toying with the scammer... Better to keep the e-mails predictable and tired. That way only the most unsuspecting suckers respond. "*

Despite the poor construction, the Post continues, *"the scammers must be doing something right. In 2009, these "advanced-fee fraud" efforts 'managed to pry'$9.3 billion out of unwitting victims around the world. And the business is growing at a 5 percent rate each year — especially as more people in developing countries get connected to the Internet.* That statement speaks volumes about intelligent people; even marginally intelligent people, seeing through what should be an easy delete from their e-mail, and this quote only involves those messages who ask for some kind of fee.

Poor construction, especially when also naming government or organization leaders incorrectly, is always a good indicator of a fraud, as you will see in the chapters which follow.

Crude English Translations The construction of messages, is often crude, usually due to the inability of the person creating the message to understand the particular idioms of either British or American English. Many messages are not originally created to look crude. Rather, the problem is even worse, as all too often the message is first written in a foreign language, then passed through a translator of some type, to create the same message in English. Sometimes, the message is translated automatically through the e-mail service, leaving a translation, which is generally similar to the original, but only to the extent it mimics as closely as possible the words used within the original message, even though the reader's understanding may be different.

Unfortunately, the customs and idioms of language, especially English, are quite different from those in many other

---

[2] Herley, Cormac, Microsoft Corporation, *Why Do Nigerian Scammers say they are from Nigeria?* Retrieved from:
http://research.microsoft.com/pubs/167719/WhyFromNigeria.pdf

countries, particularly in Africa and Asia. But then, if the Post article noted above is correct, perhaps the creator of the message does not really care. Personally, I think a middle ground exists here; there are those that know they are not using correct grammar, and those that do not.

The message writers, those who are unaware of the language idioms of the country or area where they are directing their message traffic, simply look foolish. However, they still get responses from some unsuspecting recipients. In most of the book, we look at the messages from an English-speaking perspective, since many of these messages target the English-speaking world, but the people who wrote them are simply, in my view, not sophisticated enough to either realize, or take the time, to do good translations, ones which may produce better results, even among the very few respondents desired by the scammers.

Very large amounts of money are involved one interesting aspect of these types of e-mail message traffic, is the amount of money cited as the 'unclaimed' inheritance, illegal fund, or whatever the description might be of the funds.

Herley seems to feel that the more egregious the claim, the less likely the majority of those targeted will respond; leaving only the most gullible, and, therefore, the most likely to 'fall for' the scam. Citing very high amounts of money certainly could contribute to this view of messaging, to include the lack of concern over proper idiom and sentence construction from translation. It is simply a matter, according to Herley, of spending little on the initial message blast, and reserving costs to cater to those most likely to respond positively.

What Harley said is true; with one possible caveat. Some of these messages generate responses as a means of creating sellable lists of valid e-mail addresses, and other supporting information. Developers of these lists would want to maximize their investment to generate as many respondees as possible to create large lists for other, future scams. As you will see throughout the book, these 'list-makers' create quite different messages than those who want a quick nibble from someone unsuspecting or gullible.

Getting more respondees is a function of making the message more believable; that is, making the recipient a willing partner, still for a good amount of money, but not so egregious an amount, that it would be obvious the message is a scam. Getting even one response, who initially believes in the message, and provides their information, generates a validated source to add to the mailing list for later sale.

Fewer valid responses in these types of scams, makes the job harder. Thus, in my view, the address scammer has to be smart enough to capture what is desired in volume, at least initially, without turning everyone off from the start, before selling to someone else. The sale is the real start of a conversation.

Naming high-level political or international figures Virtually no one would respond to a message offering millions from someone they don't know, from a source they don't recognize, or a country they might not even know exists. There will always be a few extremely gullible people, but the response rate goes up exponentially when the e-mail message creator is also a 'name dropper'.

You will see throughout the book that messages drop the names of well-known political figures, especially from the United Nations Secretary-General, or the name of some well-known banking institution, or even, perhaps, the Director of the FBI. You will also see throughout that scammers drop the names of leading political figures, president of countries, or other well-known persons.

In many cases, when the name or the institution is cited, there will also be the name of a 'contact' to work with the responder to claim their millions. In most cases, the 'contact' will not use an e-mail address of the organization, but an address from some third-world free internet mail site, catering to those who want to send these types of e-mails. You will see a number of examples of this throughout the book.

Tales of illegal, hidden, family, and 'official' riches Each e-mail scam has a 'story', a scenario, which is often almost heart-wrenching for the reader. There are military, who took money from occupied countries (e.g. Iraq, Afghanistan, Libya, Egypt, Nigeria) and hid it, or spirited it out of the country to unnamed third countries, where it is often locked in a vault.

Others hid their wealth as the country's leaders were overthrown (The most common scenario in the 'Nigeria' scams), the money was hidden away, and just waiting for your help in getting it out of the country.

Some writers pretend they are actually in the current government, working at a major bank with trust accounts, or lawyers representing people, who have secreted away large sums, they now want to 'share' with others. Commonly, these involve rich widows or wives of political leaders, now dying of some mysterious disease or condition, have 'seen the light of religion', and they don't want to die without passing their wealth to others who will, of course, use it well.

Then, there are 'official' stories, and some of these are really the most interesting. They involve organizations that have decided to compensate people for their previous hassles in other schemes, or scams, for which their government, organization, or agency, has established a compensation fund. These can be the most insidious, since the messages often exhibit a tremendous sense of reality and honesty; even though they are as false as all the others.

A processing fee for completion of the transaction One common trait of the scammer is the 'fee', by whatever name it is called, which the scam artist expects as their reimbursement to help process the funds transfer. Some will call it a transaction fee; several messages in this book speak of a fee for issuance of a debit card with money posted to it, for example. In one case, I have seen the debit card fee goes even further; they expect a fee every time the card is used to take funds (Most say up to $5,000US per day), and they want several iterations of the fee upfront. Others have additional mailing and processing fees as well.

Some messages speak to the need to 'grease' the transaction, with a bribe or payment to an official to release the funds to you. Others expect you to pay a small amount of outstanding taxes before the funds can be released; still others expect an outright percentage of the take, often upfront, as their cut of the transaction. You send the money and they disappear, along with your money, of course.

One final, and most common, cash requirement is the 'administrative fee' for filling out and filing the official paperwork, usually with other, unnamed officials, to get the funds released. There are many variations of this; one of the most interesting involved a banking official in one of the African republics, requiring over $400 US for processing the official documents needed by the panel in that country responsible for 'making right' all the previous scams perpetrated on people. If this kind of situation were real, you would expect the government involved would at least pay the fees associated with their own legal requirements, since they (the government) claim to be the original scammers.

Whatever it is called, sending money to these people is just like flushing it down a toilet. The only money ever transferred is yours, and, when you send messages to find out what is happening, you never hear from them again. You have been completely scammed.

There are other factors you may commonly see as you read these messages; I have given you a few of the most common. Also, be aware that most of this book involves money scams, similar to the so-called 'Nigerian 419 Scam'; it does not include the myriad other scams, occurring daily on the Internet, and which bear careful scrutiny as well.

I will mention one such scam, currently in vogue. It is a message, which appears to come from someone you know, who is caught overseas or in some distant location, and is in trouble. He needs you to wire him money immediately. Sometimes they want it via Western Union, or sometimes they send bank information for you to transfer the funds. BE WARNED on these type scams. These appear to be legitimate, and, since they involve someone you know, there is a natural impulse to want to respond immediately to get them out of their trouble.

I received one, not too long ago, as I was reading my e-mail on my Blackberry, talking to a friend sitting next to me. The incoming e-mail, supposedly from my friend, the one sitting next to me, related that he was in Paris, his wallet lost, and he needed $500US right away to get home. We both laughed; in fact, he received one as well, on himself. Had he not been there at the time, I undoubtedly would have read the message at least one more time, and perhaps considered whether I needed to help.

The more ominous thing here is how both of our e-mail addresses were on the scammer's list for sending his messages. It almost has to mean that the scammer, or the person he bought his e-mail lists from, had access to our e-mail contact lists, especially since both my friend's e-mail service and mine were from two different services, our addresses have nothing in common, and my friend seldom even uses the address by which he received the scam message We'll speak more about these kinds of problems later on, when I discuss avoiding these traps.

Right now, read carefully what follows; a number of scams using various techniques are discussed, and each is shown for the fraud that it is.

The book is divided into several parts, and includes; Personal appeals (Part Two), U. S. Organizations (Part Three), foreign organizations (Part Four), and a part I call 'Other Ridiculous Opportunities (Part Five). There is an Epilogue, discussing 'Saving Yourself from Fraud', and some Appendices, from the Secret Service, and the Internal Revenue Service, with their issuances on e-mail fraud.

> **ALERT:** A word about G-Mail, Hotmail, and Yahoo Mail, the major free internet e-mail providers. These are generally reputable e-mail providers, and they will remove an e-mail account if they are notified it is being used for scams, such as those described in this book.
> Always feel free to notify one of these if you have a question about a message you receive.

PART ONE – THE WORLD OF FRAUD

Chapter 1 Scams 101

Scams present themselves in coats of many colors. There are simple, plain vanilla scams, which are simple, straightforward, and direct. They want to hook you into responding quickly (so they can draw you in even deeper), with details which will seem to be overwhelmingly true (the easiest way to entice you into participating, often at considerable financial risk, and damage to yourself); and do it quickly, before you catch on to the possibility of fraud.

Look at this message from a Mister Jacob Molotsi of Lesotho:

DEAR SIR/MADAM,

I AM MR. JACOB FROM LESOTHO KINGDOM BUT PRESENTLY IN LONDON UK. I HAVE A BUSINESS PROPOSAL OF ($ 5 MILLION USD) WHICH I WOULD WANT TO DO WITH YOU.

KINDLY RESPOND SOON FOR FURTHER DETAIL IF YOU ARE INTERESTED TO PARTNER WITH ME.

YOURS,

MR. JACOB M. MOLOTSI
E-MAIL: molotsi_m@yahoo.co.uk

This scam is simple; 'Mr. Molotsi', of Lesotho has a business proposal involving millions of dollars. He does not give specifics, but, if you e-mail him, you will know all. When you return the e-mail, he is validating your e-mail address for sale to other scammers. Mister Molotsi is a well-known scammer, going back at least two years, with at least one known alias, and several variations of his 'yahoo.uk' e-mail address.

Mister Molotsi, or whatever his name really is, uses the benefit of an overseas subsidiary of a well-known US internet e-mail provider, Yahoo, to try to cajole you into responding. Most people would think that having a Yahoo e-mail address somehow makes your activities legitimate; nothing could be more from the truth. Yahoo will let virtually anyone, who provides them with minimal information, and an alternate e-mail for 'verification', get an e-mail address on their servers. [See page 23 for more information on US Internet providers.]

This type of message is designed for a quick, unthinking reply from someone gullible enough to believe the message presented by 'Mr. Molotsi'. Whoever created the message will snare a number of people by the request.

When you reply, the scammer knows the e-mail address is genuine, and also that the person might be gullible enough to fall for the scam. There is NO LOSS for the scammer; the only loss is whatever you might send to the scammer to participate, or, at least, the use of your e-mail address as a part of a list of gullible responders, which the scammer can then re-sell to others.

Most often, the scams are more complex. In the next example, the scammer wants you to know that he/she has done research into your background and profile, and you are just the person he/she wants to participate in their venture. Notice the range of areas where this person's interests lie.

Dear Friend
Sir:
I have gone through your profile from the peoples search database on the web during my discrete search for a foreign partner who can assist me in taking this business to it success, I am a business man and politician based in United State (USA) and I am currently seeking means of expanding my business interest in the following sectors: Real Estate, Stock Speculation, Furniture Making, Crude Oil, Manufacturing and various trading.

If you think you have a solid background and an idea of making good profit in any of the mentioned business sector in your country: Please write me for possible business co-operation, I am ready to facilitate and fund any business that is capable of generating good % annual returns on investment (AROI) reply me on this email address, Dr.Heward.Wilson@myonline-usa.com

Looking forward for possible business collaboration with you
Yours sincerely
Dr Heward Wilson
Philadelphia
United States of America

Here, there are several giveaways. The spelling of the 'United State', and the signature block on the bottom should both ring out loudly as a scam, as should the e mail address. This guy didn't even put his own address into the spot where the template address had been placed. The e-mail address is a fraud—you get switched to another site, which collects information on you.

One of the most telling points is the poor sentence and syntax construction of the message, a clear indicator that this message was probably written in a foreign language, and translated into English, giving it, like many others you will see in the book, their 'broken language' sense when read. This is a person to stay away from if you receive this, or a similar e-mail.

'Dr Wilson', by the way, is a well-known scammer; often uses a webmail service in the Philippines for his e-mails to other countries, which he redirects through his 'myonline-usa.com' address. Be careful if you use a search engine to find him. His blog site, also in the Philippines, 'cabis-ngeblogtoz.blogspot.com' has a curious bot attached to it that appears to try to access information on your hard drive, probably contact information in your e-mail contact list.

As I noted in the preface, some scammers use the approach of apologizing for earlier scams you may or may not have received. These messages make interesting reading, such as the one that follows:

Dear friend,

It's been quite long since we heard from each other. Betrayal they say is the willful slaughter of hope. I have betrayed you my friend from the moment you responded to that email I sent to you some time ago. From that moment you accepted that lotto wining notice and then you sent me your name, address phone and account details.

From that moment I choose to betray you when you choose to trust me. I diverted the wining to myself. I am so sorry that you have lost a lot of money to claim this prize.

I am in a poor state of health now and i may have died from cancer before my Son send you this letter, but please accept the Two hundred and sixty thousand dollars compensation as an atonement for my sin against you. Please contact my legal adviser Barr.Paul based in Malaysia because I have given him instructions to deliver this money to you as soon as possible.

You can contact my legal adviser Barr.Paul his email [infoIqbalChambers1941@mail.mn] just tell him that you are contacting him under instruction from Code:AUYYR456 he will honor my WILL and pay you within 48hours. Forgive me this is all i ask for. Please send him your I.D, phone and address for verification and payment processing. My spirit will be uplifted once you get this compensation.

Regards
AUYYR456

> **ALERT:** Mail.MN is a fraud. The ISP is located in Mongolia, and is well-documented as a source for a number of spam and phishing messages

Aside from being an outright fraud, personal appeals, such as this one, can really twist a heart. Here is a person that wants you to know they have betrayed you, and they want to make amends, since they are now in poor health, and feel that they need to expiate their sin. So, they give you a secret code (shared, by the way, with many thousands who also receive the e-mail directed to 'undisclosed recipients') and ask you to contact their 'legal advisor'.

At first reading, the story is heart-wrenching. It cries out for response, and you really want to help. The amount of money is just enough to peak your interest, but not enough to cause you to dismiss the message outright. So, what do you do? The smart person will delete it from their e-mails, and move on to the next message.

Speaking to next messages, what follows is about outright theft—or so he admits in his message. At least this guy appears honest—he wants to rip someone off, and wants your help to do it. Enjoy the read.

Dear Sir,

Confidential Business Proposal

Having consulted with my colleagues and based on the information gathered from the Ghana Chambers Of Commerce And Industry, I have the privilege to request for your assistance to transfer the sum of $47,500,000.00 (forty seven million, five hundred thousand United States dollars) into your accounts. The above sum resulted from an over-invoiced contract, executed commissioned and paid for about five years (5) ago by a foreign contractor. This action was however intentional and since then the fund has been in a suspense account at The Bank Of Ghana Apex Bank.

With our links we have been able to transfer the funds overseas to a third party financial Institution with branches in USA and United Kingdom and U.A.E and where you come in is that we would need your assistance to move the money from the account with the Financial Institution to your private account in your country. It is important to inform you that as civil servants, we are forbidden to operate a foreign account; that is why we require your assistance. The total sum will be shared as follows: 70% for us, 25% for you and 5% for local and international expenses incident to the transfer.

The transfer is risk free on both sides. I am a Senior accountant with the Ghana National Petroleum Corporation (GNPC). If you find this proposal acceptable, we shall require the following documents:

(a) your banker's name, account, telephone, and fax numbers.

(b) your private telephone and fax numbers -- for confidentiality and easy communication.

(c) your letter-headed paper stamped and signed.

Alternatively we will furnish you with the text of what to type into your letter-headed paper, along with a breakdown explaining, comprehensively what we require of you. The business will take us fifteen (15) working days to accomplish.

Please reply urgently.

Best regards,

M.J Ola.

Ola's letter has all the earmarks of a great scam. He offers a huge amount of money; asks for a lot of information, including your bank, your letterhead, and a bunch of personal information, and mentions freely some government and corporate names to sway you into replying.

Once again, you are faced with a dilemma. Do you respond, even if taking the claims with the proverbial 'grain of salt', or do you move on, delete the message, and protect yourself from possible fraud, or even prosecution for theft? The rational, honest person will move on, even if the amount cited is a lot of money; because this scenario, as with the others in this book, cannot possibly be real.

Two things are wrong with these types of e-mails. First, they are almost always addressed to 'undisclosed recipients'. That is a bit like getting a letter to 'resident' or 'occupant' in the mail. Just like those types of mail, throw out the e-mail and don't bother with it, since it is a scam. Above all, do not even reply to say you are not interested. If you do, the scammer now has a verified e-mail address, and that is a saleable item in the underground world of e-mail scams.

Before we go on to other topics, be aware there is no limit to the either the source of the scam, or the persons they propose to represent. There are ample examples on a large number of Internet sites that provide literally thousands of e-mails, all scams, from virtually every country across the globe. These messages represent both private solicitations, and governmental ones, one of which I have reproduced just below, from the 'Federal Bureau of Investigation' in Washington DC.

Of course, the source e-mail address is not a US Government address for Mister Robert Mueller; it is from 'info@websouls.com', which ought to cause any person reading it to ask about its legitimacy, or maybe not. A second copy of the message arrived in my in-box a couple of days later, this time from an e-mail address at 'fbi@investi.ca'. Clearly not a real e-mail address used by the FBI, unless they are doing undercover work in Canada. Read and enjoy.

J. Edgar Hoover Building
935 Pennsylvania Avenue,
NW Washington, D.C. 20535-0001, USA.

We sincerely apologized for sending you this sensitive information via e-mail instead of a certified mail, post-mail, phone or face -to- face conversation, it is due to the urgency and importance of the security information of our citizenry. We the Federal Bureau Of Investigation (FBI) Washington, DC in conjunction with some other relevant Investigation Agencies here in the United states of America have recently been informed through our Global intelligence monitoring network that you presently have a transaction going on your name with the Remittance Department of the Central Bank of Nigeria as regards to your over-due contract payment which was fully endorsed in your favor accordingly by the FEDERAL GOVERNMENT OF NIGERIA.

It might been of your interest to know that we have taken out time in screening through this project as stipulated on our protocol of operation and have finally confirmed that your contract payment is 100% genuine and hitch free from all offends of law which you have the lawful right to claim your fund without any further delay.

Having said all this, we will further advise that you go ahead in dealing with the Director Remittance Department of the Central Bank of Nigeria with due Banking protocols as we will be monitoring all their services with you as well as your correspondence at all level. In addendum, also be informed that we recently had a meeting with the Executive Director of the Remittance Department of the Central Bank in Nigeria, in the person of Mr.Tunde Lemo along with some of the top officials of the Ministry regarding your case

file in their management and they made us to understand that your file has been held depending when you will personally come for the claim.

They also told us that the only problem they are facing right now is that some unscrupulous element are using this project as source of revenue from innocent people off their hard labor money by impersonating the Executive Governor of Central Bank of Nigeria and Director of the Remittance Department of the Central Bank of Nigeria. We were also made to understand that a lady name Mrs. Joyce Q. Tyreses from Florida has already contacted their management and also presented to their management all the necessary documentations as evidence to claim your fund which those documents tender to the bank has been purported signed personally by you prior to the release of your contract fund valued of US$10,000,000.00 (Ten Million United States Dollars.), but the Remittance Department of the Central Bank of Nigeria did the wise thing by insisting on hearing from you personally before the go ahead on wiring your fund to the Bank information's which was forwarded to them by the above named Lady so that was the main reason why they contacted us so as to assist them in making the investigations as the Authority on Security and protecting the citizen of this Great Nation.

They further inform us that we should warn our dear citizens who must have been informed of the contract payment which was awarded to them from the Remittance Department of the Central Bank of Nigeria, to be very careful prior to these irregularities so that they don't fall victim to this ugly circumstance. And should in case you are already dealing with anybody or office claiming to be from the Remittance department of the Central Bank, you are further advised to STOP further contact with them in your best interest and then contact immediately the real office of the Remittance department of the Central Bank only with the below information's accordingly:

BANK NAME: Central Bank of Nigeria.
Email: *tundelmemo11@live.com*
EXECUTIVE DIRECTOR: MR. Tunde Lemo

NOTE: In your best interest, any message that doesn't come from the above official email address and phone numbers should not be replied to and should be disregarded accordingly for security reasons. Meanwhile, we will advise that you contact the Remittance Department of the Central Bank of Nigeria office immediately with the above email address and request that they attend to your payment file as directed so as to enable you receive your contract fund accordingly. Ensure you follow all their procedure as may be required by them as that will further help hasten up the whole procedures as regards to the transfer of your fund to you as designated. Also have in mind that the Remittance department of the Central Bank equally have their own protocol of operation as stipulated on their banking terms, so delay could be very dangerous.

Once again, we will advise that you contact them with the above email address and make sure you forward to them all the necessary information's which they may require from you prior to the release of your fund to you accordingly. All modalities has already been worked out even before you were contacted and note that we will be monitoring all your dealings with them as you proceed so you don't have anything to worry about. All we require from you henceforth is an update so as to enable us be on track with you and the Remittance department of the Central Bank. Without wasting much time, will want you to contact them immediately with the above email address so as to enable them attend to your case accordingly without any further delay as time is already running out.

Should in case you need any more information's in regards to this notification, feel free to get back to us so that we can brief you more as we are here to guide you during and after this project has been *completely perfected and you have received your contract fund as stated.*

Thank you very much for your co-operation in advance
Await your urgent response to this matter.

Best Regards,
Robert Mueller III
Federal Bureau of Investigation

Just a quick note about 'Mr. Tunde Lemo', the Remittance Executive Director of the Central Bank of Nigeria. As you will see in the more extensive chapter on the 'Nigerian 419 Scams', the e-mail address of the Central Bank of Nigeria is 'cbn.com', and not live.com, another of those free e-mail servers around the world. Mr. Lemo, or at least the person impersonating Mr. Lemo, is a fraud.

This last message leads us quite well into a broader discussion of the impact of Nigeria on the overall development of the e-mail scam industry, since it is an industry in current days. The following chapter discusses the original Nigerian scams, and how they have evolved.

Chapter 2 Nigeria – Scam Capital of the World

Somewhere there must be an old movie, "It all Started in Nigeria,", or something close. Nigeria has the dubious distinction of being one of the first, and most frequent, of the scamming locations, especially the e-mail scams. That distinction is not really true, since the United States and the United Kingdom, actually produce more scams, but the appellation has stuck over the years.

Wikipedia[3] has a good description of the historic connotations, and it is reproduced here:

> *The Nigerian 419 scam is a form of advance fee fraud similar to the <u>Spanish Prisoner</u> scam dating back to the late 19th century. In that con, businessmen were contacted by an individual allegedly trying to smuggle someone connected to a wealthy family out of a <u>prison</u> in <u>Spain</u>. In exchange for assistance, the scammer promised to share money with the victim in exchange for a small amount of money to bribe prison guards. One variant of the scam may date back to the 18th or 19th centuries, as a very similar letter, entitled, "The Letter From Jerusalem" is seen in the memoirs of <u>Eugene François Vidocq</u>, a former French criminal and <u>private investigator</u>. Another variant of the scam, dating back to circa 1830, appears very similar to what is passed via email today: "'Sir, you will be doubtlessly be astonished to be receiving a letter from a person unknown to you, who is about to ask a favour from you . . .' and goes on to talk of a casket containing 16,000 francs in gold and the diamonds of a late marchioness."*
>
> *The modern 419 scam became popular during the 1980s during the hyper-corrupt "<u>Second Republic</u>" governed by President <u>Shehu Shagari</u>. There are many variants of the letters sent. One of these, sent via postal mail, was addressed to a woman's husband and inquired about his health and a long, unexpected silence. It then asked what to do with profits from a $24.6 million investment, and ended with a telephone number. Other official-looking letters were sent from a*

---

[3] The full story of the 'Nigerian 43219 Scam is located on Wikipedia, at: http://en.wikipedia.org/wiki/Nigerian_scam

writer who said that he was a director of the state-owned Nigerian National Petroleum Corporation. He said that he wanted to transfer $20 million to the recipient's bank account – money that was budgeted but never spent. In exchange for transferring the funds out of Nigeria, the recipient would get to keep 30% of the total. To get the process started, the scammer asked for a few sheets of the company's letterhead, bank account numbers, and other personal information. Yet other variants have involved mention of a Nigerian Prince or other member of a royal family seeking to transfer large sums of money out of the country.

The spread of e-mail and email harvesting software significantly lowered the cost of sending scam letters by using the Internet. While Nigeria is most often the nation referred to in these scams, they may be originated in other nations as well. For example, in 2006, 61% of Internet criminals were traced to locations in the United States, while 16% were traced to the United Kingdom and 6% to locations in Nigeria. Other nations, known to have a high incidence of advance fee fraud include, Côte d'Ivoire, Togo, South Africa, the Netherlands, and Spain.

These scams, as indicated, cover a broad range of topics, use the names of virtually every major public figure on the international scene, and most are so outrageous, and poorly constructed, it defies comprehension that people could fall for them.

Nonetheless, people being people, many do fall for these scams, and some harder than others, as you will see in many of the examples below, and even throughout the book. The Nigerian scams are often used as 'templates' for other scams, which numerous others have tried to foist over time on the unsuspecting reading public.

Much of the success of these scams is due to the increasing reliance on e-mail, as a primary form of communication, replacing letter-writing. People have come to rely on their e-mail as factual communications, and too many have fallen into a trap, leaving their pride, and their money, in the hands of the unscrupulous.

The pages below show examples of the variations in theme and content built over time, and all based on a similar theme earlier letter form scams. Both direct and indirect approaches are described below, starting with the more subtle, indirect approaches, and progressing to the more direct, almost 'in your face' approaches, which seem to be more common today.

The Indirect Approach

Let's start with one of the more well-known 'Nigeria' scams to show you how all this works. The real Mrs. Mariam Abacha was the wife of the late dictator of Nigeria in the 1990's. There are a large number of messages attributed to her, and members of her family, most of them documented on a myriad of Internet sites devoted to e-mail scamming. This chapter has a representative set to show the depth to which the scammers will go to achieve their desired results.

CONFIDENTIAL

Dear Sir,

Good day and compliments. This letter will definitely come to you as a huge surprise, but I implore you to take the time to go through it carefully as the decision you make will go off a long way to determine the future and continued existence of the entire members of my family.

Please allow me to introduce myself. My name is Dr. (Mrs.) Mariam Abacha, the wife of the late head of state and commander in chief of the armed forces of the federal republic of Nigeria who died on the 8th of June 1998.

My ordeal started immediately after my husband's death on the morning of 8th June 1998, and the subsequent takeover of government by the last administration. The present democratic government is determined to portray all the good work of my late husband in a bad light and have gone as far as confiscating all my late husband's assets, properties, freezing our accounts both within and outside Nigeria. As I am writing this letter to you, my son Mohammed Abacha is undergoing questioning with the government. All these measures taken by past/present government is just to gain international recognition.

I and the entire members of my family have been held incommunicado since the death of my husband, hence I seek your indulgence to assist us in securing these funds. We are not allowed to see or discuss with anybody. Few occasions I have tired traveling abroad through alternative means all failed.

It is in view of this I have mandated DR GALADIMA HASSAN, who has been assisting the family to run around on so many issues to act on behalf of the family concerning the substance of this letter. He has the full power of attorney to execute this transaction with you.

My late husband had/has Eighty Million USD ($80,000,000.00) specially preserved and well packed in trunk boxes of which only my husband and I knew about. It is packed in such a way to forestall just anybody having access to it. It is this sum that I seek your assistance to get out of Nigeria as soon as possible before the present civilian government finds out about it and confiscate it just like they have done to all our assets.

I implore you to please give consideration to my predicament and help a widow in need.

May Allah show you mercy as you do so?

Your faithfully,

Dr (Mrs.) Mariam Abacha (M.O.N)

N/B: Please contact Dr Galadima Hassan on this e-mail address for further briefing and modalities

As you can see, she is in a terrible quandary, trying to get her husband's ill-gotten gains out of the country in trunks. It is truly a heart-warming possibility that you might help her in this matter. Just contact her representative to get the scam going. By the way, we are talking about a very large amount of money here; 'Mrs. Abacha' routinely leads the list for the sheer numbers she quotes that is available for you to assist her to spend.

Of course, if you are not fully convinced of her sincerity and desire to get this 'problem' resolved, then this message from 'Mrs. Abacha' should do the trick in convincing you that she needs your help. She and her family are going through a terrible ordeal. The Nigerian Government found over $700 Million in 'Dutch marks' and confiscated it, along with other accounts. Thankfully for her, as is often the case in these African dictatorships, she still has a lot of money, we think.

She claims about $89 Million (Probably interest plus principal since 1998) and wants your help. This could a great, illegal venture, if it were real. By the way, the money has apparently moved from Ghana to somewhere in the Americas.

As far as I can research, there is no firm evidence that Mrs. Abacha, or her surviving children are directly involved in any of the scams that use their name. For a number of years, she was under house arrest in Nigeria, and prevented from leaving the country, or having much contact with the outside world.

Nonetheless, so many scams were developed, particularly those which ask outright for an advance fee to help get her money out of the country that a large part of the 'Nigeria Scam' is named after the Abacha family. You can be assured that anything you receive with her name, that of any of her children or relatives, her lawyers, or anyone claiming to represent her, are frauds.

Read the next message, also from 'Mrs. Abacha', but with a twist. In the first message, she, and her family were being held 'incommunicado', but now the son is in jail, under interrogation about his father's mysterious 'cardiac arrest', the one which occasioned his death. The amount of money is down to $58M US, but she still wants your help.

FROM THE DESK OF MRS MARIAM ABACHA,
29th April, 2001.
 Attn: Managing Director,
 Dear Sir,
 I salute you in the name of the most high God. I am Mrs. Mariam Abacha, the widow of the late Gen. Sani Abacha former Nigerian Military Head of State who died mysteriously as a result of Cardiac Arrest. Since my husband's death, my family has been under restriction of movement and that notwithstanding, we are being molested and constantly been harassed by the so called security officials, above all, our Bank accounts here and abroad have been frozen by the Nigeria Civilian Govt. Furthermore, my eldest son in detention by the Nigerian Government for more interrogation about my husband's assets and some vital documents.

 Following the recent discovery of my husband's bank account by the Nigerian Government with my son's bank in which a huge sum of US $700 million Dutch Mark, & another $450 million was also lodge and 1.6Billion Pounds Sterling belonging to my late husband, all the said fund was seized by the Government of Nigeria.

 I therefore wish to personally appeal to you seriously and religiously for your urgent assistance to transfer the sum of $58million US Dollars into your account in your country where I believe it will be safe, since we cannot leave the country due to the restriction of movement imposed on the members of my family by the Nigerian Government or can you receive for the Abacha family the funds already in Europe & America about $89million USD , already deposited with a security firm you can advise us on areas where and what to invest on abroad, already we are presently nursing real estates or any other blue chip investment you can reach my lawyer(DR ISA MUSA.) on his direct Tel lines as a copy of this letter is equally sent to him in confidence .Any advise should be directed to my lawyer for security reasons thank you,

 You can contact me through my lawyers Tel Number : +871-762336687 or Fax +871-762336689. Upon receipt of your good response. My lawyer shall arrange a meeting to facilitate the smooth transfer of the fund , that is to liase with him towards effective *compromise of this transaction. However, arrangement have been put in place to remove more of the family fund amounting to$114 million US$ from a security firm were it is deposited , Before moving the remaining fund out of the country with the assistance of my husband's friend's that's some(some top government functionaries) still in government through a diplomatic means, and deposited in a security company, as soon as you indicate your interest. My lawyer shall send to you the Security Deposit Certificate and Airway Bill of the luggage and other related documents so that you can arrange how and where the luggage tagged _Family Treasures_. From an African king will be deposited. Conclusively, we have agreed to offer you 30% of the total sum while 70% in collaboration with my lawyer to be held on trust by you until we can decide on what to do next , subsequent to our free movement by the Nigerian Government. Please reply urgently and treat with absolute confidentiality and sincerity.*

Yours sincerely,
Mrs. Mariam Abacha.(alhaja)

But 'Mrs. Abacha' isn't finished quite yet. She still wants your help, if you have not already replied to her previous messages, or those of her sons, daughters, and solicitors. This is one of her more recent requests. Now, she has only $70 Million, and has them securely protected in a Museum Trust Account, instead of the security company she described in the last message. This time, she is willing to give 20% for any help she can get. You also get more information on the General and his billions, which are back somewhere in Nigeria from Ghana (I thought the Government had taken them earlier, but maybe not).

MRS. MARIAM ABACHA MALLAM ISSA ABBA ABACHA
TEL/FAX: 234-1-7597515

Dear Sir,

STRICTLY URGENT AND CONFIDENTIAL

I am Mrs. Mariam Abacha, widow to the Former MilitaryHead of State,Late General Sanni Abacha, who died suddenly as a result of Cardiac Arrest on 8th of June 1998.

One early morning, I was called by my Late Husband General Sanni Abacha, who at that time was the Commander in Chief of the Army and the President of Nigeria. He conducted me round the apartment and showed me three metals boxes of money all in Foreign Exchange, my husband told me he was to use the money for the settlement of his Personal Royal Guards on his self Succession Bid and campaigns.

Upon his tragic and unexpected death, the new civilian Government of Chief Olusegun Obasanjo, has insisted on probing my family's financial resources and has gazetted all our properties, also. They recently seized all the known family's fund abroad with the assistance of the British Government. It is only this money US$70,000,000.00 (Seventy million US Dollars Only) that he deposited with a security company vault, that they cannot trace because the funds were deposited as (ANTIQUITY) African Art Work from the National Commission for Museum and Monuments (N. C. M. M.) Nigeria, the family intended to use this money for investment purpose to enable the family start life all over again.

Therefore, the family is urgently in need of a "Very competent and investor participant" that we could entrust with the certificate of Deposit and (PIN) Personal Identification Number Code to help us remove the funds from the security company "Since no names were used in securing the vault.

I got your contact address and name from our Chamber of Commerce, Agriculture and Industry Office in Lagos - Nigeria, if the proposal is acceptable to you, after getting the money out from the security company vault to your country, my family have agreed to offer to you 20% of the total sum for the kind assistance you rendered to us. And in addition bank the family's own part of the funds and assist us in investing (with my approval on project) as a front for us until the situation becomes more favorable for us to now meet and discuss the way forward, most especially now that my elder son, Mohammed Abacha and I are under pressure from the Government, despite the fact that my family had already returned the sum of US$3 Billion my late husband's Account in the U.S.A, Europe and other countries.

Please kindly state your early response immediately on this email: abbkabat@yahoo.com or the above fax number for more details on the logistics and modalities.

NOTE: I do not need to remind you of the absolute secrecy and confidentiality that this transaction demands. You are free to speak directly either with me or my son Mallam Issa Abba Abacha on the phone.

Communication is strictly on the above Tel/Fax Numbers only. If you are not interested, please kindly reply me immediately to enable me search for another interested partner.

I await your kind reply.

Thanks and accept my regards. MRS. MARIAM ABACHA TeL: 234-1-7753803

'Mrs. Abacha's' messages are classics in the scam traffic out of Nigeria, and, later on, many other countries. These messages still 'travel the circuit', and come up in one form or another several times a year. In addition to Mrs. Abacha, there are a wealth of messages attributed to her two sons, a daughter, and a nephew, along with a slew of 'barristers' or 'solicitors' who represent her interests.

More often, however, the pleas are much simpler and more direct. They involve banks, and museums, cultural organizations, and others, all of whom have very corrupt individuals who want you to help them escape with their funds, perhaps for a fee or percentage, but more often than not, they want to relive you of your funds.

Let's look at several other interesting variations in this historic scam. One of the newer variants involves notification to you (as one who has already been scammed), that the Nigerian Government is determined to put the money previously scammed or stolen from you back into your account.

From Mr Lucky Kadiri

Chairman Payment Committee
Presidential Villa Abuja

Dear Beneficiary

This letter is written to you in order to change your Life from today as you have been listed as one of those VICTIM who lost huge sum of money while trying to receive your payment from Nigeria, London, USA etc, we also want to inform you that during the last Head of States Meeting in the African Union (AU) in which Nigeria is a Leading Member Country, we were directed to refund to you the sum of $900,000 which covers the money you lost plus accrued interest generate. Further Investigation carried out on your payment revealed that effort made in the past to pay you through Bank to Bank transfer was not successful as a result of so much money requested from you to secure numerious transfer documents thereby causing long delay in carrying out the bank to bank transfer which never took place up till now.

In order for you to receive this $900,000 without any delay, we have decided to pay you through a Specialized atm card which is one of the fastest, reliable and convenient means of receiving payment worldwide. As soon as this Specialized atm card arrives your delivery address, you will be able to use it to withdraw money from any atm machine without any delay or difficulty.

We wish to inform you that the members of Payment Committee are honorable men of Great Repute and Intergrity who have served the Government of Nigeria in both local and International capacities, we also wish to inform you that the Committee members were appointed by our respected President to pay foreign Debt such as Contract Debt, Inheritance/Next of Kin Debt, Compensation Debt, Lottery Debt, Purchase/Sales of Good Debt, and all other Foreigner debt own by Nigeria Government, in order to restore good image to international communities. You are advice to reply to therealways@yahoo.cn immediately you receive this mail, so that you will receive your own payment. THE FEDERAL GOVERNMENT OF NIGERIA HEREBY ADVICE YOU TO HENCEFORTH STOP COMMUNICATING WITH THOSE PEOPLE WHO HAVE BEEN DECEIVEING YOU FOR TOO

LONG AND WORK WITH THIS COMMITTEE TO RECEIVE YOUR PAYMENT BECAUSE THIS IS THE ONLY COMMITTEE APROVED BY NIGERIA GOVERNMENT AND *In case you want to receive your payment this week, you are advice to reply with ANSWERS to the Questions below.*

Your Full Name
Your Contact Address
Your Direct telephone. Fax Number (if any) Your AGE What You Do For A Living How Many Months Or Years in which You Have Been Expecting your Payment The Place you sent Money Last whether Nigeria or London etc The Last Amount of Money You sent to Nigeria and What Month or Year

Mr Lucky Kadiri
Chairman Payment Committee
Presidential Villa Abuja Nigeria

This message, together with some others, and in Chapter 11, is typical of the current wave of traffic from Nigeria. In many ways, they are similar to those in the past; they require 'proof' of who you are, and want you to know how disgusted the government is with those who have been scamming in the past.

What is most interesting, of course, is how much money must have been scammed if they can pass out to some large list anywhere between $10M and $30M to each potential victim. The only money they really have is whatever they can scam from you.

Scams attributed to 'Mr. Kadiri' have been out for nearly two years. He has used both an overseas Yahoo address (from Congo) and one from gmail.com, both in his own name.

Indirect scam approaches are a great way to encourage you to get involved, perhaps out of compassion, or at least out of a desire for wealth. If only that were possible. Those who have usually contacted 'Mrs. Abacha', or 'Mr. Lucky Kadiri' either never hear anything in return, or suddenly find they need to 'invest' their own money, in varying amounts, for a short time, and as proof of their sincerity and dedication to the task.

None had their money returned, although we will see later in the text that one variation on this theme is directed toward those who have been scammed previously, and are about to be scammed again, if they believe there are agents in these governments who will help them get their money back.

The Direct Approach

Before leaving Nigeria (or at least its scammers), I want to share some recent e-mails; one from yet another 'officer' of the Central Bank of Nigeria, another message, supposedly from an officer of the Nigerian National Petroleum Corporation (NNPC), a third message from a supposedly 'satisfied' customer with advice for all of us, if we choose to take it, and a fourth from the Nigerian Financial Crime Commission. The first man, Julius Tomari, is very direct in his request; he will get you money from the bank if he gets a bribe. As he says in his last lines, *"YOU HAVE TO LET ME KNOW HOW MUCH YOU WILL GIVE ME AT THE CONSUMMATION OF THIS DEAL."* Nothing could be more direct.

(CENTRAL BANK OF NIGERIA)
OFFICE OF THE DIRECTOR
TELEX / COMPUTER DEPARTMENT
TINUBU SQUARE
ABUJA - NIGERIA

I AM SENDING THIS PRIVATE EMAIL BASED ON THE CONFIDENTIALITY OF THE TRANSACTION.
PLEASE, I WILL LIKE TO ADVISE IF AFTER GOING THROUGH MY PROPOSAL AND YOU DO NOT ACCEPT IT, KINDLY KEEP IT TO YOURSELF. AS OF THIS MOMENT, I AM STILL IN SERVICE WITH (CENTRAL BANK OF NIGERIA).AND I WILL NOT BY ANY MEANS LIKE TO LOSE MY JOB, IF YOU ARE NOT INTERESTED.

I HAVE PUT IN OVER 23 YEARS IN THIS BUT I DO NOT HAVE ANYTHING TO SHOW FOR IT. THIS IS JUST MY OPPORTUNITY TO MAKE SURE THAT I GIVE MY CHILDREN A DECENT TRAINING SINCE MY

GOVERNMENT WHICH IS CORRUPT HAS REFUSED TO TAKE CARE OF ITS RESPONSIBILITY. INFACT I AM SICK AND TIRED OF EVERYTHING HERE I NEED TO GET OUT. I FOUND OUT THAT YOU ALMOST MET ALL THE STATUTORY REQUIREMENTS IN RESPECT OF YOUR PAYMENTS. PLEASE BE EQUALLY ADVISED THAT NO SECURITY COMPANY IN AFRICA CAN HANDLE YOUR CONTRACT PAYMENTS/INHERITANCE FUND WITH ANY WITHOUT THE INSTRUCTIONS OF THE CENTRAL BANK OF NIGERIA

I WISH TO ASSURE YOU THAT WITH MY POSITION HERE AT CENTRAL BANK OF NIGERIA, I CAN ACCOMPLISH THIS UNDER FIVE WORKING DAYS. BUT WE HAVE TO REACH AN AGREEMENT. FIRST OF ALL, YOU HAVE TO LET ME KNOW HOW MUCH YOU WILL GIVE ME AT THE CONSUMMATION OF THIS DEAL.

MR. JULIUS TOMARI

His e-mail address is: mr.pauldou23410@e-mail.ua and that brings out even more interesting facts. The e-mail URL is real; it belongs to a Russian e-mail service that is free, accepts all comers, and provides little real protection against frauds such as you see above.

> ALERT: e-mail.ua. A Russian-based e-mail service, which provides anonymity for all comers. Signup is easy, storage space is limited, and forwarding is their best service.

Anyone want to guess why Mister Tomari has to use the address of Mister Pauldou, whatever his name is, from Russia, and not Nigeria. The average person would not know the country code 'ua', but should be concerned at such an obvious fraud, since this is not one of the extensions normally seen in the US, or in Europe. I kept the message to show in the book; others should delete it quickly to avoid getting scammed.

Nigerian National Petroleum Commission

The second e-mail scam is from a Mister Johnson George, who, as I indicate earlier, is supposedly from the NNPC. Read what this guy has to say.

> I am Johnson George of the Nigerian National Petroleum Corporation (NNPC) Portharcourt office. we want to quietly transfer the sum of ?21.5m from NNPC offshore account to over-sea trust account.
>
> This ?21.5 Million arose from over-invoicing of contract receipts for the Turn Around Maintenance (TAM) of the Port Harcourt and Kaduna refineries in Nigeria and also the rehabilitation of Petroleum pipelines, depot and jetties.
>
> The Federal Government and the Federal Ministry of Petroleum resources have approved the total value of ?280m, and the payment of foreign contractors from Japan, France and U.S.A. has already started, because most part of the work for the Turn Around Maintenance (TAM) has been fully completed, we will use your company as a consultant and job costing contractor to NNPC so that the ?21.5m can be transferred into your account without any hitch whatsoever.
>
> If you are interested in assisting us in this transaction, kindly, provide us the following immediately to enable us discuss further details for the successful completion of this transaction. Your full Name:
>
> Your full address:
> Age:
> Marital status:
> Gender:
> Occupation:
> Country:
> Phone number and fax #:
>
> Regards.
> Johnson George

'Johnson George' is, of course, a fraud. His messages have been coming into unsuspecting mailboxes for several years, and using both the name 'George Johnson' and the name 'Johnson George', as in this e-mail. The current one, shown above, has been out there at least since 2010, and probably earlier. He uses several e-mail addresses, one of the most common being 'ericbates@voila.fr'. This address is not always shown publicly; George masks it with a phony address, and simply redirects to his real address.

The next message is from 'Mrs. Connie Dutton' of Florida. She readily admits, she says, that she was a Nigerian scam victim, and went to Nigeria to get her money. Lo and behold, she found Barrister George Alex, who immediately made everything right for her, and at a cost of only $270 for 'papers', after which everything was fine.

It should be obvious, after reading the message that 'Mrs. Dutton' is a scammer of the first degree.

Attn: My Dear,

I am Mrs Connie Dutton, I am a US citizen, 51 years Old. I reside here in Silver Springs Florida. My residential address is as follows. 7008 E Hwy 326 Silver Springs FLorida 34488, United States, am thinking of relocating since I am now rich. I am one of those that took part in the Compensation in Nigeria many years ago and they refused to pay me, I had paid over US$20,000 while in the US, trying to get my payment all to no avail.

So I decided to travel down to Nigeria with all my compensation documents, And I was directed to meet Barrister George Alex, who is the member of COMPENSATION AWARD COMMITTEE, and I contacted him and he explained everything to me. He said whoever is contacting us through emails are fake.

He took me to the paying bank for the claim of my Compensation payment. Right now I am the most happiest woman on earth because I have received my compensation funds of $1,500,000.00 Moreover, Barrister George Alex, showed me the full information of those that are yet to receive their payments and I saw your email address as one of the beneficiaries, that is why I decided to email you to stop dealing with those people, they are not with your fund, they are only making money out of you. I will advise you to contact Barrister George Alex.

You have to contact him directly on this information below.

COMPENSATION AWARD HOUSE
Name : Barrister George Alex(Esq)
Email: barristergeorgealex@yahoo.cn

You really have to stop dealing with those people that are contacting you and telling you that your fund is with them, it is not in any way with them, they are only taking advantage of you and they will dry you up until you have nothing.

The only money I paid after I met Barrister George Alex was just US$270 for the paper works, take note of that.

As soon as you contact him he will send you the payment information which you are to use in sending the payment to him in order for him to obtain the document from the court of law there in Nigeria so that your fund can be transfer to you without any delay just the way mine was being transfer to me.

Send him the following details if you know you are ready to have your FUNDS so that as soon as he receive your information he will send to you the payment details for sending him the $270USD that is needed for him to get the document that is needed to make the transfer a successful one and that is that only payment i made to Barrister George Alex and he help me in the transfering of my FUNDS and i most say that you have to countact him so that he will help you the way he help me to Get my FUNDS without any further payment.

Fill Out the information to him if you are ready to get your FUNDS

Your Full Name:...............
Direct Phone:....................
Country.................
Occupation:.....................

Gender:..........
Age:...............

Once again stop contacting those people, I will advise you to contact Barrister George Alex so that he can help you to Deliver your fund instead of dealing with those liars that will be turning you around asking for different kind of money to complete your transaction.

Thank You and Be Blessed.

Mrs Connie Dutton.
7008 E Hwy 326 Silver Springs
FLorida 34488, United States

Mrs. Dutton's hope is that you respond with enough information that they (She and whoever she works with) will be able to sell the information or bilk you out of your money. That's the only money that changes hands—yours to them.

Barrister George Alex is also a fraud, and has been used in these messages for several years. One of his first appearances was in a very similar message, with the same appeal, but from a woman named Mrs. Christy Richard. Be warned, these are very dangerous, but typical Nigerian scammers.

Nigerian Economic Financial Crime Commission (EFCC)

The final message is from Mr. Ibrahim Lamorde, who claims to be from the Economic Financial Crime Commission (EFCC) in Lagos, Nigeria, where he is the 'Legal Chairman'.

FROM THE OFFICE OF MR. IBRAHIM LAMORDE
CHAIRMAN
ECONOMICAL FINANCIAL CRIME COMMISSION (EFCC)
9/10 ADEOLA HOPEWELL STREET,
VICTORIA ISLAND
LAGOS,NIGERIA.

DATE: 1/04/2013

TO WHOM IT MAY CONCERN.
Attention: Beneficiary,

I am Mr. Ibrahim Lamorde the legal chairman of ECONOMICAL FINANCIAL CRIME COMMISSION (EFCC) in alliance with economic community of West African states (ECOWAS) with head Office here in Nigeria.

We have been working towards the eradication exercise of fraudsters and scam Artists in Western part of Africa. With the help of United States Government and the United Nations we have been able to track down so many of this scam artist in various parts of West African countries which includes (NIGERIA, REPUBLIC OF BENIN, TOGO,GHANA, CAMEROON, SENEGAL AND LONDON) and they are all in our custody here in Lagos Nigeria.

We have also been able to recover so much money from these scam artists. The United Nation Anti-crime commission and the United State Government have ordered that the money recovered from these Scammers should be shared among hundred Lucky people around the globe.

This message is been directed to you because your email address and your personal information was found in one of the scam Artists file and computer hard disk in our custody here in Nigeria. You are therefore to be compensated with $700,000,00) Seven Hundred Thousand United State Dollars Via a U.S BANK OR LONDON BANK OR A NIGERIAN BANK PENDING ON YOUR CHOICE .

Consequent to the record we have here, this Scam Artists has defrauded a lot of people of their hard earned currencies, as they claims to be Barristers/Bank officials, Lottery Agents who has money for transfer or want you to be the next of kin of such funds which do not really exist.

Since your name appeared among the beneficiaries who will receive this compensation offer of Seven Hundred Thousand Dollars (US).

Thanks and we appreciate your kind response.
WE ARE AT YOUR SERVICE.
BEST REGARD

MR. IBRAHIM LAMORDE
CHAIRMAN
ECONOMICAL FINANCIAL CRIME COMMISSION (EFCC)
Tel: (+234) 802-813-8216

Replies to this e-mail go to lamorde63@gmail.com, although the original address provided to the 'undisclosed recipients' says senders@email.com. Mr. Lamorde cites a number of supporting characters in his e-mail message, including the United States Government, and the United Nations Anti-Crime Commission, along with the Economic Community of West African States (ECOWAS), as his supporters. In fact, his message indicates the US Government has ORDERED his commission to send you the money. What could be better proof that this is not the usual scam!

Seriously, there is no US Anti-Crime Commission, and the ECOWAS does not chase Nigerian (or other country) scammers. This is just another group of Nigerians trying to make a buck. Beware.

United Nation Office of the President in Nigeria

This is a newer version of the Nigerian scam, and bears many similar characteristics to its older brothers:

- Claims to be from a very senior official of the Government
- Makes at least a vague claim to the United Nations, or some other world organization
- Offers 'proof' that the claims in the message are real, and that you should reply

- Makes the document 'official-looking' with references to Government addresses, agencies, and other reference points
- Asks you to stop working with others, who are illegally contacting you
- Offers a lot of money for your efforts

Read the message, and then we'll discuss it further before moving on to other scams. Be prepared, it is a long, and sometimes thoroughly ridiculous message.

UNITED NATION OFFICE IN
OFFICE OF THE PRESIDENT
FEDERAL REPUBLIC OF NIGERIA
F.C.T ABUJA NIGERIA.

FROM THE DESK OF DR CHARLES WILLIAMS
OUR REF: FGN/UN/XXVBCH147/2013

DEAR BENEFICIARY,

This is to officially inform you that we have verified your contract file presently on my desk, and I found out that you have not received your ATM CARD due to your lack of co-operation and not fulfilling the obligations giving to you in respect to your contract payment.Secondly,you are hereby advised to stop dealing with some non-officials in the bank as this is an illegal act and will have to stop if you so wish to receive your payment immediately.

Now your new Payment,United nations Approval No; NG567P, Reference No.-30295, Allocation No: 3426 Password No: 7644, Pin Code No: k875 and your Certificate of Merit Payment No: 875, Released Code No: 059; Immediate Activation confirmation No: -8575; Secret Code No: XXTN554, Having received these vital payment code, therefore You are qualified now to received and confirm Your payment with the Federal Government immediately within the next 72hrs

Below are few list of tracking numbers you can track from USPS website(www.usps.com) to confirm people like you who have received their ATM CARD payment successfully in the year 2011 physical payment scheme.

www.usps.com

James R.Wersinger EO 993 080 241 US
ELIZABETH S. PETTIT EO 993 080 238 US
Simene' Walden EO 993 080 215 US
Rachael Hocevar EO 993 080 224 US
Joanne Chun EO 993 077 905 US
Mildred Elizabeth Cagle EO 993 077 888 US ANDREW T SLACK EO 993 077 891 US Erica Carboni EO 993 077 914 US William A. McWilliams EO 993 082 993 US Rebecca Marie Frye EO 993 082 962 US sonya emery EO 993 082 980 US Alfred st.dic EO 993 082 976 US Marjorie J. Steffke EO 993 082 959 US Charles Gallagher EO 993 169 289 US Stacey Williams EO 993 169 275 US Ronald Highsmith EO 993 169 261 US Erica D. Blanks EO 993 170 684 US James B. Roosa EO 993 170 401 US Mary T Wiggins EO 993 170 432 US loghin grigorescu EO 993 170 415 US Ron Mazzocco EO 993 170 429 US Lanece White EO 993 170 675 US Hazel Foxworthy EO 993 171 000 US Bobbie Jo Stradling EO 993 171 035 US Jacinta Glenn EO 993 171 027 US Ralph Hodge, EO 993 077 874 US Brian Morrissey EO 993 170 707 US Catina L Cota EO 993 170 667 US Vitolina Key EO 993 170 698 US

If you like to receive your fund this way, Kindly reconfirm your.

Full Name.........
Full residential address.........
Phone/country code And Fax Number....
Company name (IF ANY)..........
Age..........
Marital Status...............

To effect the release of your fund valued at $8.3 million you are advised to contact me immediatelly

Name:. Dr Charles Williams

Email:.atmnotification2013@rocketmail.com
Tel: +234 816 934 7245

We shall be expecting to receive your information as you have to stop any further communication with anybody or office.Thanks for your co-operation.

BEST REGARDS,

Dr Charles Williams
Cc: Senate President.
Cc: All Foreign Payment Offices.
Cc: Board of Directors .
Cc: Accountant General Of The Federation
CC: Central Bureau of Interpol
CC: United Nation Office
cc: Federation President

  I hope you will agree that this message, as egregious and officious as it sounds, is a fraud – a SPAM – and, if you received it, don't reply. If you do reply, your response will go to w.drcharles@yahoo.com.hk, a YAHOO e-mail address in Hong Kong. In our searches, we found a number of references to Dr. Williams, all of them tying the name to the 'Nigerian 419' scheme, where the person sending the messages has been working for quite a while. In this case, the message is so obviously a fraud, little more needs to be said, but all messages similar to this one are not so blatant.

  Other similar messages can be found in Chapter 9, where the scammers claim that the FBI is involved, or in Chapter 12, with other 'barristers. 'As you read the chapters that follow, many of the things you read are similar to the original Nigerian scams; nothing changes after all.

Part Two — Personal Appeals

Going a bit more into the 'personal' appeals introduced in Part One, let's look at some of the more interesting forms of this type of scam, to see the broad scope of people's efforts to part you from your money or information. The first example is one that is seeking to confirm a good e-mail address, which they will probably sell to others for their own scams.

Personal appeals take many forms, as you will see below. Some, however, are seemingly simple appeals that you might fall for, if you don't take the time to look further into their appeal, such as the message below from someone claiming to be a Mister Kulman Smith. The messages, ostensibly from Togo, are rarer than those from Nigeria.

Hello Beneficiary

I will like to introduce myself to you my name is Mr.Kulman Smith am from Lome Togo I am the legal adviser to my late client with this I seek your presence to present you as the beneficiary to my late client. I will give you more details as soon as I get to read or hear from you.You can contact me directly on my email kulsmith00@yahoo.com. I will also request for details.

Your Contact Address
Your Date Of Birth
Your Mobile Number
Your Marital Status
Your Full Name
Your Private Email
Your Skype Id

I await to read from you

Regards
Kulman Smith
00228 98634001

Mr. Kulman Smith is found in the search engines, has an account on Linkedin.com, but with little information, other than his graduation from Lome, Togo High School, and a Degree in Law from the Lome University. His e-mails (There are two of them, both similar) show differing e-mail addresses, all from overseas subsidiaries of yahoo.com.

Here is another, more recent 'offering' from the elusive person masquerading (we think) as Mister Smith.

Dear Beneficiary

It is my pleasure to get across to you, please do not be offended receiving this message from me as we have not met before. My name is Kulman Smith, a renowned Togo based solicitors. I am writing in connection to late client who died with his wife and only child in an auto accident. Ever since the finance firm has asked me to provide his relative and I was unsuccessful, so I decided to track his last name, hence I contacted you. I have contacted you for the repatriation of the money valued at seven million five hundred thousand dollars. Get back to me for more clarification with the following information

!. Your full name......................
2. Your telephone number..................
3. Your resident address...................
4. Your profession......................
5. Your age............................
6. Your Email Address.............

Best regards,
Kulman Smith
00228_986_34_001

--
Este mensaje ha sido analizado por MailScanner en busca de virus y otros contenidos peligrosos, y se considera que está limpio.

There are several problems with Mister Smith and his e-mails. First, judging by his messages, everybody he seems to represent is dead, and they all left a lot of money. Second, he readily admits his client, the client's wife, and their only child died in a car accident; he has been trying ever since to find an heir. Lacking that, he has turned to you to help him create a scam to get the money.

In other messages, this theme of misrepresentation is also quite common, lending a new dimension to the otherwise honorable term 'solicitor'. So, is Kulman a lawyer, or a huckster? You have to figure that out; hopefully before you send him any information, which just might give your identity away forever.

Another, even more sympathetic approach, is to play the grieving relative who wants to settle a family estate, preferably by investing his money into a worthwhile venture, such as the one described below. This person, Mister John Martin, is also from Togo.

> *Dear Friend,*
> *I have a close uncle of mine by name Mr. Jose Manuel Flavior originally from Angola but resides in Lome, Togo. Unfortunately, he has Cancer! According to his doctors, his days are numbered in this earth. He has mandated me to look for a successful foreign business man from Asia who will invest his fortune for his young son. The man made his fortune during the civil war in Angola. He made his fortune in the sales of Diamonds and Crude Oil during the war in Angola. He left Angola immediately the war ended and relocated with his family to Lome, Togo. This man has an inexperience son who is not yet ready for international business while his wife died two years ago.*
> *He has mandated me to look for a successful foreign business man who will invest his fortune for his young son.. I solicit for your assistance in the investment of a large sum of money in the neighborhood of $48,000,000.00 (Forty Eight Million United States Dollars Only). My friend wants an investor who will make a long term investment of the fund in a profitable business venture. The economic and political instability in Togo and Africa is the main reason why my client wants the funds to be invested in Asia because the Asian economy is fast growing.*
> *I request for your assistance in the investment of this fund. I have spent several days in Dubai, the United Arab Emirates looking for a*

reliable investor who will invest this money before I came across you. My instinct has never failed me. I am presently in Lome, Togo however, I intend to travel to London soonest in order to discuss with the Financial consultant of Mr. Jose Manuel Flavior who is based in the United Kingdom.

I look forward to hearing from you soonest so that I can give you a complete picture of this transaction.

Thank you for the understanding.
Regards,
John Martin
Email: john.martin.office@superposta.com

According to 'Mister Martin', his uncle, a man named Flavior, made several requests, including investments for his own son, preferably in Asia. There is a lot of money involved here, and that should pique your interest. It should also concern you that the e-mail is not addressed to you, but to the more usual 'undisclosed recipients', especially since Mister Martin indicates his confidence in you, based on his own instincts, and believes you to be a reliable investor.

Mister Martin's message also shows several common attributes of a scam. He mentions at least three countries, and alludes to investments in Asia as well; most recently going to Dubai in search of the elusive investment opportunity. He apparently had no luck there, so he is turning to you – the consummate expert on Asian investments. How ridiculous!

Good luck, if you choose this obvious scam as your means of acquiring wealth. You will probably get more aggravation than wealth.

Taking another turn in the wicked web of e-mail scamming, there is nothing like a nebulous, personal appeal to raise your interest, get your juices flowing, and create a desire to respond to what is almost certainly a scam. One of the most common is to instill a fear that you might have missed something.

The next e-mail is a 'second notice' to an e-mail not previously received, similar to the one I used in the preface to this volume. A bit more complex than the prior message, it has a number of common points, which might make you believe it is genuine, and should respond.

First, it is from 'overseas', if you are not in the unstated country of the writer. The phone number seems to indicate a foreign address, located in Punjab, in the city of Gudiana, using '1646' as an international calling prefix. Alternatively, it is also a valid number for a person in the Manhattan Borough of New York City. Of course, it could also be a complete fraud.

Second, it is from someone who signs their name 'Barr', which might suggest a barrister, an attorney. Everybody should trust attorneys.

Third, it involves an inheritance, and that might mean money, or at least land or a title. In this case, simply because I apparently share the same surname, 'recipients' (since the message was addressed to undisclosed recipients), and I checked with others with my surname, several of whom had received the e-mail, I have to assume this is a fraud. It is interesting reading, though.

08-12-2012 Good day,

This is to notify you for the second time in regards to an inheritance funds, you are to be the beneficiary to the funds because you share the same surname with the original depositor who happens to be my client.

Please confirm receipt of email so we can proceed with the process of release and transfer.

Name:
Address:
phone number:
occupation

Regards

Barr Stacy Russel
+16462174046

A similar approach, with a slightly different way to get you interested, is the following message from "Mrs. Robin Sanders':

> *Atten*
> *I am Mrs Robin Sanders Former USA Ambassador to Nigeria, Did you instruct Mrs Glenda F Ward to claim your fund worth $7.000.000, Below is the bank account information provided by Mrs Glenda F Ward, saying that you authorized her to claim your fund that you are terminally ill.*
> *1. BANK NAME:UNION STATE BANK*
> *2. BANK ADDRESS:Kerrville Texas 78028 USA 3.ACCOUNT #:3202650 4. ROUTING #:114922443*
> *Reply to me as soon as possible.*
> *Sincerely Yours*
> *Mrs Robin Sanders*

The real Robin Sanders is the former US Ambassador to Nigeria, and distinguished member of the US Diplomatic Corps. She has been used by various 'Nigerian 419' scammers since roughly 2008 in a multitude of e-mail messages trying to get people to respond with varying amounts of personal information, on which they hope to claim millions in stolen funds. Many of these messages are reported on various Internet sites. This message is simply the latest in this long string of scams.

Without dwelling too long on this message, there are some questions here.

First, why would a distinguished former ambassador ask you about a terminally ill woman in Kerrville Texas? Now, it could be that Ms. Sanders and Ms. Ward are friends, or associates of some kind. I really doubt that, since Ms. Ward is about to commit fraud and the average former ambassador generally does not get involved in such activities.

Second, why a state bank in Kerrville Texas? Ms. Sanders has no known connections to Kerrville, and nothing in her extensive biography would indicate any reason to be associated with the town. You would think that the bank would be larger, and in a more metropolitan area.

Third, what about Glenda F. Ward? How is she related to Ambassador Sanders? Well, the answer to that is relatively straightforward. Some form of the message above has been circulating since early 2011, and Ms. Ward has always been the person of inquiry. After a diligent search of records in Kerrville, there is no Ms. Ward in that town, or even close by. In fact one of the messages sent out by whomever is posing as the ambassador, indicates she first came upon Ms. Ward in Nigeria. Isn't that a surprise?

Finally, if this message were real, why would Ms. Sanders use her former title as a come-on to commit the fraud? That makes no logical sense either, and leaves only the possibility that the message is a complete fraud.

Investigation ended. Let's move on.

Part Two – Personal Appeals

Chapter 3 Business Claims

Claims to be a representative of some business, one which wants urgently to do business with you, are becoming very common as the e-commerce community expands. Most of the e-mails are from generally unknown overseas companies, and often fail to describe their exact business.

Many of the messages are simple in nature, and express a desire to do business with you. The ones that I see often ask for a listing of my inventory or products, because they earnestly want to do business. Most, as usual, are addressed to 'undisclosed recipients', although I have received several which clearly knew I have a business as well. Let's look at a few examples of these types of scams.

The first message is the simplest, from a 'Mrs. Hafsia Haider', and asks only for basic information and costs. It seems harmless enough. Of course, since my major business venture is as a writer, I have no inventory, or FOB (freight-on-board) prices to provide. I did respond to the e-mail, and received no response from Ms. Haider. Guess they don't want to do business after all. I gave them an e-mail address I only use for scam responses, and they have yet to respond to it nearly six months later. Enjoy the read for yourself.

Hello

My Name is Mrs. Hafsia Haider and am the Purchasing Manager of Mohammad Al Mojil Group Building, We are very much interested in your products, we urge you to send us your full products list with price quotation via our email:

- Your minimum order quantity.
- Your FOB Prices and FOB Port
- Your estimated delivery time.

Meanwhile we will like to do business with your company and will need the order very urgent.

Best regards
Mrs. Hafsia Haider
King Fahed Road , Ibn Khaldoun
P.O

This message originated in Malawi, but refers to an organization in Saudi Arabia. Mrs. Haider's e-mail address is "Mrs. Hafsia Haider cls@sdnp.org.mw", which, as you can easily see, is a Malawi-based URL, and not one associated with the Mohammad al-Mojil Group. The address following her name at the bottom of the message is not even complete, or it might have given away the company location.

Moreover, Mrs. Haider has been known for some time in the Internet community monitoring scams. Messages abound which refer to the 'Haider Group of Company, in Russia and Chechnya, among others, where she is listed as their purchasing manager. She is always looking for inventory lists, and prices, but several of the Internet blogs seem to believe she is really validating e-mail addresses for later sale. Only time will tell on that surmise. I can't give you a good answer myself, since, she has not responded yet to my message.

It is interesting to note here that messages are not always what they seem to be. You can sign up for an e-mail account from various vendors, literally anywhere in the world, and have your messages seem to come from one place, while actually originating around the world, as you will see in other messages throughout the book.

Some vendors attempt to control their subscribers; others could care less, and allow virtually anyone, real name and information or not, to gain access to their servers by signing up.

The next message is an example of how these messages, pretend to originate in one place, while they actually originate somewhere else. In this case, the message is from a person, supposedly in Ukraine. Reading the poorly composed email, with its equally poor sentence structure, and you would have to assume it is probably a translation from another language.

However, The URL cited has what is called a 'redirect' hidden in it, and you don't end up at Ms. Smith's website. A redirect is a hidden address or internet site, to which you are taken while believing you are going to arrive somewhere else. The actual address or URL is 'attached' to what is written in the message, and executed when you 'click' with your mouse on the highlighted and underlined e-mail address.

There is a real website for Jeanie Adams Smith, a noted photojournalist. The only 'products' she sells are her photographs, and she does not, as far as we can see, buy photos from others. This item starting appearing just before Thanksgiving, 2012, as I first started writing this book, but there are reports it appeared earlier.

Hello ,

Am Mrs masha Lee Purchasing Manager of SIMS GROUP,write to inform you that we are interested in your products and We require to order a particular design.

The photos of the designs has been uploaded to the below link because of the size of the gallery,You are advised to open or copy and paste the link to the URL to view our interested product sample,to confirm if you can supply exactly the designs. copy and paste the link to your address bar browser to view pictures and size. or click the link

Gallery Link : http://jeanieadamssmith.com//wp-content/themes/widescreen/includes/temp/Sample/index.html

Note: For you to be able to view the picture sample, Kindly login with the same email you use for correspondence for access to our product sample cataloger gallery below.

Kindly send us your catalog, And we would like to inquire about the following:
1. Delivery time of the product
2. product warranty
3. Minimum Order Quantity
4. Payment terms available

Looking forward to your response.

Regards,
SIMS GROUP
PURCHASING MANAGER: MRS masha Lee
ZABOLOTNOGO 76, OFFICE 35
UKRAINE 03187, KYIV
COMPANY REGISTRY NUMBER IN UKRAINE 37641588

'KYIV', formerly called KIEV, is the capital of Ukraine. While the Sims Group exists as a company in several countries, it exists in Ukraine only in the mind of Mrs. Masha Lee, a well-known scammer going back several years.

Some scams are so simply constructed, it is easy to fall into their web. The message below speaks only to a 'business proposal', which Mrs. Yahya will discuss further with you, when you respond. She wants you, and members of your family to get involved in her proposal. That's all she says about it, leaving you to let your mind wander on what kind of proposal it might be, and possibly cajole you into a response.

This type of message generally seeks information, and not a possible business opportunity. By responding, you validate your e-mail address, and provide personal information to the scammer. These scammers then ask for additional information, and it gets more personal over time. Soon enough, your identity is in jeopardy, and it's too late for you to get out of the mess you got yourself into through your initial response.

Greetings From: Mrs. Iszam R. Yahya,

A very good day to you and members of your family, I have a business proposal for you, If you are interested, you can contact me through my private Email: izam.yahya@blumail.org OR iszamyahya@hotmail.com for details.

Thanks
Mrs. Iszam R. Yahya.

These are usually easy to see as a fraud, and a quick hit to your delete key provides the only real answer to the inquiry.

> **ALERT:** BluMail "provides global e-mail accounts, educational content, employment needs, entrepreneurship, networking, story / experience sharing, mentoring and volunteering opportunities to youth and others who are coming online in developing countries."
>
> "We provide "make-a-difference content" on activism, conflict resolution, education, entrepreneurship, environment, health, human rights, humanitarian relief, news from around the world, religious understanding, women's empowerment, youth empowerment, and other areas that educate and inform, not just entertain."

The next message is a bit more complex, and even easier to fall for, since it relates to religion, missionaries, and a kindly uncle who has a lot of money. We take a world trip on this one, from Zimbabwe, to India, where the 'seminarian' is studying, and then to the United Kingdom (UK) where our religious student has an uncle with$10 Million dollars to give away located somewhere. The 'uncle' has a list of potential investments of interest to him, and he wants you to help spend the money. Be sure, he only asks for ideas on how to spend the money, and wants to remain vague on the specific details until you respond.

I checked on both Victor Chigudu, and his uncle. Victor advertises, with virtually the same message, on a website called "United Black Untouchables Worldwide" out of Delhi, (URL:Indiahttp://unitedblackuntouchablesworldwide.blogspot.com/2012/09/investment-proposal.html. His message has been floating around the Internet since early 2012, and perhaps before.

His 'uncle' is even more interesting. There is a Dr. Daniel Chigudu in Zimbabwe, the Deputy Provincial Elections Officer for the Zimbabwe Elections Commission, and a well-known and respected public servant in that country. It would appear that whoever created this message, and the nephew, relied on the reputation of Dr. Chigudu for a way to validate their fraud, as has been the case with other public figures who were the subject of similar e-mail messages. In any event, read the message, and see what you think for yourself.

> Hello,
>
> This is victor Chigudu from Zimbabwe presently living in India as a student undergoing my pastoral program in catholic Christian collage new Delhi, i am writing you on behalf of my uncle Dr Daniel Chigudu who based in London united kingdom who want to invest with $10million us dollars, here is my uncle profile link below:
> http://zw.linkedin.com/pub/dr-daniel-chigudu/36/317/773   my uncle is interested in investing with anyone who has business ideas in any of the following areas below:
>
> 1. Real estate investment,
> 2. Fore trading,
> 3. Hotel investment,
> 4. School investment,
> 5. Transportation investment,
> 6. Oil and gas investment.
>
> Agriculture or any lucrative international or national business but it must be handled by the individual or company nominated. i believe in sincerity and honesty.
> The main purpose is for investments and return of profits from investment on a long term agreement and utilization of funds.
> If you are capable to handle this; considering the funds that is involved, please do not hesitate to respond to my mail and forward to me your business ideas or job plans.
> Contact email id: {victorchigudu@live.co.uk}. Please do not disregard this mail as i have being vague with details until i receive a response and information from you.
>
> My very best regards,
> Victor Chigudu.

The e-mail has several of the hallmarks of an e-mail scam—alluding to investments, ill-health, and ill-gotten gains, which can be disbursed—are the three big ones, and you will see that many other messages have similar ingredients, and many, many variants.

Victor, the 'nephew' appears on a large number of blog sites, which document the major 'Nigerian 419' scams, and scammers. That alone, for the diligent person, should be enough to click 'delete' when receiving the message. Unfortunately, so many people, particularly in the Third World, will see the reference to Dr. Daniel Chigudu as a sign that the message is real, and they will reply, but at their peril.

> **ALERT:** One of the addresses used in this e-mail refers to **Linkedin.com,** one of the major social networking sites. This is another instance of using a good, legitimate, service for illegal purposes.
> **Live.co.uk** is another one of the free services that will allow anyone to send messages without any form of oversight or responsibility

Just as a diversion, let's look quickly at an example of another hallmark of these types of scam messages—ill-health. While covered more in-depth in Chapter 6, I put one message here, just to let you see that many of these scams differ only in the scenario used to try to bilk you out of money or information.

The following e-mail came, as usual to 'undisclosed recipients', and to an e-mail address I do not commonly use or give out. That in itself is an indicator that the message is a fraud. Many of us have multiple e-mail addresses we use for varying purposes. One address is for 'normal' e-mails, another for those sites where you might want the family or close friends to have a place where they can correspond in private, and others, where you fully expect to quickly have all the span e-mails that the system can handle.

When you get an e-mail on a private site, or more commonly one where you expect spamming, it is the result of a person 'mining' the URL, and collecting your contact list, or recent addressees, simply to identify URL's where they can mine the information of others, through scam messages, or 'phishing'.

This e-mail was generated by someone who used an e-mail provider, sending the e-mail to anyone with some part of the address group they are trying to reach. In my case, it might be everyone named 'John' that has an e-mail address with my provider. In my case, the e-mail provider services included utilities which marked the message as SPAM, and my e-mail software placed it in the SPAM folder on my desktop. Not everyone has this type of protection. Read the following e-mail message, and decide if you would reply to it.

BEWARE: *No e-mail address is completely safe from these type messages.*

> My name is Mrs. Rosella Johnson. I am a dying woman who had decided to donate what I have to you. I am 59 years old and was diagnosed for cancer about 2 years ago, I lost my husband and i was left alone i have no family and I will be going for an operation, and i pray that i survive the operation I have decided to WILL/donate the sum of (Ten million five hundred thousand dollars) to you for the good work of the lord.
>
> Presently, I have informed my lawyer about my decision in WILLING this fund to you. Kindly Contact my lawyer through this email address (s.barristerjim@yahoo.cn) or you can call his private line: Tel: +447035939722. If you are interested in carrying out this task.
>
> Thank you and God bless you.
>
> Mrs. Rosella Johnson

Mrs. Johnson hits all the major hallmarks for this type of scam — she is dying, needs to give away money, probably for the betterment of her soul, and want to give it YOU (Whoever 'you' is that answers first to get scammed). What she DOESN'T say, however, will fill volumes.

First, 'Mrs. Johnson' probably does not exist. The e-mail address is a fake, and re-directs you to another address. Importantly, Mrs. Johnson is well-known within the e-mail scam community, and has been putting out this message since at least early 2011, and probably earlier. She often uses the name Thelma Johnson as well, and if you reply to her e-mail, all you get is a response from someone claiming to be Barrister Sturman.

In the past, Johnson also used another e-mail address, this time for yet another 'barrister' who can help you at barris.jaymcheny@lawyer.com, and yet another willing person at basterjimss@email.ch. Both of these are from spurious e-mail service providers.

Second, while she refers you to her barrister, Jim Sturman, and there is a Jim Sturman, a noted Queen's Counselor (QC), with a London practice, this is not him. Sturman is referred to by Mrs. Johnson, on several e-mail addresses. One, sterjimstur4444@email.ch is actually from an e-mail service in Switzerland, with offices in Germany. Another, barrsturman@crawler.com, is also seen in several of her e-mail messages using both names, and yet another is sturmanbarristerjim@yahoo.com.hk. All lead down the same path to no money, and a lot of aggravation.

I discuss more on the myriad of medical claims in Chapter 6.

The third area of commonality in many messages is 'ill-gotten gains'. These I spend a lot of time on in many of the chapters that follow, so I will not repeat those message themes here. As you can easily see from the Table of Contents, there are a lot of areas to exploit. In the meanwhile, let's go on to the next chapter, which features messages from dictators, and other seemingly horrible people. I think you will find these messages fascinating as well.

Chapter 4 Alliances with Dictators

Everybody likes to be able to say they are a friend of a really important person. In the first message, we start with the dictator Muammar Gaddafi, late of Libya. The story is heart-wrenching, as usual, and has a lot of money involved, in two hidden accounts just waiting for you.

'Mr. Williams' claims to be in the United Kingdom, but gives an Australian address and phone number, and wants you to call him right away. There is even a disclaimer at the bottom of the e-mail to make it look more authentic. Responding only confirms you exist, and that he (whoever he or she is) can use your e-mail, sell it, or further harass you forever. Read and enjoy.

By the way, this one is particularly interesting for the last sentences in the appeal. Mr. Williams claims to have an Australian Financial Services license for his activities in trying to give you the money stolen from Libya. He follows that up with the very official-looking disclaimer of financial responsibility for the advice he gives you to come get his money.

Seasons greetings,

I know that my mail already sound very unsecured and strange to you but permit me to introduce myself, i am Mr Williams H one of the close workers to Colonel Gaddafi of which i have worked for him for 13 years before his death.

I decided to stop working for him when i saw things not going as planned again and he threatened to kill me but i had no option but to run away through a ship that came to deliver goods here in Libya, i am in united kingdom now where i am try to start a new life.

My mail aim of contacting you is of two things, i decided to contact you through this means so that i can be sure of whom and dealing with and because i have information of two accounts(6.1 Million pounds and 4.5 Million Pounds) and one security company which he deposited money with fake names and is only me that has the information's , i will like you to stand as the beneficiary of the money and when this money is out we share it equally.

At this point i am incapacitated that i cannot follow up the claims because it will need funds to get all done, please if you are ready for this deal get back to me so that we can discus more.
Waiting.

Street Address: 46 Woodriff Street, Penrith NSW 2750 (cnr Derby Street) Postal Address:
Phone: 1300 55 95 13
Direct:
Fax:
Email: mailto:williams@mail.com
Website: http://
Australian Financial Services Licencee 232706

DISCLAIMER: Any general advice in this email does not take account of your personal objectives, financial situation and needs. Read the relevant Product Disclosure Statement before acquiring any product mentioned in this email. This email is confidential and is for the intended recepient only. If you are not the intended recipient do not use or rely on this information. Please contact us on 1300 55 95 13 and delete all copies of this email If you do not want to receive any more emails from us please let us know by return email.

I went looking for Mr. Williams H, of Penrith New South Wales. At the address cited, '46 Woodriff St', there is a private home-style building, which has a financial planning company located at that address, named Financial Independence Planners, It has a completely different number from that cited in the e-mail, and very little information found on the search engines, even in local searches in Australia. **Do not assume, however, that this means the firm is the scammer; probably not.** The house is located in an area which is mostly commercial, with many other companies also in houses, rather than office buildings.

The phone number in the e-mail is the Australian equivalent of a '1-800' number in the US. It is designed mostly for local use across Australia, but, when properly switched, can be used for international calls. That makes the local number it will ring at difficult to trace.

Muammar Gaddafi had a long history as a terrorist, and exporter of terrorism throughout the world. A minor player, even a somewhat important player, as this guy claims to be, would be dead, and, if alive, not wanting to fleece his old boss. For fear of retribution, he would not be safe, even in Australia.

This is just another kind of scam to be aware of, and avoid at all costs. You can't win with these, and they are no fun to even play with on a whim.

Chapter 5 Military Claims

The ill-gotten gains scam is one that I particularly dislike, especially when it is combined with circumstances claiming involvement with military actions. The first message is one of those scams, involving a Captain Hogan, an officer serving with the 82nd Airborne Division in Baghdad, Iraq. In this message, something called the 'Trade Center Chamber of Commerce directory' somehow identified me as the very person to help this military officer steal money from Iraq.

Citing an organization, such as a Chamber of Commerce, is a common façade for a scam. Most people think the Chamber of Commerce in their area is an indicator of truth and trust. So, when they hear from someone who is quoting such an organization, they often take the time to read the message. The scammer counts on that name recognition for getting his proverbial 'foot' in the door.

This particular scam, citing the 'Trade Center Chamber' comes in many forms. Citations commonly include the Chambers in Iraq and Japan, and describe a number of different scenarios.

In the military scenario, there is "Captain Kenneth Hogan", and "Captain John Anthony", with both sets of messages essentially identical in nature. They want your help in getting some boxes out of harm's way, although Hogan, at least says the boxes are already in the UK, awaiting assistance to get them out of there as well.

Read through the e-mails first, to see if you qualify.

The composition of this e-mail makes it clear, early and consistently, that the person writing it is neither American nor a member of the US 82nd Airborne Division. What is does do is ask for comprehensive personal information to 'reconfirm' you as a person of interest (He already saw it in the directory), but wants to make sure it is you.

Dear Sir/Madam

I am sorry to encroach into your privacy in this manner, I found you listed in the Trade Center Chambers of Commerce directory here in Iraq,I find it pleasurable to offer you my partnership in business.

I only pray at this time that your address is still valid. I want to solicit your attention to receive money on my behalf.

I am Capt Kenneth Hogan, an officer in the US Army, and also a West Point Graduate presently serving in the Military with the 82nd Air Borne Division Peace keeping force in Baghdad, Iraq.

I am on the move to Afghanistan from Iraq as the last batch just left, and i really need your help in assisting me with the safe keeping of two military trunk boxes which has just arrived the United Kingdom from the Iraq. I hope you can be trusted?

If you can be trusted, I will explain further when i get a response from you. Nevertheless, reconfirm the following to me as follows.

(a) Your full Names
(b) Your physical mailing address
(c) Your direct telephone numbers
(d) Your occupation.

Please ensure to reply via my private e-mail address:captkennethhogan@globomail.com

God bless you and thanks for cooperation in advance.

Capt Kenneth Hogan

Captain Hogan does not speak of money, only to two trunks he took from Iraq and then sent to the UK. He leaves to your imagination what may be in the trunks.

The Trade Center Chamber is also mentioned in other messages, mostly from Japan, where two names pop up frequently in the message traffic. One name is 'Suzuki Kakuya Yuki,' supposedly head of accounts at Tokyo's Mitsubishi Bank, Who wants you to accept money on his behalf, and then split the loot. 'Takamuneo Tihara', with a similar. The messages are nearly identical on these two, and they can both be traced to Chinese e-mail providers.

Some e-mails do get more specific, and relate mostly to currency schemes, often by military personnel, as shown below in two e-mails. The first is from an Army Colonel who claims to have a lot of money, which he took from somewhere (he wants you to think Iraq or Afghanistan) when he was serving with his army division.

Hello,

My name is Col. Archer Reese an American soldier serving with the Third infantry Division.

During our operations we discovered some large containers of currencies which I smartly carted away some substantial amount which I deposited with the Red Cross security vault house as family valuable and also informed them that we will contact the real owner of the box. It is under my power to approve who is eligible, I need to present someone as the recipient. I have a 100% authentic means of transferring the box through diplomatic courier Service. I just need your acceptance, and everything is done. Please, if you are interested in this transaction, I give you the complete details you need for us to implement this transaction successfully. send me an email for more details if you are interested in helping me, I give you enough proof about the incident clink the below link for the BBC NEWs
   http://news.bbc.co.uk/2/hi/middle_east/2988455.stm

I need:
Your full name..
Your full address......................................
Your direct cell phone number................

hoping to hearing from you.
Col. Archer Reese

'Colonel Reese' gives you a lot of reasons to read his e-mail message, and then want to help. He tries to do a great job of reassuring you that what he wants to do—steal the money—if it exists, is completely above board. He claims the money is with the Red Cross, and he has promised them he will find the rightful owner. That is where you come in—you will be the 'rightful owner'.

This 'Colonel' is well-known on the e-mail circuit. He has a number of messages out there, and a number of e-mail addresses from which to choose for your reply. He also indicates more than one unit of assignment, wherever he was serving. In one e-mail, he is clear about being in Iraq with the 1st Armored Division, as an Intelligence officer, (Although interestingly, he spells Armored as 'Armoured', the British spelling, not American), and, as you saw in the above e-mail, with the 3rd Infantry Division. In both messages, he claims to have secured the money during a military campaign.

In another message, instead of making you the 'rightful owner', he suggests boldly that you pretend to be the owner, for a fee to be negotiated later.

The colonel does have one consistent theme through the various messages I have seen; he always mentions the use of the diplomatic courier service as his means of getting the money out of the UK, and over to the US. The diplomatic courier service, a function of the US State Department, does not usually provide courier service for military-related letters or packages.

The e-mail address often cited by Col. Reese (reese7068111@mail.com) is a fraud, from another of the 'free e-mail' sites in Europe, although several web sites have reported it from other locations as well. Beware.

The-next mail message, shown below, is simply incredible. I can't believe anyone would believe it true, at least in the United States, or some other western nation where people know and understand military ranks and what they do. This e-mail is almost certainly translated from another language; the typing is egregious; the spelling horrible; and the punctuation atrocious. In short, it is simply not believable, a perfect example of the type of message described in the introduction, and mirrors Herley's thought in the Washington Post article we discussed in an earlier chapter. I wonder how many people bit on the possibility of the millions of dollars promised.

> Dear Friend,
> My name is Captain Paul Benson from, United States. I am an American Citizen currently serving in Afghanistan. I formally served in Baghdad Iraq in 2003. I'm 37yrs old the reason I contacted you is that, I want you to help me receive a consignment Box that I deposited with a security company in Baghdad Iraq; the consignment (Box) contains 10million dollars.
>
> Please note that the security company does not know that the box contains money. I listed it as containing family belongings Anyway i think i should tell you how i came into possession of this money. In 2003, I was the one commanding the US 3rd Infantry Division in Baghdad, Iraq.
>
> On our raids of 23 and 26 April 2003 in Baghdad, we came across a huge amount of money in containers. Please visit if your willingness to assist me in receiving the consignment from the security company.
>
> Let me know if you are interested then you send me a mail in my private ,
> email address: paul_benson00010@yahoo.co.uk

Several things stick out here in 'Captain Benson's' e-mail. First, an Army Captain does NOT command a division anywhere, much less Baghdad. Second, $10M in US Dollars, even in $100 bills, would take a very large box, and it is beyond normal belief to think that any security company would not have some inkling of what was contained in the box, and simply store it away for later retrieval, without accounting for its contents. The potential liability would be extraordinary.

Then, there is the 'yahoo.co.uk' address again. Every military person these days has a military address, and most have a personal e-mail address. Very few US military members might have a UK personal e-mail address, even when they are in Afghanistan, as the Captain alleges. Rather, most have a personal

US e-mail address they use, especially if they might intend to commit theft, as the Captain alleges he wants to do.

As any person with logical intelligence would consider theft a crime, and theft from a military area of engagement is usually punished severely by the military; so it is rare that these situations occur, and are always discovered eventually.

Benson has several variations on the message themes, and several e-mail addresses, which he uses to communicate with anyone who will listen to his pitch. One of the more common variations is that he, and several other officers, found the money, took part of it, and gave the rest back to the US Command. He wants to bring the money to the US, wants your help to do it, and will want part of the money when it arrives from the security company, where it currently resides in a vault. In those messages, he provides as his e-mail address *paul.benson@bluemail.org* , one of the free e-mail services.

A simple suggestion here: Beware of Captains (?? Colonels) bearing boxes supposed to contain instant wealth.

Chapter 6 Medical Claims

Medical claims are perhaps the saddest type of claims, and also the kind of claim that people are naturally prone to read. The stories differ greatly, as you will see in the following pages. Many start simply, and ask you to do something for them, since they are ill, and their relationship with god calls out for you to help them. Read the e-mails that follows, and see what your own heart does in response. Before you act, however, put your mind in motion as well, and look again logically at the messages as well.

> *Dearest Beloved In Christ*
> *I'm Mrs. Elizabeth Dixon an aging widow suffering from long time illness. I have some funds I inherited from my late husband, the sum of 5 Million United State Dollars and I needed a very honest and God fearing Christian that will use the fund for God's work, Please if you would be able to use the funds for the Lord's work, kindly reply me back to me at my email (elizabethdixon0147@live.com) Stay Blessed*
> *Mrs. Elizabeth Dixon.*

This e-mail was supposedly sent from 'info@dixon.com', although Dixon.com actually belongs to the Dixon Company in Dixon, California, and has nothing apparently to do with an aged lady with a lot of money.

She tells the recipient to use another e-mail address, this time from 'live.com', one of the free international internet e-mail sites. Good things come from the Lord in many ways, but not generally through this type of e-mail.

By the way, Mrs. Dixon has several variations on this theme out on the airways. In some, she is a widow, and at an advanced age; in others, she is 45 years old, and dying. She also uses a number of e-mail addresses, which all end up at the same place, a free Internet e-mail service. You may get a message asking you to use Elizabeth.dixon47@yahoo.com, where she is a cancer patient, who has sold all her property, put the money into a certificate of deposit ($5M US), and wants you to invest it in charities that deal with 'motherless babies' and the deaf.

In another message, Mrs. Dixon is 49 years old, has esophageal cancer in the UK, and wants your help, although she does not mention what she expects you to do for her. You can reach her at elizabeth19665@yahoo.com, if you are interested.

Another interesting character is 'Mrs. Judith Williams', who sounds a bit like she emulates the late Leona Helmsley of New York hotel fame. Mrs. Williams puts virtually all of the heart-wrenching details into her e-mail; mentioning no fixed amount, but inviting someone to come to her for help, which she can provide from her investments. Since she is dying of lung cancer, she wants to be a good person to the end.

> From: Mrs Judith Williams.
> My name is Mrs Judith Williams am 75yrs old of age, i stay in new york city, USA.I am a good merchant, I have several industrial companies and good share in various banks in the world. I spend all my life on investment and coporate business. all the way i lost my husband and two beautiful kids in fatal accident that occur in November 5th 2003.
>
> I am a very greedy woman with all cost i dont know much and care about people, since when I have an experience of my it difficult to sleep and give rest.
>
> later in the year 2004 Febuary i was sent a letter of medical check up,as my personal Doctor testify that i have a lung cancer, which can easily take off my life soon. I found it uneasy to survive myself, because a lot of investment cannot be run and manage by me again. I quickly call up a pastor/prophet to give me positive thinking on this solution, as my adviser.

He minister to me to share my properties wealth, to motherless baby/orphanage homes/people that need money for survivor both student that need money/ business woman and man for their investment and for future rising. So i am writing this letter to people who really need help from me both student in college, to contact me urgently. so that i can make available preparation on that.especially women of the day, who are divorced by their husband, why they cannot survive the mist of feeding theirself.

please contact me and stop weeping. probably let me now what you really need the money for, and if you can still help me to distribute money to nearest orhanages homes near your town. now am so much with God, am now born again. May you be blessed, as you reach me, please to remind you, dont belongs to scammers or any act of fraudlent on internet. I will give more information to you as i await your response immediately.

Best Regards

Judith Williams

The story related by Mrs. Williams, if you can get through the poor translation, is truly heart-wrenching; she tries so hard to make amends for an apparent life of greed, and disdain for humanity.

Mrs. Williams is not what she appears to be, however. This woman is well-known to the spamming community, since about 2006, thus making her one of the 'older' e-mail spammers. She has used a number of message formats, a range of e-mail addresses, but always has a sad story to tell, usually involving some form of cancer, from which she has assuredly not yet died.

One of her early messages (from 2007) tells how she is living in Sugarland Texas, USA, and had lost her husband and children the year before in an auto accident. Her message came from an e-mail address (*dr_pookim200@virgilio.it*) in Italy, but she wants you to reply directly to her at *mrsj.4williams@yahoo.com*.

By 2009, Mrs. Williams was in London, and sending out messages with a completely different sad story. Now, she claims to have been married to a Liberian, with no children, and he died in 2003. She has cancer, is expected to live for only a few months, and also has had a stroke. In this message, sent from *help.mrsjudithwilliams@yahoo.com*, she asks that you reply to that address, with information on how she might contact you further.

In 2011, she again changed her message, to make it more generic, and, perhaps, inviting to the gullible. The address was not judith.williams21@yahoo.co.uk, and bore the cryptic message to make the contact so she could 'explain' herself to you.

The message I reproduced above is a 2012 message, which still has the cancer theme, but the death of the husband and children is back, and she needs you to get in touch quickly, because she could die at any minute. Mrs. Williams wrote the message from an address in Poland (The ISP is 'wp.pl'), another of the no-questions-asked ISPs for free e-mail.

> ALERT: WP.PL is a free internet mail service from Poland. According to Wikipedia, it is the 182nd most popular website worldwide, and the 6th most popular site in Poland. For some, that may give an air of legitimacy to the e-mail.

'WP.PL' is one of those sites that will remove an account for fraud. Send them a note, if you can write Polish. In this case, by the way, it is easy to surmise that the e-mail was originally written in Polish, and translated badly into other languages.

This person, whoever she is, has an amazing mind, and a lot of resilience for a scammer. She relies on vendors, such as Yahoo, which has a huge customer base, and a lot of smaller subsidiaries through which the scammers can make a living without being caught. If someone complains, they simply change their e-mail addresses, as they often do their stories.

In a similar way, the next e-mail from 'Roland and Aamina', is truly heart-wrenching. It has every possible combination of events and clichés, from AIDS to theft in it.

> *From: Roland and Aamina*
>
> *Attn:*
> *Compliments of the day!*
> *I and my younger sister write to seek for your assistance; we got your contact from a noble gentleman that came to our refugee camp who came to give a seminar about AIDS whom we confronted that we are looking a God-fearing person that is when your data was given to us.*
>
> *First and foremost i want to introduce myself to you. My name is Roland and my younger sister mina a Sudannes,my consignment contains 45million United States dollars and some quantity of gold and Diamond, which I cannot specify.*
>
> *The consignments are presently in States. The consignment gets to States through the help of a U.N diplomat Patrick Dankwa Anin. The fact is that Patrick Dankwa Anin is supposed to have delivered this consignment to a man called Dr. Smith Paggy in States.*
>
> *The week Patrick Dankwa Anin is suppose to deliver the consignment to him, when he got to States after clearing the consignment from the Airport,h- call Dr. Smith Paggy to tell him the description to is house for the delivery, but is wife answered the call and told Patrick Dankwa Anin that her husband Dr.Smith Paggy hard a fatal car accident which lead to hisdeath some few hours later.*
>
> *Dr.Smith Paggy has already paid the demurrages from the security company, he paid for Bullion van that took the consignment to the airport and he paid for custom check report he also assisted us in getting the DRUG / ANTI TERRIORIST CERTIFICATE, which is so expensive that he spent 25 thousand dollars to acquire it, but unfortunately he died in a car accident, that was why Patrick Dankwa Anin has to deposit the consignment with a warehouse over there in States and called us to informed us about what is happening.*
>
> *Please when you call him you will tell him that you are calling in respect of Roland and mina consignment that is in States. If Patrick Dankwa Anin asks if you have discussed with me tell him that you have discussed with me immediately.*

> *Please, get to Patrick Dankwa Anin on time and get back to me through mail. I await your urgent response.*
> *Thanks and God bless you.*

Let's take a quick look at the elements of this message, and see if it passes the span sniff test. We can read the following from the message:

- The man and his sister were referred to me by someone who visited a refugee camp to talk about AIDS
- They have $5M US in gold and diamonds, in unspecified amounts
- The gold and diamonds are in the United States from Sudan
- A United Nations diplomat got the stuff into the US, and was supposed to deliver it to someone else for safekeeping
- The person who was to receive the gold and diamonds died in an automobile crash before receiving the gold and diamonds, but had paid the demurrage charges for the stuff
- The UN diplomat deposited the stuff in a security warehouse, where it apparently resides
- He wants me to get in touch with the diplomat, say I represent the owner, and get the stuff, then get back in touch with Roland, through the mail.

That is one amazing set of circumstances, and, at least for me, makes it incredible to believe. I don't know of any friends travelling overseas to do lectures on AIDS; I have no idea, from the message how to get hold of this 'diplomat' (he is not listed on any UN diplomat list), and I have no idea how to find this guy 'Paggy' either. To me, it is not worth replying to ghosts.

Although not shown here, their e-mail address was 'Arizona@grupodelaware.com', another completely fraudulent address. However, all is not lost here; if you click on the address as given, you will go to 'roland-aamina11@gmx.com'.

> **ALERT:** We found GMX, and it's a legitimate service, which claims the following: "GMX's professional virus protection is based on a leading provider's scan engine. It locates viruses, worms, and Trojans, even in compressed file formats. GMX mailboxes are protected from spam with seven anti-spam modules, resulting in 98% less unwanted mail. GMX is secure and reliable, protecting its users from malware and spam with a guaranteed webmail accessibility of over 99%"
> Regrettably, the Spam filters don't seem to work outgoing, only incoming.

GMX.com is a listed ISP, but it probably goes to yet another address somewhere, and you name is forever registered as one of those who will answer anything. Better to simply stay away from this one.

Another, similar situation is that of 'Sheerah King', who gives an even more specific diagnosis, which, for her, has defied medical treatment, and now she wants to give away her money before her death. What a good person you would be if you helped her do that. Unfortunately, she will probably continue to live a very long life, with a very good income, coming mostly from the funds of those who decided to 'help' here, and, in the process were scammed instead.

Ms. King is another well-known and prolific message writer, mostly with sad tales to tell. Starting around 2009, Ms. King has had a range of diseases, from AIDS to Cancer of varying types, and her constant request is to have someone use her money (Normally around $15M US) for AIDS and cancer research. All one needs to do is get in touch, and she will start working with you to make it happen.

One line, which appears in virtually all her messages, is my nominee for the 'favorite scammer quote award'. It is "I want to donate what I have to the needy. You could be surprised why I picked you. But someone has to do it." Isn't that a beautiful sentiment? And from a scammer yet. WOW!

Going back to reality, Ms. King, by 2011, was apparently over the AIDS, since it was no longer mentioned as a specific ailment. She was now concentrating on 'cancer and blood' diseases, and one message mention cancer of the breast, which was resisting treatment. By now, her e-mail address had become *srakng@gmail.com*, but the actual return address was *ksh0r@yahoo.com.hk*, a Hong Kong subsidiary of, you guessed it, Yahoo.com. During 2011, she was also using the e-mail *Sheerah@wish.org*, with a similar message.

The 2012 message, similar to those generated in 2011, is below. The e-mail addresses changed during 2012-2013, and the reply is now *skroh0g@wish9.org*. Read the latest below.

Dear friend

My name is Sheerah King, I want to donate part of what I have to the needy through you, you could be surprised why I picked you but someone has to do it. I have been diagonalized with Breast and Blood disease which has defiled all forms of medical treatment and I have been told by my doctor that my days are numbered on earth.

I have been touched to donate from what I have made from this World to charity through you for the good work of humanity and business bequest for you to Handle with me. Please email me with your contact information such as Your Full Names, Country, Direct Telephone number and direct email address so I can tell you what you need to do and also give you more details about my intentions.

Best Regards,
Sheerah King

Anyone got any idea what 'diagonalized with Breast and Blood disease' means?

One final medical e-mail is the one below. Very direct and a lot of money for the lucky recipient. Just contact the 'lawyer' to get your money. Good luck on this one. Mrs. Perkins will bless you forever, for helping her get your money.

> Hello,
> My name is Mrs. Beatrice Perkins. I was diagnosed for cancer about 3 years ago. I will be going in for an operation today. I decided to WILL/donate the sum of (Fourteen Millions Two Hundred Fifty Eight Thousand United States Dollars) to you for the good work of the lord.
>
> Contact my lawyer with this email:
> Name: Joe McDonald Esq
> Email: 2375565053@qq.com
>
> Tell him that I have WILLED 14.258M to you by quoting my personal reference number BRW/876/430//U765S/UK.
> As soon as you contact him with this details quoted above, he should be able to recognize you and help in claiming this amount from my Bank. Be informed also that i have paid for the state tax on this money to be transferred to you.
> Meanwhile you are advised to keep this mail and it contents confidential as i really want my wish accomplish at the end of the day. Please do pray to God for my recovery. My friend please do not send me any email as you are to send my barrister an email directly.
>
> God Bless
>
> Regards,
> Mrs. Beatrice Perkins

ALERT: 'qq.com' says " QQi (QQ International) connects you to over 700 million Chinese QQ Accounts and many of your favorite websites and useful tools. It's the best place to stay in touch with friends and make new ones.
I try to steer clear of sites originating in China. You never know what information they are collecting, and they have a long history and reputation for having no protections at all.

Among the more recent medical scams is one from a 'Mrs. Imilda Elkousy', supposedly the widow of the late Bello Wisdom, who died in the Egypt Air Flight 990 crash in 1999. Look at the deal she offers, apparently to everyone named 'john' she could find among Internet addresses.

Good day.

I am mrs lmilda Elkousy a widow suffering from long time illness. I have some funds I inherited from my late husband,.bello wisdom who died in an Air crash on the 31st October 1999 in an Egyptian airline 990 with other passengers on board (http://news.bbc.co.uk/1/hi/world/americas/502503.stm).

I was a month pregnant when I received the sad news of his sudden death, but I lost the pregnancy because of the trauma and have vowed not to remarry. I dedicated my life to minor charity work, but because of the trauma of his death and my childlessness, I became ill of the Cervix Cancer With other complicated health issues because of many years of loneliness. Sincethen, I have been in and out of the hospital and had never had time to fulfill a dream.

However, believing God to see me through in the operation which the doctors are deciding upon because of my age and fear of medical complication due to the deteriorating state of my health , I have decided to give out the deposit which my late husband had left me and the ever hoped child since years of protracted illness did not allow me to embark on the mission.

The deposit is valued US$15,500.000.00 (Fifteen million, five hundred thousand U.S dollars) and I am in need of a very honest and God fearing person that will use the fund for God's work to help the less privileged out there.

Please bear in mind that my concern is your personal commitment towards any project that you will embark upon to ensure that its benefit is well distributed among the less privileged in our immediate society.

I have mapped out $2, 500.000.00 for your personal use in this work, while I pray that the rest will be used for the mission. Please if you know that you will sincerely use the fund to fulfill this dream, kindly reply for further details with your information.(1) Your full Name (2) your contact address (3) Telephone Number (4) Country of Residence (5) Nationality (6) Occupation (7) Age / Sex (8) Marital Status.

Be blessed.
Mrs..lmilda Elkousy

She offers a great opportunity to take here money (Over $15M US), and invest it in whatever project you wish, and keep $2.5M (US) for your own, as a commission of sorts. All you need to do is send her every bit of personal, which she can then use for whatever purpose she chooses.

If you are going to get caught by this scam, better do it quickly, because she claims to be dying of cervical cancer, and you probably won't find her, if you do try.

Over the past several months, the number of cancer-related messages seems to have dramatically increased. Perhaps global warming, and the melting of the North Pole is responsible. Whatever the reason, there are increases in letters, such as the one from 'Sarah Bin Rasheed' which follows. Ms. Rasheed, also a widow, is suffering from Cancer of the breast, and, unfortunately, it has progressed to the point she cannot, on her doctor's orders, discuss the possibilities of using her $18.2M (US) legacy from her late husband, Khalifa bin Rasheed, former Owner and Chairman of the Petroleum and Gas Company in Dubai, United Arab Emirates (UAE). A truly tragic story, even if it were true.

Read the message for yourself, and see what you think.

From:Mrs. Sarah Bin Rasheed
Adress: Dubai, UAE.
Email: sarah.binr80@yahoo.com.ph

Dear,

I'm Mrs. Sarah Bin Rasheed a Christian married to a Muslim, now a widow to late Khalifa Bin Rasheed former owner of Petroleum & Gas Company here in Dubai, United Arab Emirates. I am 59 years old, suffering from long time Cancer of the breast. From all indications my condition is really deteriorating and it's quite obvious that I won't live more than 2 months according to my doctors. This is because the cancer stage has gotten to a very bad stage. I don't want you to pity me, but I need your assistance and trust.

My late husband died early last year from Heart attack, and during the period of our Marriage we couldn't produce any child. My late husband was very wealthy and after his death, I inherited all his business and wealth. The doctor has advised me that I will not live for more than 2 months, so I have now decided to spread all my wealth to contribute mainly to the development of charity in Africa, America, Asia, Africa and Europe. Am sorry if you are embarrassed by my mail, I found your e-mail address in the web directory, and I have decided to contact you, but if for any reason you find this mail offensive, please you can ignore it and please accept my apology.

Before my late husband died he deposited the sum of Eighteen million, Two Hundred Thousand United States dollars ($18.200.000.00 Million) in a Bank some years ago, that's all I have left now, I need you to collect this funds and distribute it yourself to charity, so that when I die my soul can rest in peace. The funds will be entirely in your hands and management. I hope God gives you the wisdom to touch many lives. That is my main concerned 30% of this money will be for your time and effort, while 70% goes to charities that will appreciate your assistance for this projects.

Please contact me through my private e-mail: sarah.binr80@yahoo.com.ph , The doctor has stopped me from receiving and making calls due to my health condition.

I look forward to your respond and cooperation toward this great charity work..

Truly Yours,
Sarah

According to her letter, you get 30% for yourself, and 70% goes to charity. How generous! Her e-mail address is interesting in itself. It's another of the national 'Yahoo' accounts, but the 'ph' on the account is from the Philippines. She wants you to use that address, as her 'personal e-mail' address, but the message was originally sent from "mail@mail.8hy.hk", an e-mail domain originating in Hong Kong, with two Internet protocol servers, one in Hong Kong, and one in Delhi, India.

So, if you want to believe this e-mail, we have a grieving widow, with a lot of money, who inherited the business, and his wealth, from the husband on his death. One would estimate she still lives in Dubai. Would not one ask why, a person in Dubai is writing an e-mail from a Hong Kong server, and giving you a Philippines-based e-mail address, on which to reply confidentially to her?

I might add one thing on this one: the web domain '8hy.hk' has a very poor Web-of-Trust (WOT) rating, the international rating for trustworthiness of the domain. A number of these sites are on international blacklists, according to the WHOIS, and other reporting agencies. Be aware on this one.

Chapter 7 Partnering Scams

Another approach makes you think you are partnering with someone on a great deal – one too good to miss. Perhaps oil exploration is your ultimate dream. If so, then the next best thing to doing exploration yourself is to work with someone else. They get the customers and sources for you; all you have to do is get a license, and sit back to reap in the profits. The best of all worlds, maybe.

The first e-mail message, from an engineer named 'Frank Thabi', could take you into the lucrative oil exploration business, and reap you immense profits. In this case, the 'National Oil Company' will do the actual drilling, and you will be involved in securing customers for their products, after the gushers occur in their oil fields. You get a 'lifting license', which allows you to legally solicit customers, and a commission on each barrel of oil sold. Could anything be easier than this?

There are some 'minor' catches to this seemingly endless gushing of profits for you. First, you will need a 'seller's agent' who will help you find customers. That agent is, presumably, Mr. Thabi, who will undoubtedly take a commission—a large commission—for his efforts. Then, of course, the license is for 500,000 barrels of crude per month, and that license must be procured from the government.

Now none of this 'participation' is going to be cheap. But then, since you will be getting about $3 US per barrel for your efforts, according to the message, sharing should still give you a large profit, or at least you would think that to be the case. Read the message to see what you think about the 'opportunity'.

Hello,

I choose to reach you through e-mail, as it is the fastest medium of communication irrespective of the fact that it has been greatly abused. I deem it necessary to introduce you to a lucrative business opportunity. I'm talking of crude oil trading! This is considered as the most legitimate and fastest money making machinery anyone can setup.

A crude oil "lifting license" gives the owner the mandate of the National Oil Company (Suppliers of the crude oil), to locate crude oil buyers and arrange a buy/sale crude oil transaction between the oil company and the crude oil buyers. The "lifting license" syndrome came into place because the national oil company does not deal directly with the buyers of the crude oil rather; they prefer to issue oil "lifting license allocations" to individuals/companies to assist them to market the crude oil which they produce. Anyone that owns an ?lifting license" from the local National Oil Company is entitle d to a $2.00 commission from the oil company on each barrel of crude sold to the buyer and another $1.00 commission from the buyer. In total, oil lifting license owners receives a $3.00 commission on each barrel of crude sold by the oil company. Please note that the commission rates of
$2.00 and $1.00 normally increases in times of crude oil scarcity.

The smallest license allocation/quantity one can procure from the National Oil Company is for the sale of 500,000 barrels of crude monthly/per transaction.

This implies that 500,000 barrels of crude oil will be assigned to the license owner for sale per month. This allocation size will earn the license owner about ($3.00 multiply by 500,000 barrels) which is $1.5 million gross commissions monthly. If one is lucky to secure a bigger allocation that means you will be earning more commissions monthly. These commissions will be calculated and paid to the license at the end of the sales transaction.

In case you decide to invest in this money spinning project; I will personally reveal to you a well packaged procedure to acquire an oil lifting license. I will personally assist you to locate the buyers of the crude oil and facilitate the sales transactions for you while the resulting commissions will be wired into your overseas nominated banking co-ordinates as the license owner. You need a "seller agent" to assist you to sale the crude since you are alien to this business and do not know the buyers for the crude oil and also because you are not locally resident here.

Feel free to ask for clarifications.

Engr. Frank Thabi

'Frank' is another well-known scammer on the Internet. He is cited in several other e-mails, all related to oil exploration, some more specific than others.

In 2011, working from an e-mail address out of mynet.com (*frankthabi12@mynet.com*), Frank made a big splash, with a message similar to the one above. He asked that you return with a response to *frankthabi@mynet.com*. As expected from one of these scammers, he registered at least two separate e-mail addresses for his schemes.

By 2012, Thabi changed services, and had migrated to 'BTCONNECT.COM', a British internet provider, with a large e-mail offering. Thabi's e-mail address became *btba@btconnect.com*, although he continued to ask that people respond to *frankthabi@mynet.com*. During 2012, Thabi, or whoever claimed to be this person, also used two other addresses, all linked to the others previously used in his ventures on oil exploration, *sunny@btcxonnect.com*, and *frankthabi1@mynet.com*.

BT.com, the parent company, claims to be a reputable service, and will deny continued service to scammers. They probably are, in the main, but the message I received came to my e-mail in January, 2013, so they have not yet been completely successful.

Here is another, even more interesting example of this scam. The writer wants you to believe he is a Slovak, living in Libya, who is having real problems with the Government there. Other e-mail messages show he also claims to be Moroccan, living in Nigeria. You pick what you choose to believe, as you read the message below.

Dear Friend,

I got your email on my search for a reliable business partner on the internet.

> I am interested in establishing and operating a very viable business as a means of investment abroad. I do not know too well how this is done in your country, so I will need you to help me in this regard.
>
> My preference is any good profit yielding business and I would appreciate any viable ideas you could come up with. I will also need you to help me look for properties like homes and lands for sale as I am proposing to invest the sum of Twenty Million United States Dollars (20,000,000.00 USD) for this.
>
> I do not know if you can and will be of help to me. For a brief on my personality; my name is Alhaji Hussain Ahmad, a Slovakian based in Libya.
>
> I am a retired Business man, formally into Oil and Gas business. I am 62 years of age, married with awife and 4 lovely kids. I have had so much problems with the Libyan Authority just because am a foreigner I believe. My need for this business proposition and to acquire these properties is very urgent as I am planning to move out of this country with my family down to your country. I want you to also help in finding a good home where my family and I will live in. Please you can reply to my personal email as soon as you receive this message so we can communicate further: bbhussain2@gmx.com
>
> Sincerely,
> Alhaji Hussain Ahmad

Mr. Ahmad is an interesting character, well-known in scamming circles. He has been operating at least since 2011 Ahmad has pretty consistently used the 'gmx.com' domain, which was previously described as a free service with no apparent legitimacy rules. He has, on occasion, used some other addresses, including aljhuss77@arab.net, bbhussain2@hotmail.com, and aljjhg@live.com. Beware of this guy.

One last example of this specific type of scam, before we go to the variations on the theme, is the following recent message. It involves a set of trunks, locked up inside a security company in Ghana.

The owner is dead, and the writer of the message, a Mister Bannerman, wants your help in getting them claimed. You and Mister Bannerman each get 50%. All you have to do is arrange for the deal, and go to Ghana to claim your set of trunks. What could be easier than that?

There are several clues to this fraud. First, the address this guy Bannerman uses in the e-mail header is John Bannerman 'bernie46@live.com' That would be interesting in itself, but the actual e-mail for this guy, the one you reply to, is quite different and not from live.com; instead, you are replying to an address (jbannerman@zing.vn), still for Bannerman, but the domain is in Vietnam's Ho Chi Minh City.

So, there is the usual question; why is a man, who claims to be in Ghana working for a security company, sending his e-mails from Vietnam, and covering up his real address, at that.

The answer is simple: IT IS A SCAM, AND YOU ARE THE INTENDED VICTIM mister 'Undisclosed Recipient', whoever you are.

TO WHOM IT MAY CONCERN:

A Cash Sum in the amount of US$91million was concealed in a 5 Trunk Boxes and tagged Family Valuables and Treasures. The aforementioned Cash Funds have been in the Vault Room of our Security Company unclaimed as at 14 years ago till date. My investigations confirm that the Original Depositor is dead while the Depositor's Family knows nothing about the Cash Fund and its Deposit. I therefore wish to collaborate with you to lay claims on the Funds on condition that you will be able to make a trip to Republic of Ghana where the 5 Trunk Boxes that contained the Cash Funds will be released to you for possible Bank to Bank Transfer by the Security Company. Our Sharing Ratio is 50/50.If you are interested; I will appreciate if your Telephone Numbers will be sent to me for discussion of this offer in full details. There is no legal implication attached.

Thank you.
John Bannerman

You may recall earlier messages where a security company reference was used to give a sense of validation that the money (the $51M US) actually existed, and could be transferred to you, or more directly, your bank if you work out a sharing arrangement with the person creating the message.

Let's look at 'John Bannerman from Ghana' briefly. The message says he is in Ghana, working for a security company, and has control of five boxes containing over $51M US dollars, which have lain unclaimed for over 14 years. There is also a 'John Bannerman' John Bannerman (e-mail: *capp@difacooper.com*), who claims to be the Director of Foreign Operation of a Bank in Accra, the capital of Ghana, and has over $120M US in his vaults.

What I believe, however, is the several messages, those which claim to have originated from Ghana, refer to another John Bannerman, a well-known name in that country from the Soccer world; used by someone actually located in Hong Kong (e-mail: *karl_ericp@yahoo.com.hk*) and actually running the scam.

Looking in another direction, we have seen a number scam devices described in this book, and I want to address as well the proverbial 'little old lady' out there, who has a deal you will not want to miss. Now, not all of these are women; in fact, the majority of those I have seen are probably men, trying to foist a good scam on the recipients of their messages, as you will see in the messages below. Nonetheless, using a woman may seem more plausible to some, as we have already seen in the medical and 'poor widow' scams.

Take a look at the first one, from a person named 'Dofle Bernard', from the Republic of Benin, who claims to be an advisor to the former President of the Ivory Coast, now on trial at the International Court, the Hague, Netherlands.

> *Dearest one,*
> *With due respect, please permit me to inform you of my desire of going into partnership relationship with you, am also very sorry if i intrude your privacy.*
> *'am interesting to invest on your domain.*

I am very aware of so many scam messages going around and this is why i will be very careful in my statement to you.

I am not forcing you accept this proposal but simply make your choice and let me know what you decide.

My name is Dofle Bernard and I am currently leaving in neighboring country of Republic of Benin but i am a citizen of Ivory coast.

I work as an adviser to the former president of ivory coast who is currently on trial at International Court of Justice Hague, Netherlands.

I spent three years in United State of America before i came home to take appointment in government.

I do not want to explain much to you now until i receive your reply but my main reason why i contacted you is about some fund in-care of me.

The fund was deposited in my name in one of the prime bank in Europe which i will give you the full details when i receive you reply. I received a letter from the bank some months ago confirming me as the beneficiary of the fund.

All i want you to know is that this is not the kind of scam letter you usually received in your email box but a reality and i will like you to treat it as such, i know it will be very difficult for your to believe in me but just give me chance to proof myself to you.

I have all the documents relating to this transaction is with here.

All i want from you is how this fund will be transfer to any special account provide by you.

I will give you more details about myself and my family, also i will will give more details about the fund and how everything happened but i will have to wait for your reply to see if you are interesting in this transaction.

Expecting your reply as soon as possible.

Thanks.
Dofle Bernard

'Dofle Bernard' claims to have money—and will tell you how much when you reply to the e-mail sent (By the way, the e-mail address is <u>dofle_bernard@yahoo.com</u>) as you can see, another Yahoo account.

Dofle has been working his/her scams since at least 2008, and many of the early messages are in French. Bernard also has Facebook and Linked-in accounts, but they are basically empty — a normal occurrence with spammers who want to establish themselves, without giving out real information.

The second message is from a man in Rumania, who wants a 'trusted advisor' for an investment partnership, and so he writes to 'undisclosed recipients' to seek the best possible person (for his scam). I guess if I wanted to run a scam with a trusted advisor, I might look for an unknown quantity as well (just kidding here.)

> Hello,
>
> I am Morgan Solomon. I am seeking for investment opportunities and I need a trust worthy person/investor whom I can talk to on how to invest, why to invest, as well as sound financial planning advice.
>
> Basically, all I need is sincerity, authenticity, integrity protection, virtue, accountability and honor which bring trust in business. As you already know, nothing can undermine a business relationship more completely than lack of trust because trust is the essential precondition upon which all real success depends and the key to trust is action and commitments. Commitments made and commitments honored.
>
> Once you agree to this, we shall prepare an Equity Investment Agreement where we shall state the profit sharing pattern and all other conditions.
>
> Waiting for your response.
>
> Best Regards
>
> Morgan Solomon

If you want to respond to this message, simply tell Mister Solomon that you are an undisclosed recipient, who wants to be scammed. His e-mail is test@konsolavto.ru.

Here is another common scam message. 'Ruth Kokoma' wants help investing money she inherited from her husband, and you get 20% for your trouble. Not unlike a number of others currently making the rounds.

> MY DEAR FRIEND,
>
> I AM RUTH KOKOMA THE ONLY CHILD AND DAUGHTER OF LATE MR AND MRS HENRY KOKOMA,I KNOW YOU WILL BE SURPRISE TO GET THIS REQUEST MAIL FROM ME BUT IS IMPORTANT YOU READ AND TELL ME IF YOU CAN DO WHAT I STATED ON IT.
> THEREFORE CAN I INVEST $25 MILLION UNDER YOUR CARE IN YOUR COUNTRY?
> IF YOU ARE CAPABLE TO ASSIST ME INVEST AND CONTROL THIS FUND IF I HAND IT OVER TO YOU REPLY SWIFTLY AND 20% OF THE FUND WILL BE YOUR OWN FOR YOUR ASSISTANCE.
>
> GOD BLESS
> MISS.RUTH KOKOMA.
> EMAIL: ruthkokoma@ymail.com

One amazing thing about this message is the complete invisibility of the writer, given that she inherited over $25M US from her parents. You would expect some small inkling or reference, somewhere in the Internet about the Kokoma family, even if sparse. There is none. Stay away from this message, if you get it. There is no way to confirm the story as true.

One final message concerns those with convoluted stories, where the author wants you to believe that several actions have already been taken to bring the money to the US, but an unfortunate set of circumstances have occurred which require your help.

> From: Rita and Morooe Gamez
> Attn:
> Compliments of the day!
> I and my younger sister write to seek for your assistance; we got your contact from a noble gentleman that came to our refugee camp who came to give a seminar about AIDS whom we confronted that we

are looking a God-fearing person that is when your data was given to us.

First and foremost i want to introduce myself to you. My name is Morooe Gamez and my younger sister Rita Gamez a Sudanese,my consignment contains 12.5million United States dollars and some quantity of gold and Diamond, which I cannot specify.

The consignments are presently in States. The consignment gets to States through the help of a U.N diplomat Edward Ortiz. The fact is that Edward Ortiz is supposed to have delivered this consignment to a man called Smith Paggy in States. The week Edward Ortiz is suppose to deliver the consignment to him, when he got to States after clearing the consignment from the Airport, he call Smith Paggy to tell him the description to is house for the delivery, but is wife answered the call and told Edward Ortiz that her husband Smith Paggy hard a fatal car accident which lead to his death some few h ours later.Smith Paggy has already paid the demurrages from the security company,he paid for Bullion van that took the consignment to the airport and he paid for custom check report he also assisted us in getting the DRUG/ANTI - TERRIORIST CERTIFICATE, which is so expensive that he spent $25 Thousand dollars to acquire it, but unfortunately he died in a car accident, that was why Edward Ortiz has to deposit the consignment with a warehouse over there in States and called us to informed us about what is happening.

Please when you call him you will tell him that you are calling in respect of John Gamez's consignment that is in States.If Edward Ortiz asks if you have discussed with me tell him that you have discussed with me immediately.

Please, get to Edward Ortiz on time and get back to me through mail.

I await your urgent response. Thanks and God bless you.

Have you ever heard anything this foolish? Probably not, but I bet that a number of people replied to the Gamez pair, in the hopes of a big fortune.

These messages all tell a single story—there are a lot of people out there, who will wave large numbers before you, and hope you will bite. If they do, they get a sucker, information, and usually make some money for themselves, as they benefit from scamming you. Any personal message, particularly ones such as those above, and whose 'to:' address is 'undisclosed recipients', or something similar is a SCAM, and should be treated as such. Any legitimate offer would be more direct, and to you, from a source you know, or a context you are aware you have entered.

Chapter 8 Other Personal Claims

Personal appeals often take an approach that involve money, winnings, and helping people achieve their lofty goals. This appeal to wealth is the subject of the next e-mail, also recently received, which encapsulates some part of virtually every major scam ever used, including an attempt to capitalize on the fraud on the Internet.

People Dying

Let's return for another look at the 'I'm dying' scams, but from a different perspective. We saw briefly in the earlier messages how people seem to discover God and want to do a lot of good when they think they are dying, or, more correctly, when they want YOU to think they are dying.

Here the lady is claiming to be dying, but has a lot money ($10.5M US). She takes a different approach, and is certainly concerned with pleasing God, and she is knows the Internet is being abused with scams. Still, she feels that a message to my e-mail address is her only way to get to me (or anybody else, since, as usual, this is addressed to 'undisclosed recipients; at least she got that right). She wants to be sure I know that she has a lot of money to give before her soon-to-be untimely death. Her message makes the heart simply throb with sympathy.

> *Hello Dear,*
>
> *Though this medium internet has been greatly abused, but I chose to reach you through it because it still remains the fastest medium of communication .However, this correspondent is unofficial and private.*
>
> *Please give me this little chance to explain myself to you, I would have like to meet you face to face before departing from this mother earth but my illness continue to deprive the chance, but I know I am strong even if I die on the process of this operation I will still praise ALMIGHTY.*
>
> *My name is Mrs. Maria Mark I am a dying woman and i decided to donate what I have to you which is to be used to assist poor people*

and charity homes. I am 49 years old and I was diagnosed for cancer for about 2 years ago, immediately after the death of my husband, who has left me everything he worked for and because the doctors told me I will not live longer than some weeks because of my health, I decided to WILL/donate the sum of $10,500,000(Ten million five hundred thousand dollars) to you for the good work of the lord, and also to help the motherless and less privilege and also for the assistance of the widows in general.

I wish you all the best and may the good Lord bless you abundantly, and please use the funds well and always extend the good work to others should encase I did not survive this major operation I am about to go through now, but all I need now is prayers.

I will like you to Contact my lawyer for all the assistance you need to get this money transferred to you. (Bar William Johnson) with his specified contact and let him knows all I just said about this money, ($10,500,000.00) although he is aware of my intention. Please send him all the below information for easy communication.

Your full name
Your phone number
Your age
Your sex
Your identification proof
Your occupation
Your country and city.

NB: I will appreciate your utmost confidentiality and trust in this matter to accomplish my heart desire, as I don't want anything that will jeopardize my last wish. Always write me with below email address:

mariamark70@live.co.uk
Thanks.
From Mrs. Maria Mark

Several major elements of traditional scams appear evident here. Mrs. Mark is dying of cancer, her husband is also dead, she wants to please God before she dies, and she has a barrister to handle her affairs, if only you will contact him.

As I said, there is a lot of really heartbreaking information in this message. She wants to be sure you are the very person that she should give the money to, so she asks for a lot of personal information, including a 'proof of identification', whatever that might be, and she wants you to contact her 'bar' (sic) William Johnson, but doesn't tell you how to do so. All you have is the lady's e-mail address to a *live.com* address in England.

This is her last wish, but e-mail her back at your peril. You will soon find your information has been sold to others, your bank account may be gone, and your e-mail account is certainly full of similar scams for you to answer.

Before you go too far, though, there are some 'things' about Mrs. Mark you should know. She has been in the scamming business since at least 2006 (That's a long time beyond the two years dying of cancer she claims), and has a long string of similar messages, from several e-mail addresses around the world. Several of those documented include:

- mariamark70@freewilldonor.org,
- mariamark70@live.co.uk
- mariamark11@56788.com
- mariamark@56788.com
- mariamark545@yahoo.com

Several Internet sites have identified Mrs. Mark as Maria Mark Jones, AKA Diego Borja, another known scammer. Whoever writes the e-mail messages, they continue to arrive in mailboxes, and need to be avoided, deleted, identified as Spam, and as quickly as possible.

One last note, Mrs. Mark also seems to have a confederate, who claims to be her son, and who sent out one of his own messages in 2006, which I remembered I had in my archives, and have reproduced below.

FROM: DAVID AND MOTHER MRS MARIA MARK
13 RUE DE JARDIN PLATEAU
REPUBLIC DE COTE D'IVOIRE
SIEGE SOCIALE
IVOIRY COAST
ABIDJAN

WEST AFRICA

Dearest in the Lord,

My name is David Mark, the only son of Late Mr Browers Mark a nationality of Kuwait, who worked with Kuwait embassy in Ivory Coast fornine years before he died last year October 2005, He died after he waspoisoned by his wicked brothers, illness that lasted for long four days.Before his death he made some will to his fund do to my mothers cancer and stroke which has kept me and my mother miserable because my fathersbrothers after us to claim everything my fathers has since they havemade my mother a widow with paralysed stroke, because when my latefather was alive he deposited the sum of $5.5Million dollars with myname in one of good banks here in Cote d'Ivoire, Presently, this moneyis still with the bank. Recently my mother instructed me here in the hospital to source for travelling out since am 18yrs for now before she die do to enemies and that she can not survive her sickness which the Doctor has told us that she would not last for the next three months due to cancer problem and deadly stroke,

Having known all this condition my mother decided to donate this fund to church or better still a God fearing individual that will take care of me both in education and also utilize this money the way my mother is going to instruct here in, so we want a person or church that will use this fund to any missionary school I will attend, use some for orphanages, research centres and widows propagating the word of God and to ensure that the house of God is maintained. The Bible made us to understand that blessed is the hand that giveth. My mother took thisdecision because I have fully devoted to God and vowed to her that Iwill be a servant of God since my late father was killed because ignorance and evil in our family let vengeance be for God himself,

Since my fathers brothers and relatives are not God fearing and I don't want our family hard earned money to be misused by the wicked once. I don't want a situation where this money will be used in an ungodly manner. now my mother is lying critically ill here in the hospital, ideally need your advice and sincere help for her cure I don't want to loose my mother after all this painfull days, hence she has taking this bold decision's, am not afraid hence I know where she will go to if shdoesn't survive . I know that she will be going to the bosom of the Lord. Exodus 14 VS 14says that the lord will fight my case and I shall hold my peace. I want your telephone communication in this *regard because of my mothers health because of the presence of my family relatives around me always, I don't want any of my late fathers family relatives to receive this money. With God all things are possible,*

As soon as I receive your reply I shall give you the contact of the Finance/bank. we will also issue you a letter of authority and the **certificates** *which am the next of kin that will empower you as the new beneficiary of this fund. I want you and the church to always pray for our family because the lord is our shepherd. My happiness is that we live a life of a worthy Christian. Whoever that wants to serve the Lord must serve him in spirit and truth. Please always be prayerful all through your life. Any delay in your reply will give me haste insourcing for a church or a cincere individual for this same purpose, Please assure me that you will act accordingly as I stated here.Expecting hearing from you urgently with your contact information,*

NB!! you can reach us here in the hsopital through this number below,

PHONE CONTACT! 0022508165007
YAHOO EMAIL ID! davidmkdvine@yahoo.co.uk
Remain blessed in the name of the Lord.
David and mother Mrs Maria Mark
davidmark
davidmkdevine@jubii.dk

'Mrs. Lucy White' is another poor woman, dying of cancer, but wanting to make right before she passes away. She has $50M (Euro) to give you, if you will only share it with a worthwhile organization that does well, and, by the way, they have to be Christian and god-fearing.

Dear Beloved Friend.

Greetings in the name of Lord Jesus Christ, I am Mrs.Lucy White, a widow to late Dr.John White, a Christian suffering from long time cancer of the breast and have only six months, presently I am in a Hospital in Ghana taken my treatment. My late husband, was killed during the USA raid against terrorism in Afghanistan, he was very wealthy, and I inherited all his business and wealth after his death because during the period of our marriage we couldn't produce any child, so I decided to divide this wealth to churches in Africa, America, Asia and Europe and for humanity in general.

I am willing to donate the sum of Euro 50,500,000.00 million to you or if you have any organization to lend a hand in reaching out to the less privileged and the development of the gospel of our lord Jesus Christ. This fund is in presently in Bank Accredited Agent in HSBC BANK LONDON, in Europe that will move my fund to you for safe keeping custody. So upon your reply I will instruct my attorney to file in an application of Withdrawal of this fund to your favor from the Bank Accredited Agent with the HSBC BANK LONDON in Europe.

So please confirm these items as below if you are interested to assist:
1, your full name
2, your mailing address
3, your telephone and fax numbers.

On receipt of the confirmed items, I will forward it to my Attorney, so that some necessary changes will be made on the documents to enable you have claim to the Donation fund with the Bank Accredited Agent in Europe , but note that until this Donation of Euro 10,500,000.00 million is release to you, I will strongly insist that this transaction most be keep a top secret, as I wait your gentle and kind response.

God bless you and your family.
Mrs.Lucy White

Solicitors

As you have already seen in other e-mails throughout the book, the English-style 'solicitor' is so often the person writing the e-mail to the unsuspecting. Look at the one below, from England, and the set of circumstances provided in the message. It has a number of the clichés, such as we often mention as common in e-mail scams:

- Client died
- Rich person (Oil Magnate)
- Immediate family all gone with him
- Already tried to find legitimate living relatives
- Property will be considered abandoned
- Bank is trustee

- He wants to help you convince the bank you are an heir
- You get a percentage, and he gets the rest
- You can be assured by him that this is a legitimate deal the two of you are working

Of course, the e-mail is addressed, as expected, to 'undisclosed recipients', but then, Mister Austine Morris, the 'writer' only says that your name is 'close' to the spelling of the dead man. He wants to help you perfect the claim. I sent Mr. Morris a return message, using the name 'Recipient' as my last name, but unfortunately received no reply. Perhaps I had misspelled it from what he expected.

In all seriousness, what we have here, if you want to believe the story, is a solicitor, a lawyer, asking you to get involved in a scam on a bank which holds the funds of his late client. As we often see in these messages, the solicitor alleges that the client, and his family, all died in an auto crash. It would seem that a large number of auto crashes throughout the world involve very wealthy people, most of whom never seem to leave legitimate relatives.

In any case, read this message for yourself, and see what you think. Would you reply?

>AUSTINE MORRIS
>THE COUNTING HOUSE,
>53 TOOLEY STREET,
>LONDON BRIDGE CITY,
>LONDON, SE1 2QN

>Good day,

>This is a personal email directed to you and I request that it be treated as such. I am Austine Morris, a solicitor at law. I am the personal attorney/sole executor to the late Mr Norbert,hereinafter referred to as 'my client' who worked as an independent oil magnate in my country and who died in a car crash with his immediate family on the 4th of oct,2006. Since the death of my client in oct,2006, I have written several letters to the embassy with an intent to locate any of

his extended relatives whom shall be claimants/beneficiaries of his abandoned personal estate and all such efforts have been to no avail.

Moreso,I have received official letters in the last few weeks suggesting a likely proceeding for confiscation of his abandoned personal assets in line with existing laws by the bank in which my client deposited the sum of 4.8 million U.S.D.On this note i decided to search for a credible person and finding that you bear a similar last name, I decided to contact you, that I may, with your consent, present you to the "trustee" bank as my late client's surviving family member so as to enable you put up a claim to the bank in that capacity as a next of kin of my client. I find this possible for the fuller reasons that you bear a similar last name with my client making it a lot easier for you to put up a claim in that capacity. I propose that 35% of the net sum will accrue to you at the conclusion of this deal in so far as I do not incur further expenses.

Therefore, to facilitate the immediate transfer of this fund, you need, first to contact me via signifying your interest and as soon as I obtain your confidence, I will immediately appraise you with the complete details as well as fax you the documents, with which you are to proceed and i shall direct on how to put up an application to the bank. HOWEVER, you will have to assent to an express agreement which I will forward to you in order to bind us in this transaction.

Upon the reciept of your reply, I will send you by fax or E-mail the next step to take. I will not fail to bring to your notice that this proposal is hitch-free and that you should not entertain any fears as the required arrangements have been made for the completion of this transfer. Like I have implied, I require only a solemn confidentiality on this. I will like you to provide me immediately with your full names and address direct telephone number is very much needed to enable us have heart to heart discussion.

Best regards,
Austine Morris

Mister Morris, a more recent entrant to the scamming biz, at least under that name, claims to be from London, England. He uses two e-mail addresses for his schemes, *austinemorris24@yahoo.com*, and another registered with the Philippine subsidiary of *Yahoo. Com* in the Philippines, *austinemorris78@yahoo.com.ph*. A new guy on the net, but expect to see more from him.

Here is another similar e-mail, this time from a 'lawyer' in Libya, who will tell you he used to work for an associate of Muammar Gaddafi, the late tyrant of that country. Now living in Burkina Faso, Mister Hall claims to have a lot of money which he wants to send to you as quickly as possible. Read, and enjoy.

From Mr.John Hall.
Ouagadougou,
Burkina Faso.

Dear Friend,

Good day to you. I am Mr.John Hall a lawyer and personal confidant to Abdullah Senussi who was the intelligence chief of Colonel Muammar Gaddafi. I need your urgent assistance in transferring the sum of ($39.5) million to your account within 14 banking days from a bank in Burkina Faso. This money belongs to my master Abdullah Senussi and was deposited in the bank on the name of his son. The urgent need for the transfer of this fund is to avoid confiscation by the Libyan government as they quest the seizure of every related assets belonging to Late Colonel Muammar Gaddafi and his aides. I am contacting you in a good faith so that the bank will release the money to you for safe keeping/investments till the release of my master who is now in custody.

So if you are capable of receiving this huge amount of money, let me have a positive response from you via return mail for more personal discussions on how we are going to go about it.

Best.Regards,
Mr.John Hall.

John Hall is another customer of Yahoo.com, using the e-mail address of *john_hall00@yahoo.com*. He also is known through this e-mail, *pandian_sp2004@yahoo.co.in*, an address from the Indian subsidiary of Yahoo. There are probably others as well. All of the messages seen to date, including at least one on a Yahoo group site, carry the same message.

To show that no subject is unfit for spam, here is an interesting one concerning a dairy farm:

> Dear friend,
>
> Sorry for contacting you on this manner, I am Mrs. Abir Joyce, from United Kingdom, i wish to inform you that my company have outline for mutual and furtherance investment of Diary Milk Farm,real estate in buildings, hotel and to erect ultramodern hospital in your country and we are looking for an investment manager in your country who will direct us concerning the yielding details for the investment, we contacted you because we know that you are capable of handling this. We are ready to invest in your country and we urge you to get back to us as soon as you read this message. We will give you the full details immediately we get your reply.
>
> For fast response to your email .kindly reply to the below email *abirjoyce1@rediffmail.com* *fxdepartment@inmail24.com*
>
> Thanks,
> Mrs Abir Joyce

Mrs. Joyce uses an interesting ISP, 'rediffmail.com'. We found them too, and the 'ALERT' below tells you about them as an ISP.

ALERT: Rediffmail.com is an ISP from INDIA, which has an extensive 'Terms of Use' agreement that subscribers to their free service are supposed to follow, including not putting scams online. This is the only message of its type I have found from them. They say in their agreement, "Rediff.com is under no obligation to monitor or review the user contributed content. Rediff.com assumes no responsibility for the content, no obligation to modify or remove any inappropriate messages/content and no responsibility for the conduct of any user of this service."

Using Rediffmail.com fits in with what I have been able to find out about Mrs. Joyce. Some of her first e-mail message came from Nepal, and are documented on various Internet blog sites, and she eventually expanded her message circle late in 2012, when she started targeting the US and Europe.

Mrs. Joyce has several e-mail addresses, although the two in her message to me are the most common. Her other e-mail address is registered to yet another of the 'free' services, inmail.com, and we are able to provide some information on that vendor as well, in the alert box which follows.

> **ALERT:** Inmail24.com is another free internet e-mail service that has few rules, and not a great reputation for removing those who put out their spam to the world.
> Look at what you get with Inmail24:
> • Your mailbox is **accessible** from anywhere on the Internet, not just your own computer. Travelling abroad? As long as you have Internet access, you have access to **Zoner inMail24**.
> • Your mailbox name is **unchanging and valid forever** no matter what Internet provider you choose.
> • You can **forward** incoming messages to a different email address.
> • You can add any number of **attachments** to the messages you send.
> • **Zoner inMail24** supports all European **accent marks**. If you can write it, you can send it through Zoner inMail24.
> • **Zoner inMail24** is completely **free** and there are no conditions on its use.
> [From their web page]

The next message is much more direct in its approach. It involves an 'advocate' from Malaysia, a person similar in function to a solicitor, just like the others, but it is more direct, has a lot of money involved, and doesn't initially ask to do anything but contact 'Advocate Thomas Phillips'.

These messages are dangerous because they seem more real, and less possibly a scam, than those which offer immediate gratification, if only you will send all the information on your personal identity. There is still the nagging question, though, how the 'advocate' will determine that, the person receiving the e-mail 'undisclosed recipient' is the true beneficiary of the legacy.

>THOMAS PHILIP LAW CHAMBERS
>LEGAL SOLICITORS/PRIVATE
>56 JALAN RAJA CHULAN
>KUALA LUMPUR MALAYSIA
>
>Dear Sir/Madam,
>
>My name is Advocate Thomas Philip (Esq). A personal attorney to my late client Mr. Ronald Owen who worked with an oil firm here in Malaysia, Mr. Ronald Owen a well known Philanthropist, before he died, he made a WILL in my law firm stating that US$17,000,000.00 (Seven Million U.S. Dollars) only should be donated to any Philanthropist of our choice outside Malaysia (Overseas).
>
>It is my utmost desire to execute the WILL of my late client. You are required to contact me immediately to start the process of transferring this money to any of your designated official bank account. I urge you to contact me immediately for further details bearing in mind that the Bank has given us a date limit.
>
>Please contact me urgently for reply to this message immediately stating your details.
>
>CONGRATULATIONS ONCE AGAIN.
>
>Regards
>Advocate Thomas Philip
>Attorney-at-Law

One final solicitor/barrister letter is the one from 'Barrister Melvin Casey' from London, England. He says he represents Mr. Ronald Stewart, who left a great deal of money ($8M US) that is to be divided 30% to you, 30% to a charity of your choice in Africa, and $40% to Barrister Casey for his efforts.

While lawyers are known for requiring large fees, I believe, as you read the message which follows, you also will realize this is a major rip-off—of you. Enjoy!

> BARRISTER MELVIN CASEY'S LAW CHAMBERS
> LEGAL PRACTITIONERS AND PRIVATE LAWYER
> 111 CRAVEN HILL GARDEN
> LONDON, W1F 8GJ
> UNITED KINGDOM
> LATE MR. RONALD STEWART'S PHILANTHROPIC FUND
> Attn: Sir/Ma,
> My name is Barrister Melvin Casey; I am a native of England, and president in the Chambers Melvin Casey Law Chambers here in London United Kingdom. I am a legal practitioner, called to the U.K Bar in 1986. I used to be the personal Attorney to late Mr. Ronald Stewart.
> Mr. Ronald Stewart was a great philanthropist before death; before he died, he made a philanthropic will of Eight Million Dollars (US$8,000,000.00) which was meant to be donated to charity organizations in Africa to support African children living with HIV/AIDS.
>
> We conducted an electronic email random draw in our chambers today, and your email address was picked as the beneficiary to this philanthropic fund of $8m.
> It is our great desire to claim this fund so that it can be used for the purpose for which it is meant, because the bank where the money is currently deposited has instructed that we produce the beneficiary of this fund within 14 working days else the money will be confiscated to the Government's treasury as unclaimed funds.
> You have to get back to me immediately so that we can begin the process of transferring the fund into any of your designated bank accounts. As soon as I receive your reply message I shall give you further information on the process.
> With your full co-operation, this transaction shall be concluded within 7 days, and after the funds have been transferred into your account, you shall keep 30% of the money ($2.4m) to yourself as the beneficiary, donate 30% to any Charity Organization of your

choice, while the balance of 40% comes to me as the attorney in this transaction.

Also, this transaction is highly confidential and should remain as such until the funds must have been transferred into your account, so do not discuss this transaction with ANYBODY.

I wait to hear back from you immediately, so that I can give you all the necessary information needed to proceed, and don't forget to include your name, location and phone numbers in your response.

Regards,

Barrister Melvin Casey(Esq.)

Copyright ? 2013 Melvin Casey Law Chambers, all rights reserved.

If you do respond to 'Barrister Casey', you will responding to a 'Yahoo.com' subsidiary address in the Philippines, hardly the place for an established English barrister to be maintaining an e-mail account for his business. You can also note in his message how he wants you to carefully refrain from telling anyone else about this. In fact, the message subject line is 'Urgent and Important', while it is addressed to the usual 'undisclosed recipients.' BEWARE!

Indirect Claims

While we have been seeing solicitors for many years, more recently, the tide has turned a bit toward 'investment counselors' of many stripes. The message that follows is from a scammer impersonating as one of these counselors (or perhaps not, since his job is to raise money for his client, even if that client wants him to scam for them).

This guy covers a lot of ground. He is a Frenchman, based, he says, in the United States and the United Kingdom, who is a financial consultant for a client in England. The 'client' is from the United Arab Emirates (UAE), and has deposited a large sum ($8M (US)) in an investment company in Spain. Oh, and she is now on her sickbed.

Read the message, and you too will probably be amazed at diversity of the scam. The message, by the way, is addressed, as usual, to 'undisclosed recipients'.

> Dear Sir/Madam
> I am Brian Edmond (French National),a Financial consultant (Brian Ed Nation-wide Financial Consultant)based in UNITED KINGDOM/AMERICA
>
> .I have a client here in England (a widow, from United Arab Emirate 78yrs old, and on sick bed now) who deposited the sum of Eight Million United State Dollars ($8,000,000.00 USD) with a private Equity Investment Trust Company in Spain for safekeeping and Future Investment. This fund was realized from the business of Petroleum And Natural Gas Export.
>
> My client is now seriously looking for a trustworthy and business idealistic person whom she can invest with the fund in trust. She wishes to invest the fund in your country's economy and Her interest is in individual/companies with potentials for rapid growth in long terms.
>
> This fund could be delivered to you cash in your country if you wish. So i went through your internet products companies and got your contact, then decides to contact you for this investment purposes My client is interested in placing her fund in your company in your country or any other company that you may assist her in, if your Company/country`s bi-laws allows such foreign investment. if you are interested in this proposal, send me
>
> (1) YOUR FULL NAME,
> (2) YOUR CONTACT ADDRESS,
> (3) YOUR AGE AND OCCUPATION,
> (4) THE NAME OF YOUR COMPANY (IF ANY),
> (5) YOUR IDENTIFICATION/INT'L PASSPORT,(6) (6)YOUR PRIVATE HOUSE PHONE AND MOBILE NUMBERS.
> You can contact me for more details via my E-mail address:
> Yours faithfully,
> Edmond Brian

Mister Brian (Or is it Mister Edmond, the message has it both ways) has managed to keep himself well below the radar, too far, in fact, to have the clients and the reputation he claims.

One thing I always tell people who receive this type of message is to go to the search engines, and see what they find. In the vast majority of cases, somebody has already reported on the illegitimacy of the message writer making the claims. In other cases, you come upon a person with impeccable credentials, well-known and respected in their country, and advertising their business or trade openly, and above board.

When you come upon this type of person, you really have to ask yourself a key question before you respond. Would a person, with the kind of reputation the person seems to have, be conducting business in this way, especially asking you to participate in something illegal in most countries?

If the answer you get to that question is NO, then what you probably have is someone using the name for their own purposes, and to include you in their scam, possibly to harm you as well. It's always better to err on the side of caution, especially where there are seemingly large amounts of money being discussed, since invariably the money doesn't exist, and you are the real target.

Non-Existent Follow-up Claims

There are those out in the Ethernet world who will never give up their scamming efforts. Most simply send their messages, change the message content, their names, and e-mail addresses, and push right on to find enough gullible people who will bite on their schemes. It takes a lot of hard work to be a successful scammer, and they know it.

There are others, however, who try to cut corners in the process. These people claim to be following up on previous messages, which no one seems to be able to find in their archives. In fairness, most people look over their e-mails, and delete those that are not important to them at that moment. So many messages bombard the internet these days that keeping every message makes any internet e-mail service run incredibly slow over time, and causes whatever storage limit to be exceeded quickly.

Many who have received the type of messages which follow, often, so they tell me, scratch their head to try and remember a similar, previous message. Usually they cannot, and for a good reason—they never received any 'previous message' from the writer.

These messages still have the money angle, and the God angle, and the large dollar amounts to offer you as encouragement to respond to them. These people often go a step further, however, and suggest they are trying to do the 'humane thing', as you will see below, by giving you a lot of money, and generally through a cleric in Nigeria, who they want you to believe is very trustworthy.

Mrs. Sophia Jacob's message below is a good example of this type of scam. She would like you to believe that she has corresponded with you before, tried to give you some of her money, and somehow the scam both of you were working fell through, for a considerable time. Thus, you might not remember her, she alludes, but she hopes you will forgive here, and take $850K US for your trouble.

She has asked a friend, Reverend Attmash Josan to help her, since she is occupied in China, and cannot help you directly. Now having the Reverend Josan in the picture certainly makes it a better deal. Who could possibly thing a cleric would scam you? He even has a web address, through 'saintly.com' that should somehow reassure you that everything will go according to plan.

Yes, this is another variant of the original 'Nigeria 419 Scam', but it does a much better job of getting to a person's heart, and making them want to help this person out of the kindness of their heart. Everything will go according to their plan, if you respond, send them the required information, and then just wait for your 'cheque'.

My Dear Friend,

I am happy to inform you about my success in getting those funds transferred under the co-operation of a new partner, Mr. Abdullah Bin Hamad Al-Attiyah, The Deputy Prime Minister of Energy and

Industry Qatar Petroleum. Although you might find it difficult to remember me, since it has indeed been a very long time. However, I am much elated and privileged to contact you again after this long time.

While it takes faith and courage to remember old friends and at the same time, to show gratitude to them in spite of circumstances that may have disrupted our transaction ultimately not to work out as we projected.

Nevertheless, I take this liberty to inform you that, the transaction we were pursuing then together, finally worked out by the infinite mercy of God Almighty and I've decided to contact you, just to let you know the present situation.

I must inform you also that I am presently in China for business negotiations and establishment, and, with a sincere heart, I have issued a cheque to the tune of US$985,000.00 in your name as COMPENSATION for your dedication and humane contribution as it were.

Reverend Attmash Josan is the only person I instructed on how to deliver the check to you. Therefore, I implore you to contact him immediately you read this message for the collection of your cheque, for I have conscience as a human being, and I really appreciated your tremendous effort and contribution made to make things work out but which we couldn't complete due to circumstances beyond our control.

I want you to accept this token with good faith as this is from the bottom of my heart. Get in touch with Reverend Attmash Josan for the collection of your cheque.

1: Name: Reverend Father Attmash Josan (of Roman Catholic Church, Nigeria)

2: E-mail Address: *revattmashjosan@saintly.com*

Note: He is waiting to hear from you for the collection of your Cheque.

Take note and bear in mind that the cheque has a validity period of 30 banking days as such it is expedient you contact him and thus have modality put in place to conclude this arrangement in the earliest possible time.

Yours Sincerely,
Mrs. Sophia Jacob
Principal partnership with QP.
http://www.qp.com.qa

NOTE: *Do not reply to me, rather you are to contact Reverend Attmash Josan through e-mail Address: revattmashjosan@saintly.com*

> **ALERT:** Saintly.com is a trademark of World Media Group LLC, and a free, un-monitored e-mail ISP. It has no apparent connection to any religious

> **ALERT:** QP.COM.QA is the e-mail server for Qatar Petroleum, and, although the name is false, the webmail domain is real.

Using a real website domain, such as that for Qatar Petroleum, adds some level of validity to the claims made by Mrs. Jacob. However, re-directing the reply to another domain is perhaps one of the most common indicators of a fraudulent message. If the person can actually (and legally) produce what they claim, there would be no need to route someone through another person, or another site. Caution is the watchword here.

Outright Theft

Sometimes the e-mail scam is simply a matter of trying to cajole you into working an outright theft, with part of the processed 'loot' going to the scammer, as in the next message. There are two principles of scamming worth noting here;

- No scammer is going to make things work for you at their expense;
- They always get the money, not you.

Taking those two principles into account, why would any reasonable person want to answer this e-mail? The only possible results is to get themselves involved in what cannot be a winning situation for anyone but the scammer. If you do want to get involved, then write to *esmereldaevitove17@yahoo.com*, and get what is coming to you.

Let's go to a specific example of what I mean by this heading. 'Mr. Mahama' is a bank branch manager of a bank not named in the text, who indicates he has stolen money earned by the bank, which he moved to another account, one which the bank supposedly knows nothing about. He wants you to share in his theft. All he needs is information, and a response from you, to get the ball rolling. Of course, he cannot be directly involved in the theft, so you will be the fall guy.

This e-mail message originated in China, from a Yahoo subsidiary (yahoo.cn). There seem to be increasing numbers of these scams coming out of Internet providers over there. Nonetheless, enjoy the message, for what it is worth. You too could be one of the 'undisclosed recipients'.

Dear Friend,

My Name is Mr.Simeon.K.Mahama,I am the General Manager of A BANK BRANCH with a business.

It may interest you to hear that I am a man of PEACE and don't want problems, I only hope we can assist each other. If you don't want this business offer kindly forget it as I will not contact you again.

I have packaged a financial transaction that will benefit both of us, as the General Manager, Finance and Administration of the BRANCH; it is my duty to send in a financial report to my head office at the end of each year. On the course of the last year 2012 end of year report, I discovered that my branch made Ten million Seven hundred and fifty thousand dollars (US$10,750.000.00) which my head office are not aware of and will never be aware of. I have since placed this fund on what we call SUSPENSE ACCOUNT without any beneficiary.

As an officer of the bank I can not be directly connected to this money, so this informed my contacting you for us to work so that you can assist to receive this money into your bank account for us to SHARE, While you will have 30% of the total fund. Note there are practically no risk involved, it will be bank to bank transfer, all I need from you is to stand claim as the original depositor of this fund who made the deposit with our branch so that my Head office can order the transfer to your designated bank account.

If you accept this offer to work with me, I will appreciate it very much. As soon as I receive your response I will detail you on how we can achieve it successfully.

Please indicate your genuine willingness and your urgent response.

Send me your information such as:

Your full name:
Age:
Direct mobile number:
Address:
Occupation:
Nationality:

Best regards,
Simeon.K.Mahama

NOTE: *In the scams we have covered so far, you can see there are many e-mail providers who willingly, or unwittingly, abet the explosion of this type of theft. In particular, and probably due to its size, and global reach, Yahoo.com, and its subsidiaries seem to be the largest offenders. In deference to Yahoo, they will remove a registration if they find that this type of scamming, and phishing is taking place on their servers. What you have to do to get that to happen is COMPLAIN, and loudly, when you get these messages.*

Another, more recent scam involves an e-mail titled 'Can you be trusted?', where the writer wants you to participate in a scheme to transfer over $4M British Pounds to your account, with later 'settling up' between the two of you. This is an interesting read.

I am Mr.John Browns (Financial Broker & Finance Risk Control Officer)10 Sandalwood Drive, Ruislip - Middx HA4 7JT, UNITED KINGDOM,

RE- FUND TRANSFER MATTER,

Are you a business minded person, can you uphold financial transaction with utmost secrecy, sincerity and seriousness? Your ability to respond and co-operate with me, will be the beginning of more good financial deals between us. I work in the Finance Risk control/Accounts Broker Unit of a prestigious bank in the United Kingdom. I have the official duty to process and release unclaimed funds to the relatives of persons who have died without placing will/testament on their monetary assets. Recently, there are multiple funds floating in the bank treasury, these funds are what I want to shift/transfer to your account for your benefit and mine.

Can you be trusted? However, as soon as you give me a reply and we conclude necessary talks; the sum of £4,000,000.00(GBP) shall be transferred to your bank account immediately. The transfer of funds to your account shall be lawfully executed in respect to the wire regulatory ethics guiding the transfer of huge fund from one country to another.

Besides, we can achieve this success of fund transfer within 5 bank working days. Due to the confidential nature of this financial deal, please indicate your interest by simply replying to this email address: (john_browns@rocketmail.com)

I anticipate your urgent response to this financial matter, thank you.

Sincerely,
Mr.John Browns.

Widows of Dead Executed Patriots

It is always a shame to hear of someone killed by whoever took over some foreign government. It happens all the time in the African Republics, and people soon take advantage of the names of the dead to form their own scams to get either your information, your money, or both.

The message below is from a Mrs. Victoria Konan, widow of an engineer formerly working for Ivory Coast Government, now dead, after one dictatorship was replaced with another. She will soon die herself, and she wants you to have her money to put it to good use, and God bless you for it.

> Dearest One,
>
> May this mail find you well.
> My name is Victoria Konan 74yrs of age, retired process Engineer (RPE).
> I am a widow being that I lost my husband 8yrs ago.
> I have lived in a world of uncertainty before taking this bold decission to approach a complete stranger who will not take advantage of my naivety.
> My husband was a serving director of the Cocoa exporting board until his death. He was assassinated by the rebels leader following the political uprising in Cote D'Ivoire.
> Before his death he had an outlet foreign account in a bank here Cộte dʃIvoire up to the tune of USD$9,000.000.00, Nine Million united state dollars which he told the bank was for the importation of cocoa processing machine. Having known my condition, I have decided to donate this fund for charity and humanitarian purpose with help of a God fearing person.
> I know that I am going to be in the bosom of the Lord Exodus 14 VS 14.
> Please indicate your interest by replying soonest.
>
> God bless,
> Mrs. Victoria Konan

As usual, all does not meet the eye here. First, the message return address is listed an e-mail service in Hungary (Victoria.konan@mailbox.hu), however, if you decide to reply, the message is actually going to Victoria_konan@mail2world.com, a free e-mail service hosted by a firm in Los Angeles, CA (USA). Her other e-mail addresses include victoria_konan74@mkc-net.ru (A Rumanian service), victoria_konan@yahoo.com (Of course, it seems virtually anyone can get a Yahoo address). Mrs. Konan, or whatever her name actually may be, is well known on the 'Nigerian 419' circuit. Enjoy the message, just don't respond, unless you are truly adventurous.

Part Three — Using Organizations as Cover - U. S. Organizations

Now we begin a more specific journey, one that takes us into the inner workings of the spammer, and why he or she chooses to target to emulate for their spams. We start in this part with the US organizations, and then move on in the next part to the foreign organizations.

One thing is common between these parts; spammers love to use the names and organizations of very prominent individuals, much as we saw earlier with former dictators. Now, we will see US agency heads, and other prominent figures; some of whose titles and organizations are horribly mangled by people who do not know or understand the working of these Federal agencies.

In this volume, we will concentrate first, in Chapter 9, on three major federal agencies; the Federal Bureau of Investigation (FBI), the Department of Homeland Security (DHS), and the Department of Treasury (DOT), all of whom have been used in so many ways in these e-mail scams.

In Chapter 10, we show banks, social organizations, and US corporations, particularly the Microsoft Corporation, as examples of how these scams pervade even the private market in the US.

You should enjoy reading the messages which follow.

Chapter 9 U. S. Federal Departments & Agencies

US organizations are often the brunt of these international e-mail scams. Using governmental-sounding organizations, Federal agencies, and the names of large banks lends credence to the scam, and makes people a bit wary of simply deleting the message.

What makes many of these e-mails suspect is often the amount of information contained in the message. Most of the scams are not satisfied with using one agency as their source of authenticity; rather, they link several, which often makes the whole message seem overwhelming, and eventually ridiculous.

Let's start the discussion with the one agency that seems to lead the list, the Federal Bureau of Investigation (FBI).

The Federal Bureau of Investigation

What better way to create a scam scenario than to use a Government agency, particularly the one with the most charisma; the one which maintains the 'Ten Most Wanted' list, and has been the subject of countless crime-busting books and films, over many years. In some ways, it is truly amazing that in the e-mail scam world, not only is the FBI not immune from these pranksters, those who would be prosecuted by that agency seem to delight in using it for their scams.

In organizing this section, I have tried to show how the scammers use the large number of divisions, teams, and bureaus, within the FBI as their basis, some of which may not even exist. Most of the messages you will see are complex; not the proverbial 'little old lady' asking you to contact her to discuss an inheritance. What you will see instead is often a well-thought out message with a complex scenario. Most are longer than you would expect, but make good reading, even if you do see them as scams right from the beginning.

The first message is a good example of how these scams work. First, they establish the FBI as the agency that really wants to solve a problem—your problem, and make things right for you. Can anyone remember when the FBI has ever been a party to that kind of beneficial action? Probably not.

Then, the scam artist, to really make this message seem to be important, often cites the United Nations and INTERPOL as partners in the effort. Together, these agencies are going make right what the corrupt officials in Nigeria (heard from them again!) or other countries have tried to do in the past with their swindles. So, let's head off, first, to the 'Anti-terrorism and Monitary (sic) Crime Division' for our message. (NB: Please remember that I said early on that I have left the messages exactly as provided to me – including spelling and grammar, before you jump all over me for misspelling 'monitary'. There is no such division in the FBI)

Anti-Terrorism and Monitory Crime Division

Setting the scene for you, the writer wants you to understand that there has been a series of meetings between the FBI, The United Nations (UN), and something called the 'National Central Bureau of Interpol', which resulted in the President of Nigeria being directed to issue you a check for any lottery winning, inheritance, or gambling winnings that may previously been denied you by that country. An interesting thought.

For clarity here, the National Central Bureau of Interpol is that part of the INTERPOL operation in a particular country. There is a Bureau in Washington DC, managed by the US Department of Justice. The INTERPOL Washington website describes themselves as:

> *"INTERPOL Washington, the United States National Central Bureau, serves as the designated representative to the International Criminal Police Organization (INTERPOL) on behalf of the Attorney General. INTERPOL Washington is the official U.S. point of contact in INTERPOL's worldwide, police-to-police communications and criminal intelligence network.*
>
> *A component of the U.S. Department of Justice (DOJ), INTERPOL Washington is co-managed by the U.S. Department of Homeland Security (DHS) pursuant to a Memorandum of Understanding that ensures a continuing commitment to the*

guidance and oversight of the organization and reinforces its role in effectively sharing and exchanging international criminal investigative and humanitarian assistance information."[4]

One more thing before we go to the message. In some ways, the interesting part of the message below is its payment method; money to an ATM card, which can be used to get $5K per day up to $850K, the amount for which you were swindled. That amounts to 177 days of effort to get your money, if you try to collect every day. Of course, as you will see, there is a small fee for your effort.

[NOTE: Appendix B has a recent advisory from the IRS on these types of scams. That advisory and descriptions of other found on the IRS Website can be found there.]

Here's the message, as it arrived in my inbox.

Federal Bureau of Investigation (FBI)
Anti-Terrorist And Monitory Crime Division.
Federal Bureau Of Investigation.
J.Edgar.Hoover Building Washington Dc
Customers Service Hours / Monday To Saturday Office Hours Monday to Saturday:
Dear Beneficiary,

Series of meetings have been held over the past 7 months with the secretary general of the United Nations Organization. This ended 3 days ago. It is obvious that you have not received your fund which is to the tune of $850,000.00 due to past corrupt Governmental Officials who almost held the fund to themselves for their selfish reason and some individuals who have taken advantage of your fund all in an attempt to swindle your fund which has led to so many losses from your end and unnecessary delay in the receipt of your fund.

The National Central Bureau of Interpol enhanced by the United Nations and Federal Bureau of Investigation have successfully passed a mandate to the current president of Nigeria his Excellency President Good

---

[4] INTERPOL Washington, United States Department of Justice, Washington DC. Retrieved from: http://www.justice.gov/interpol-washington/about.html

luck Jonathan to boost the exercise of clearing all foreign debts owed to you and other individuals and organizations who have been found not to have receive their Contract Sum, Lottery/Gambling, Inheritance and the likes. Now how would you like to receive your payment? Because we have two method of payment which is by Check or by ATM card?

ATM Card: We will be issuing you a custom pin based ATM card which you will use to withdraw up to $5,000 per day from any ATM machine and the card have to be renewed in 4 years time which is 2016. Also with the ATM card you will be able to transfer your funds to your local bank account. The ATM card comes with a handbook or manual to enlighten you about how to use it. Even if you do not have a bank account.

Check: To be deposited in your bank for it to be cleared within three working days. Your payment would be sent to you via any of your preferred option and would be mailed to you via TNT parcel Service. Because we have signed a contract with TNT which should expire by October 16TH,2012 you will only need to pay $250 instead of $440 saving you $190 So if you pay before October 16TH,2012, you save $190 Take note that anyone asking you for some kind of money above the usual fee is definitely a fraudsters and you will have to stop communication with every other person if you have been in contact with any. Also remember that all you will ever have to spend is $250.00 nothing more!

Nothing less! And we guarantee the receipt of your fund to be successfully delivered to you within the next 48hrs after the receipt of payment has been confirmed.

Note: Everything has been taken care of by the Federal Government of Nigeria, The United Nation and also the FBI and including taxes, custom paper and clearance duty so all you will ever need to pay is $250.

DO NOT SEND MONEY TO ANYONE UNTIL YOU READ THIS: The actual fees for shipping your ATM card is $440 but because TNT parcel Service have temporarily discontinued the C.O.D which gives you the chance to pay when package is delivered for international shipping We had to sign contract with them for bulk shipping which makes the fees reduce from the actual fee of $440 to $250 nothing more and no hidden fees of any sort!

To effect the release of your fund valued at $850,000.00 you are advised to contact our correspondent in Africa the delivery officer Mr.Michael Kingston with the information below,

Email: michaelkingston@qq.com
Tel.Number: +23481 7646 6438

You are advised to contact him with the information as stated below:

Your full Name............
Your Address:.............
Home/Cell Phone:.............
Preferred Payment Method (ATM / Cashier Check)

Upon receipt of payment the delivery officer will ensure that your package is sent within 48 working hours. Because we are so sure of everything we are giving you a 100% money back guarantee if you do not receive payment/package within the next 48hrs after you have made the payment for shipping.

Yours Sincerely,
Mr. JAMES POWELL
FEDERAL BUREAU OF INVESTIGATION
UNITED STATES DEPARTMENT OF JUSTICE
WASHINGTON, D.C. 20535

Note: All correspondences and Questions should be directed to Mr.Michael Kingston and Do disregard any email you get from any impostors or offices claiming to be in possession of your ATM CARD, you are hereby advice only to be in contact with Mr.Michael Kingston of the ATM CARD CENTRE who is the rightful person to deal with in regards to your ATM CARD PAYMENT and forward any emails you get from impostors to this office so we could act upon and commence investigation.

So, having read the message, are you ready to jump in and claim your money. All you have to do is contact 'Mr. Kingston' to get it. It will only cost $250 US, and that is a discount from the normal price for the ATM card, all taxes and other fees paid by the FBI.

Believable?

Probably not.

Clearly, from much of the sentence construction and spelling, this message is another one of those written by a foreigner, who clearly understood what he/she wanted to say in his own language, but then had the message translated into English for transmission to US targets. It should be completely clear, by the end of the message, if you read that far, that this message could not possibly be real. Investigative agencies do not require you to get an ATM card; pay your fees, or work through a private intermediary to get your money. Stay clear of this type of message.

One word, as well on Mister Michael Kingston. This man is known on the various scammer blogs, and has been peddling the current message since at least early 2012. His two e-mail addresses, *michaelkingston@qq.com* and *jamespowell@qq.com*, are fronts for his current operation. Little more is known, but there was a person using the same name, also peddling a form of the Nigerian 419 scam, operating out of London and Lagos, Nigeria, several years ago.

> ALERT: qq.com is another of the free, unmonitored e-mail ISP sites, and is used frequently by a number of the perpetrators of scams and phishing in Europe and Africa.

A more recent version of this message has come out, this time from a Mr. Nicholas Story, of the same FBI Division, the money has increased to over $8M (US), and the fees have changed. This time, please reply to 'Barrister David Johnson.'

Federal Bureau of Investigation . (FBI)
Anti-Terrorist And Monitory Crime Division.
Federal Bureau Of Investigation.
J.Edgar.Hoover Building Washington Dc
Customers Service Hours / Monday To Saturday Office Hours Monday to Saturday:

Dear Sir/Madam ,

Series of meetings have been held over the past 7 months with the secretary general of the United Nations Organization. This ended 3 days ago. It is obvious that you have not received your fund which is to the tune of $8.5 USD million due to past corrupt Governmental Officials who almost held the fund to themselves for their selfish reason and some individuals who have taken advantage of your fund all in an attempt to swindle your fund which has led to so many losses from your end and unnecessary delay in the receipt of your fund.

The National Central Bureau of Interpol enhanced by the United Nations and Federal Bureau of Investigation have successfully passed a mandate to the current president of Nigeria his Excellency President Good luck Jonathan to boost the exercise of clearing all foreign debts owed to you and other individuals and organizations who have been found not to have receive their Contract Sum, Lottery/Gambling, Inheritance and the likes. Now how would you like to receive your payment? Because we have two method of payment which is by Check or by ATM card?

ATM Card: We will be issuing you a custom pin based ATM card which you will use to withdraw up to $3,000 per day from any ATM machine that has the Master Card Logo on it and the card have to be renewed in 4 year's time which is 2016. Also with the ATM card you will be able to transfer your funds to your local bank account. The ATM card comes with a handbook or manual to enlighten you about how to use it. Even if you do not have a bank account.

Check: To be deposited in your bank for it to be cleared within three working days. Your payment would be sent to you via any of your preferred option and would be mailed to you via UPS. Because we have signed a contract with UPS which should expire in next three weeks you will only need to pay $200 instead of $450 saving you $250 So if you pay before the three weeks you save $250 Take note that anyone asking you for some kind of money above the usual fee is definitely a fraudsters and you will have to stop communication with every other person if you have been in contact with any. Also remember that all you will ever have to spend is $200.00 nothing more! Nothing less! And we guarantee the receipt of your fund to be successfully delivered to you within the next 24hrs after the receipt of payment has been confirmed.

Note: Everything has been taken care of by the Federal Government of Nigeria, The United Nation and also the FBI and including taxes, custom paper and clearance duty so all you will ever need to pay is $200 for shipping.

DO NOT SEND MONEY TO ANYONE UNTIL YOU READ THIS: The actual fees for shipping your ATM card is $450 but because UPS have temporarily discontinued the C.O.D which gives you the chance to pay when package is delivered for international shipping We had to sign contract with them for bulk shipping which makes the fees reduce from the actual fee of $450 to $200 nothing more and no hidden fees of any sort!

To effect the release of your fund valued at $8.5 USD million you are advised to contact our correspondent in Africa the delivery officer Barrister David Johnson with the information below,

CONTACT PERSON: Barrister David Johnson
CONTACT ADDRESS: *barristerdavidjohnson@yahoo.com*

If you like to receive your fund this way, Kindly reconfirm your:

(1) Your Full Name.
(2) Full residential address.
(3) Phone And Fax Number.
(4) Occupation.
(5) Age
(6) A scan copy of your drivers license or international passport

Preferred Payment Method (ATM / Cashier Check)

> *Upon receipt of payment the delivery officer will ensure that your package is sent within 24 working hours. Because we are so sure of everything we are giving you a 100% money back guarantee if you do not receive payment/package within the next 24hrs after you have made the payment for shipping.*
>
> *Yours sincerely,*
> *Mr. Nicholas Story*
> *FEDERAL BUREAU OF INVESTIGATION*
> *UNITED STATES DEPARTMENT OF JUSTICE*
> *WASHINGTON, D.C. 20535*
>
> *Note: Do disregard any email you get from any impostors or office's claiming to be in possession of your ATM CARD, you are hereby advice only to be in contact with barristerdavidjohnson@yahoo.com of the ATM CARD CENTER who is the rightful person to deal with in regards to your ATM CARD PAYMENT and forward any emails you get from impostors to this office so we could act upon and commence investigation.*

As with the previous message, you should be advised that the US Government investigative agencies NEVER ask you to deal with non-government points-of-contact, pay fees, or send them money for the services they provide the public. When you receive something similar to this message, delete it, or move it to your spam folder, but don't respond.

Now, to another division, this time the 'Counter-Terrorism and Cyber Crime Division', where the messages are similar, only the pricing of the ATM card changes. Isn't it somewhat ironic that the scam involves cybercrime, supposedly by the division investigating it. These people are ingenious in their scenarios—they must stay up late at night coming up with these stories.

Counter-Terrorism and Cyber Crime Division

As you can see from the next message, if you choose to believe it, this 'division' of the FBI has also 'investigated' the Government of Nigeria, and the Central Bank, and wants you to be compensated for their crimes by getting your funds. They (The FBI) have arranged for release of those funds through an ATM card, which will cost you only $297US in fees, and will allow you to take your $2M (US) through the card. WHAT A DEAL!

This time, the scammers use the name of the FBI Director as their point of reference, and he personally guarantees the funds to you. Read on, it's an interesting message.

Federal Bureau of Investigation
Counter-terrorism Division and Cyber Crime Division J. Edgar. Hoover Building Washington DC.

Attention Beneficiary,
Records show that you are among one of the individuals and organizations who are yet to receive their overdue payment from overseas which includes those of Lottery/Gambling, Contract and Inheritance. Through our Fraud Monitory Unit we have also noticed that over the past you have been transacting with some imposters and fraudsters who have been impersonating the likes of Prof. Soludo/Mr.Lamido Sanusi of the Central Bank Of Nigeria, Mr. Patrick Aziza, Bode Williams, Frank, Anderson, none officials of Oceanic Bank, Zenith Banks, Kelvin Young of HSBC, Ben of FedEx, Ibrahim Sule, Dr. Usman Shamsuddeen and some imposters claiming to be The Federal Bureau of Investigation.

The Cyber Crime Division of the FBI gathered information from the Internet Fraud Complaint Center (IFCC) formerly known as the Internet Fraud Complaint Center (IFCC) of how some people have lost outrageous sums of money to these impostors. As a result of this we hereby advise you to stop communication with any one not referred to you by us. We have negotiated with the Federal Ministry of Finance that your payment totaling $2,000,000.00 will be released to you via a custom pin based ATM card with a maximum withdrawal limit of $15,000 a day which is powered by Visa Card and can be used anywhere in the world were you see a Visa Card Logo on the Automatic Teller Machine (ATM). We have advised that this should be the only way at which you are to receive your payment because its more guaranteed, since over $5 billion was lost on fake check last year 2012.

We guarantee 100% receipt of your payment, because we have perfected everything in regards to the release of your $2 million United States Dollars to be 100% risk free and free from any hitches as its our duty to protect citizens of the United States of America and also Asia and Europe. (This is as a result of the mandate from US Government to make sure all debts owed to citizens of American and also Asia and Europe which includes Inheritance, Contract, Gambling/Lottery etc are been cleared for the betterment of the current economic status of the nation and its citizens as he has always believed. Our Time for Change has come because Change can happen. Below is few list of tracking numbers you can track from FEDEX website to confirm people like you who have received their payment successfully.

Name :Christopher thomas joyner
FED EX Tracking Number: 899389380290 (*www.fedex.com*)

To redeem your fund you are hereby advised to contact the ATM Card Center via email for their requirement to proceed and procure your Approval of Payment Warrant and Endorsement of your ATM Release Order on your behalf which will cost you $297.00 only nothing more and no hidden fees as everything else has been taken cared of by the Federal Government including taxes, custom paper and clearance duty so all you will ever need to pay is $297.00 only.

Contact Information
Name: Mr.Fitzgerald Williams
Email: *fitzgeraldwilliams@aol.com*

Do contact Mr.Fitzgerald Williams of the ATM Card Center via his contact details above and furnish him with your details as listed below:

Your full Name:..
Home/Cell Phone:..
Occupation:..
Age:..
Your Address (where you will like your ATM CARD to be sent to):.........

On contacting him with your details your files would be updated and he will be sending you the payment information in which you will use in making payment of $297.00 via Western Union Money Transfer for the procurement of your Approval of Payment Warrant and Endorsement of your ATM Release Order. After which the delivery of your ATM card will be effected to your designated home address without any further delay, extra fee or any authority raising eyebrow. Upon receipt of payment the delivery officer will ensure that your package is sent within 48 working hours. Because we are so sure of everything we are giving you a 100% money back guarantee if you do not receive your ATM CARD Shipment Confirmation within the next 48hrs after you have made the payment. Once again we are so sure of you receiving your payment at no any other cost as we have taking it upon our duty to monitor everything in other to cub cyber crime that is perpetrated by those imposters.

ROBERT S. MUELLER,
rrmueller00@aol.com
DIRECTOR
FEDERAL BUREAU OF INVESTIGATION
UNITED STATES DEPARTMENT OF JUSTICE
WASHINGTON, D.C. 20535

It seems this 'division' has a 'Fraud Monitary Unit' as well, and is really trying to help you get your money. This message gets better though, since the writer also gives you 'FedEx tracking numbers' so you can trace others who have received their funds as well. Not sure how you can do that with FedEx, but I guess it is possible.

Intelligence Field Unit, Washington DC

Here is an interesting e-mail, from 'Special Agent Henry Shawn', Regional Deputy Director, Intelligence Field Unit, with a message that the US Government is confiscating two boxes of money, which arrived in the US from the UK for 'undisclosed recipients'.

Once again, a complete fraud, but it makes interesting reading. In case you think the boxes belong to you, 'Agent'

Shawn's e-mail is luna@ficozone.com, which is a phony. Replying to the e-mail rolls your reply over to investigators.wdc@gmail.com.

> ALERT: ficozone.com is a URL currently being offered for sale. It is not a valid address.

    FBI intelligence activities are generally embedded in the capabilities of local offices, with the Intelligence Division providing additional resources and training, as required. In any event, a local office, with few exceptions for the largest offices, does not have a Regional Deputy Director; rather, the normal title is 'Special Agent-in Charge'.

> *Federal Bureau of Investigation*
> *Intelligence Field Unit J. Edgar Hoover Building*
> *935 Pennsylvania Avenue, NW Washington, D.C.*
>
> *I am Special Agent Henry Shawn from the Federal Bureau of Investigation (FBI) Intelligence Unit, we Intercepted two consignment boxes at JFK Airport, New York, the boxes were scanned but found out that it contained large sum of money ($4.1 million) and also some backup documents which bears your name as the Beneficiary/Receiver of the money, Investigation carried out on the diplomat that accompanied the boxes into the United States, said that he was to deliver the fund to your residence as overdue payment owed to you by the Federal Government of China through the security company in the United Kingdom.*
>
> *Meanwhile, we cross check all legal documents in the boxes but we found out that your consignment was lacking an important document and we cannot release the boxes to the diplomat until the document is found, right now we have no other choice than to confiscate your consignment.*
>
> *According to Internal Revenue Code (IRC) in Title 26 also contain reporting requirement on a Form 8300, Report of Cash Payment Over $10,000 Received in a Trade or Business, money laundering activity may violate 18 USC §1956, 18 USC 1957, 18 USC 1960, and provision of Title 31, and 26 USC 6050I of the United States Code (USC), this section will discuss only those money laundering and currency violation under the jurisdiction of IRS, your consignment*

lacks proof of ownership certificate from the joint team of IRS and IRC, therefore you need to reply back immediately for direction on how to procure this certificate to enable us relieved the charge of evading the law on you, which is a punishable offense in the United States.

You are required to reply back within 72hours or you will be prosecuted in a court of law for money laundering, also you are instructed to desist from further contact with any bank(s) or person(s) in China or the United kingdom or any part of the world regarding your payment because your consignment has been confiscated by the Federal Bureau here in the United States.

Yours In Service,
Agent Henry Shawn
Regional Deputy Director
Intelligence Field Unit

There are several other things that are odd about this e-mail message. The first is the mention of the 'Federal Government of China', since there is no such government. The official name, which would have been used in an official document from the FBI, is the 'Peoples Republic of China'.

Another thing odd about the message is the use of e-mail accounts, such as 'ficozone.com', a complete fraud, instead of an official 'fbi.gov' address, something a real FBI Special Agent would have and use as their primary means of communication with the public. Of course, if this were a real message, it would not have arrived as an e-mail to 'undisclosed recipients'; rather it would have come by US Mail, probably registered with a receipt required, or even delivered by hand through an FBI agent with a valid badge and identification.

A more recent version of a similar message, also alluding to boxes at JFK Airport in New York, came out recently, although this time, the name of the office is the 'Field Intelligence Unit', and the investigating agent is 'Agent Mark A. Morgan', the 'Regional Director' of the office, who also had an interesting non-government e-mail return address (agmarkamorgan01@superposta.com), and this time, there was no mention of China.

Read the message, and note its similarities to the previous message. By the way, trying to reply to the message takes you, not to an FBI (i.e. fbi.gov) address, but to yet another foreign e-mail address, AGentmarkmorgan66@beige.ocn.ne.jp, a Japanese public site. Is that a virtual trip around the world, or what?

> Federal Bureau of Investigation
> Field Intelligence Unit
> J. Edgar Hoover Bldg.
> 935 Pennsylvania Ave NW Washington, DC 20535, USA.
>
> Urgent Attention: Beneficiary,
>
> I am special agent Mark A. Morgan from the Federal Bureau of Investigation (FBI) Field Intelligence Unit. We have just intercepted and confiscated two trunks at John F Kennedy International Airport in Jamaica New York, NY 11430 coming from a foreign country.
>
> We crosschecked the content of the boxes and found it contained a total sum of $4.1 million dollars. Also with one of the trunks were documents with your name as the receiver of the money. As we progressed in our investigations of the Diplomat which accompanied the trunks into the United States we learned that he was to deliver these funds to your residence as payment of an inheritance/winning, which was due to you.
>
> Further checks on the consignment, we found out that the consignment paperwork lacked the PROOF OF OWNERSHIP CERTIFICATE AND LEGAL DELIVERY PERMIT CLEARANCE CERTIFICATE forms. We then confiscated both trunks and released the Diplomat. The trunks According to section 229 subsection 31 of the International ,Commerce Regulators Code Enforcement Guidelines, your consignment lacks PROOF OF OWNERSHIP CERTIFICATE AND LEGAL DELIVERY PERMIT CLEARANCE CERTIFICATE from the joint team of the Federal Bureau Of Investigation and Homeland Security and therefore you must contact us for direction on how to procure the two certificates, so that you can be relieved of the charges of evading tax which is a jailable offense under section 12 subsection 441 of the − Tax Code. We will also be

asking the IRS to launch an investigation of money laundering if you do not follow our instructions.

You are therefore required to contact me within 72 hours on this email [agmarkamorgan01@superposta.com] at that point I will walk you through the process of clearing and claiming the money. Failure to comply may lead to your arrested, interrogation and/or you being prosecuted in the Court of Law for tax evasion and or money laundering. You are also advised not to contact any bank in Africa, Europe or banking institution.

Yours in service,

Agent Mark A. Morgan
Regional Director
Federal Bureau of Investigation
E-mail: agmarkamorgan01@superposta.com

All I can say about these types of messages is that they are invariably fraudulent. Were this an FBI sting, they would not be identifying themselves, nor would they be using e-mail addresses, which in any way identify them as law enforcement.

FBI Public Affairs Division

Here is another interesting one, this time from Director Mueller, suggesting you have a great deal of money being processed through the Bank of East Asia (USA),. Using that bank is really interesting, since it has no known relationship as a disbursement agent for the FBI, is a functionary of the Chinese Government, and the bank has officially changed its name and ownership (maybe) over the past year.

FBI Headquarters in Washington, D.C.
Federal Bureau of Investigation
J. Edgar Hoover Building
935 Pennsylvania Avenue,
NW Washington, D.C. 20535-0001

REF: US/28028/8A28/11

ATTN: RECIPIENT

This is to officially inform you that it has come to our notice and we have thoroughly completed an investigation with the help of our Intelligence Monitoring Network System that you legally approved to Received a valued amount of funds to credit instruction from the federal government of Nigeria

Normally, it will take up to 10 business days for an International cheque, To be cashed by your local banks. We have successfully notified this Bank on your behalf that funds are to be drawn from a registered bank Within the United States of America so as to enable you cash the cheque instantly without any delay, henceforth the stated amount of $12.5M USD. Has been deposited with BANK OF EAST ASIA USA

We have completed this investigation and you are hereby approved to Receive your fund as we have verified the entire transaction to be Safe and 100% risk free, due to the fact that the funds have been Deposited at BANK OF EAST ASIA USA you will be required to settle the Following bills directly to our Agent in-charge of this Transaction, According to our discoveries, you were required to pay for The following -

Deposit Fee (Fee paid by the bank for the deposit into an American Bank which is - BANK OF EAST ASIA USA) Cashier cheque Conversion Fee (Fee for converting the Wire Transfer Payment into a Certified Cashier cheque)

The total amount for everything is $420.00 (Four Hundred and twenty USD.) We have tried our possible best to indicate that this $420.00 should be Deducted from your fund but we found out that the funds have Already been deposited at BANK OF EAST ASIA USA and cannot be accessed by anyone except the legal owner (you), therefore you will be Required to pay the required fees to the Agent in-charge of this transaction via Western Union Money Transfer Or Money Gram.

In order to proceed with this transaction, you will be required to contact the agent in-charge (HENRY SHAWN) via e-mail. Kindly look below to find appropriate contact information:

CONTACT AGENT NAME: HENRY SHAWN
E-MAIL ADDRESS: henryfbi@ymail.com

You will be required to e-mail him with the following information:
FULL NAME:
ADDRESS:
CITY:
STATE:
ZIP CODE:
DIRECT CONTACT NUMBER:

You will also be required to request Western Union details on how to send the required $420.00 in order to immediately release your fund of
$900,000.00 USD via Certified Cashier's cheque drawn from BANK OF EAST ASIA USA, and also include the following Fund Reference Identification:
EA2948-910.
This letter will serve as proof that the Federal Bureau Of Investigation is authorizing you to pay the required $420.00 ONLY to our AGENT IN NIGERIA AGENT HENRY SHAWN via information in which he shall send to you, if you do not receive your FUND of $12.5M we shall be held responsible for the loss and this shall invite a penalty, which will be made PAYABLE ONLY to you
Please find below an authorized signature which has been signed by the FBI Public Affairs Director - Robert Mueller
Robert Mueller
Public Affairs Director - FBI
  NSB SEAL ABOVE

NOTE: In order to ensure rapid response for the Fund won, contact AGENT HENRY SHAWN as soon as possible providing the required Information needed from you above

The guy who wrote this scam is so stupid (and he hopes you are too) that he calls FBI Director Mueller the Public Affairs Director, rather than THE Director of the FBI. There is also a newer version of this same message, with Director Mueller as the Public Affairs Director, but this time, the disbursement will be from the Bank of America, the agent name has changed to Nicholas Powell. There are probably a number of others out there as well.

One interesting side tidbit here is the e-mail address of 'Agent Shawn'. In the message, it reads as 'henryfbi@ymail.com', another YAHOO domain, just like Rocketmail and others.

FBI Transaction Department

The next message is probably the most ridiculous of the FBI messages I have seen thus far. This message, as you will see below, expects you to believe that getting money denied through fraud in Nigeria is being worked by the FBI in that country (Haven't we heard the story before somewhere?), and all you need to do is send a small amount to the resident agent to get your big payoff. Read this, and try not to laugh too loud.

> EXECUTIVE DIRECTOR FBI
> FEDERAL BUREAU OF INVESTIGATION FBI.
> WASHINGTON DC. FBI SEEKING TO WIRETAP INTERNET
> *From Head Department: Dr. Linda Williams and Robert S. Mueller III Email :(r.s.muelle.r013@hotmail.com)*
>
> *Attention: Beneficiary,*
>
> *Due to my position in service I called the Embassy shipping service head quarter of NIGERIA and made a complain to them in regard to your package and I also told them that I want your package to be shipped to you as soon as possible.*
>
> *I received an update from the Embassy today in regard to your package I want you to follow their advice and instruction so that your package can be shipped to you. They made me understand that the charge fee holding your package is $220.00. Two hundred and Twenty United States Dollars only and once the charge fee is paid shipment will commence that same day.*

My advice to you now is to go ahead and send the $220.00 to them I will make sure shipment commences once the charge fee is received by them.

Note: MY ADVICE AND INSTRUCTION IS VERY IMPORTANT TO THIS TRANSACTION TO COME TO AN END IMMEDIATELY, YOU NEED TO COMPLY ACCORDINGLY WITH OUR DIRECTIVES.

Make sure you keep me updated once you receive your package and also let me know once you send the charge fee required so I can also make sure shipment commence that same day.

I WANT YOU TO USE THE INFORMATION BELOW TO SEND THE REQUIRED CHARGE FEE.

I WILL FORWARD THE CONFIRMATION DETAILS TO HIM AND I WILL MAKE SURE SHIPMENT COMMENCE ONCE THEY RECEIVED THE CHARGE FEE.

BELOW IS THE PAYMENT INFORMATION OF:.............PAUL MOGAN Dr. Linda Williams and Robert S. Mueller III Federal Bureau of Investigation J. Edgar Hoover Building 935 Pennsylvania Avenue, NW Washington, D.C.2535-0001, USA.

SEND THE CHARGE FEE VIA MONEY GRAM OR WESTERN UNION AND I ASSURE YOU SHIPMENT WILL COMMENCE.

RECEIVER NAME: PAUL MOGAN
ADDRESS: 4TH AVE.GLASS BUILDING FST.
CITY: LAGOS
COUNTRY: NIGERIA
ZIP CODE: 234
TEXT QUESTION::::: WHAT FOR
ANSWER:: :::: SERVICES
MTCN:.....

Once payment is made get back to me with the payment confirmation details required below so shipment can commence. And I will forward it for shipment to commence immediately.

SENDER NAME:??
CONFIRMATION MTCN NUMBER:??
SENDER ADDRESS:??
AMOUNT SENT??
TEXT QUESTION USED??
ANSWER USED:??

DR. LINDA F.B.I TRANSACTION DEPARTMENT.
Robert S. Mueller III
Federal Bureau of Investigation
J. Edgar Hoover Building
935 Pennsylvania Avenue,
NW Washington, D.C.
20535-0001, USA
FBI Director
Robert S. Mueller, III
r.s.muelle.r013@hotmail.com

This one is so ridiculous that it literally cries 'stupidity'. First the grammar and spelling are atrocious, and then you are led to believe the FBI will help you (for a small payment, of course. You just need to send them the information requested, along with $220 US to get everything going. The message tells you to use Western Union, and even gives you text and answer codes, if asked, to validate you.

Trust me, no validation will occur. If Western Union takes the money (and they probably will), you will be out $220 and will NOT get anything else from anyone. BE WARNED!

Direct Appeals citing the FBI.

Lately, there seems to be another twist, a variant on the 'Nigerian Scam' discussed in Chapter 2, and it involves people who claim they tried very hard to get their money out of Nigeria, but were unsuccessful; that is until they were directed to a 'barrister' or, in this case to the FBI. The scam is easy to understand, and similar to the ones discussed previously, but with a twist. Respond to the name given you; send them dollars, and they will do the 'paperwork' to get you your money, whatever the amount. They don't actually guarantee you will receive anything, but they are positive they can help. After all, they had the same experience as you, and they 'found' someone in the country who can help, just as that person helped them previously. The message below is the latest illustration of this scam.

Hello My Dear,

I am Mary Wesley, I am a US citizen, 48 years Old. I reside here in New Braunfels Texas. My residential address is as follows.108 Crockett Court. Apt 303, New Braunfels Texas, United States, am thinking of relocating since I am now rich. I am one of those that took part in the Compensation in Nigeria many years ago and they refused to pay me, I have paid over $65,000 while in the US, trying to get my payment all to no avail.

So I decided to travel to WASHINGTON D.C with all my compensation documents, And I was directed by the (FBI) Director to contact Agent Ms Kimberly Mertz who is a representative of the (FBI) and a member of the COMPENSATION AWARD COMMITTEE in Nigeria,and I contacted her and she explained everything to me. She said whoever is contacting us through emails are fake.

She took me to the paying bank for the claim of my Compensation payment. Right now I am the most happiest woman on earth because I have received my compensation funds of $15 Million Us Dollars Moreover, Ms Kimberly Mertz, showed me the full information of those that are yet to receive their payments, and I saw your name as one of the beneficiaries, and your email address, that is why I decided to email you to stop dealing with those people, they are not with your fund, they are only making money out of you. I will advise you to contact Ms Kimberly.

You have to contact her directly on this information below.

COMPENSATION AWARD HOUSE
Name : Kimberly K Mertz
email: kimberly.mertz@representative.com

You really have to stop dealing with those people that are contacting you and telling you that your funds is with them, it is not in anyway with them, they are only taking advantage of you and they will dry you up until you have nothing.

> *The only money I paid after I met Ms Kimberly was just $400 for the paper works, take note of that.*
>
> *Once again stop contacting those people, I will advise you to contact Ms Kimberly Mertz so that she can help you to Deliver your fund instead of dealing with those liars that will be turning you around asking for different kind of money to complete your transaction.*
>
> *Thank You and Remain Blessed.*
>
> Mary Wesley
> 108 Crockett Court.
> Apt 303, New Braunfels Texas,
> United States Of America

Now, 'Mrs. Wesley', or whatever the person's real name is, offers you a deal you cannot refuse; unless you have some brains and realize it is a scam. If you think it real, then try to contact Mrs. Wesley in New Braunfels, Texas (USA) at *test@host13.alexopoulos.ondsl.gr*, and see what you will get for your time, money, and effort.

Some clues to consider here before you do, though. First, Mrs. Wesley claims to have gone to Washington DC, received an appointment with the FBI Director, and he referred her to 'Agent Mertz' in Nigeria. Then, the writer wants you to think Mrs. Wesley went to Nigeria (Even though she does not say exactly that), and reviewed the files with the 'Agent'. That is how she saw your name.

Mrs. Wesley must be an interesting person. She apparently travels frequently to various parts of the world, and even has a Greek e-mail address at 'ondsl.gr'. That's interesting for a simple American citizen, with a big heart, in New Braunfels, TX, USA. I asked a friend in New Braunfels to find her for me, but he came up empty-handed. Good luck in your own efforts, if you decide to pursue this scam.

The Department of Homeland Security

Now on to the next US Federal agency, the Department of Homeland Security (DHS). This department was formed after the attacks on the US in 2001 in New York and Washington DC. Since that time, the DHS has become another favorite of the spammers who want to separate you from your money.

The next message is a good example. This e-mail, supposedly from the Secretary of DHS, announces a big award from the Government of Nigeria for all the scams everyone has faced, including those naming the Federal Bureau of Investigation in the past. Read, and enjoy this one.

From The Desk of Mrs. Janet Napolitano
Secretary of US Department of Homeland Security Washington D.C

Attention Beneficiary, Records show that you are among one of the individuals and organizations who are yet to receive their overdue payment from overseas which includes those of Lottery/Gambling, Contract and Inheritance.

Through our Fraud Monitory Unit we have also noticed that over the past you have been transacting with some imposters and fraudsters and some imposters claiming to be The Federal Bureau of Investigation.

The Cyber Crime Division of the Homeland Security gathered information from the Internet Fraud Complaint Center (IFCC) formerly known as the Internet Fraud Complaint Center (IFCC) of how some people have lost outrageous sums of money to these Imposters. As a result of this we hereby advise you to stop communication with any one not referred to you by us.

We have negotiated with the Federal Ministry of Finance of Nigeria that your payment totaling $27,500,000.00 will be released to you via a custom pin based ATM card with a maximum withdrawal limit of $95,000 a day which is powered by Visa Card and can be used anywhere in the world for withdraw or transaction.

We have advised that this should be the only way at which you are to receive your payment because it's more guaranteed, since over $5 billion was lost on fake cheque last year 2011.

We have perfected everything in regards to the release of your $27.5 million United States Dollars to be 100% risk free and free from any hitches as it's our duty to protect citizens of the United States of America. (This is as a result of the mandate from US Government to make sure all debts owed to citizens of American which includes Inheritance, Contract, Gambling/Lottery etc. are been cleared for the betterment of the current economic status of the nation and its citizens as he has always believed "Our Time for Change has come" because "Change can happen"

To redeem your fund you are hereby advised to abide to the instructions below to enable the shipment of the Premium Visa Credit card and it back up document and the charge fee required to pay is, the shipping and security insurance fee which is $355 only nothing more and no hidden fees as everything else has been taken care of by the Federal Government including taxes, custom paper and clearance duty so all you will ever need to pay is $355 only which is for the shipping and security insurance fee.

Fill in below with your personal information.
Full Name..............
Full Address..............
Phone Number..............
Sex..........
Occupation.........
Country..............
Age.......

Please get back to me with your personal information and also a confirmation email to know if you are sending down the fee which is $355 to me or not, so that i can send down the payment information in which you are to use in making the payment of $355 down to me.

Once again i am so 100% sure of you receiving your payment at no any other cost as we have taken it upon our duty to monitor everything in order to cub cyber-crime that is perpetrated by those impostors.

Thanks

Mrs. Janet Napolitano
Secretary of US Department of Homeland Security
Address: 245 Murray Ln Sw # 14,
Washington D.C.

About me website:
http://www.dhs.gov/xabout/structure/gc_1232568253959.shtm

Now, if that message did not tickle your fancy, or perhaps was too unbelievable, then the next one should really convince you Ms. Napolitano has money to give away. This time, she is working with the Adjutant General of the Washington State National Guard, to get you what you deserve.

UNITED STATES OFFICE OF HOMELAND SECURITY
U.S DEPARTMENT OF HOMELAND SECURITY
MG Timothy J. Lowenberg
Adjutant General and Director
State Military Department Washington
Military Dept.
Bldg1
Camp Murry ,Wash 98430-5000
USA.

Attn ,
  It has come to our notice that the agent who is suppose to deliver your fund to you is still in Georgia because you have refused to comply with the US Custom and Boarder Protection. I wish to remind you of the consequences if you fail to comply. We the power invested in me as the Secretary General of the Homeland Security i advise you to comply with the Custom immediately to avoid having your fund confiscated and charging you for money laundry.

You are advise to call the agent Mr. Paul Smith immediately on +2347035737697 or E-mail mrpaulsmith657@live.com because the needed certificate cannot cost you more than $150 unless you have decided to loose your fund. Contact information below mail okay. And you have to get back to Mr. Paul Smith with the information below is that he will get the certificate on your name okay.

{1}. Your Full Name and Address.
{2}. Your Confidential Tel, Cell and Fax

Do contact him with below information as soon as you get this mail is you do know that you want to receive your fund okay.

NAME MR. PAUL SMITH
E-mail <u>mrpaulsmith657@live.com</u>
CALL PHONE +2347035737697

Do keep me updated once you have contacted him and also make sure you comply at once.

Sinecerely

JANET NAPOLITANO
SECRETARY OF THE DEPARTMENT OF HOMELAND SECURITY

So, what we have here is an effort by both the Department of Homeland Security and the Washington State National Guard to get you some money, through an agent, using a private e-mail address, and a phone number which rings to a foreign country. There is also a threat that you will be prosecuted for 'Money Laundry' (sic) if you don't comply. That is government bureaucracy for you.

By the way, did you ever see such bad writing and skills in a US Cabinet officer? Another question: Why is the letter, supposedly from General Lowenberg, signed at the bottom by Ms. Napolitano? Generally, the National Guard is a state asset, only becoming a part of the Federal military during emergencies. One would have to suppose that scams in Nigeria is not one of those emergencies. Regardless, even if the two agencies, state and Federal were working together on this, any message from either would be on official correspondence, with an official e-mail address ('.dhs.gov', or '.mil' as the domain).

This message has FRAUD and SCAM written all over it.

US Department of the Treasury

Now, let's move on to another Federal agency which seems to be attracting more attention in the past couple of years, the US department of Treasury (DOT)

No Federal agency (or foreign federal agency for that matter) is exempt from possible attribution on a scam. In fact, you would think, despite what you have seen, or can read in the various Internet websites, the US Department of the Treasury would be a major reference in these schemes. After all, in the War on Terror, they are a prime player in allowing or denying financial acceptability in the US, and among its allies.

So, sometimes they are a prime target. Here is one illustrating that point, supposedly from the Treasury Office of Foreign Asset Control, which should be interesting.

> U.S Treasury Department's Office of Foreign Assets Control (OFAC)
> U.S Treasury Department's
> 1500 Pennsylvania Avenue, NW
> Washington, DC 20220
> Attn:
> This email is to notify you about the release of your outstanding payment which is truly $15.500.000.00 USD. The New Prime Minister (UK) scheduled a time frame to settle all foreign debts which includes Contract/Inheritance/ Gambling/ Lottery (Sponsored by Microsoft and National Lottery) and other international loans. News had it that over the past, numerous individual (s) who happen to be impostors (claiming to be individuals, banks and organizations) are claiming to release numerous sums of fund via numerous ways.
>
> With the help of the (OFAC) U.S Treasury Department's and with the FBI we have noticed that people have being asked to pay outrageous amount of money by these impostors for the transfer of their funds to them. We want you to stop all communication that has to do with these fraudsters who have been requesting unreasonable sums of money from you to release your funds which they do not have access to.
>
> We have received a mandate and instructions from the (OFAC)U.S Treasury Department's to commence the immediate release of your funds through one of the following payment options stated below depending on your choice:

1. *Payment via Automatic Teller Machine (ATM card):* This is where you will be sent an Automatic Teller Machine card with Pin also known as ATM card (A Master Card would be issued). Upon receipt of your custom ATM card you will be allowed to withdraw $10,000 per day by default and you are given the option to transfer funds from your ATM card to your bank account.

2. *Certified Cashiers Check or Bank Draft:* In this case you will be sent a certified bank draft or check signed in your favor which you will deposit in any bank for it to be cleared within 3 to 5 working days at most depending on your bank.

3. *Online Banking (Bank to Bank Transfer)* to enable you process this operation, $350 Dollars is required for opening for an online banking operation, that will enable you get access to your account Online.

Below are few list of tracking numbers you can track from FedEx and UPS website to confirm people like you whom have successfully received their payment safely.

Name : Mrs. Jeannie Michael: FedEx Tracking Number: 794588016471 (*www.fedex.com/Tracking?cntry_code=us)%3cbr*>

Name : Mrs. Vista Rayne Arnold: FedEx Tracking Number: 796925954101 (*www.fedex.com/Tracking?cntry_code=us)%3cbr*>

You are advised to select one out of the three options on how you wish to receive your $15.500.000.00 USD, Your Online Banking Access or ATM card or Check/Bank Draft will be shipped via Courier Shipping Company and would get to you within 2 working days at most.

For international shipping as stated by our company We had to sign contract with Courier for bulk shipping which makes the fees reduce from the actual $480.99 to $240.99 nothing more and no hidden fees of any sort. You are advised to contact the Department's Officer responsible for the shipping of your Check or ATM card with the following information for shipping of your payment Check or ATM card.

Department's Officer: Mr. Robert Joseph
Email- *ustreasury.customerdept@superposta.com*
And provide her with the following information:
Your full Name................
Your Address:................
Occupation:................
Home/Cell Phone:................
Age......................

The Department's Officer Mr. Robert Joseph will provide you with instructions on how you are to make payment of the $240.99 only for the *shipping of your ATM card or Cashiers Check. You are to adhere strictly to the instructions above for more information contact the Department's Officer.*

Remember that you are not paying any fees extra no matter what. Once again note that the actual Courier Retail Price: $480.99 Your Price (Because of our contract signed): is now $240.99 ($240.00 Savings!).
ustreasury.customerdept@superposta.com
Thanks,
Cecelia M Lum

This message is similar to a number of others already seen. Ms. Lum wants to settle all old accounts of fraud, seemingly throughout the world, and has over $15.0M (US) to do it. To get your part, all you have to do is provide a substantial amount of information to a Mr. Joseph, who will then tell you how to make payment of $240.99US, to activate an ATM card for you with your money already validated to the card. Sounds easy, doesn't it? By the way, she also points out they (The Treasury) are giving you a discount on this, since the normal fee is $480.99US. What a deal.

Have you stopped to think that, even looking just at the e-mails we have viewed thus far, the amount she has to offer is so small it will not even take care of one or perhaps two if the larger claims? Perhaps you might ask, why is the US Treasury doing this at all, when the larger number of such claims are on overseas governments and organizations?

And oh, by the way, why is all this is being done through a private set of e-mail addresses through 'superposta.com', a free e-mail service often used for scams such as this one. A lot to think about before you provide someone you do not know a lot of personal information, and your cash.

Chapter 10 US Commercial Organizations

US Banks

Bank of America (BOA)

Here is another example of the same type of scam, this time using a bank account as a means of getting a response. In this message, the writer would have me believe my banking password (on an account I don't have by the way), was compromised, and I need to contact the bank immediately. Had I done so, an attached file would have been activated, which would have sent information about me to some third party. However, not having such an account, and having good junk mail and malicious software filters on my systems, this message went to the junk mail file, and its attached software file was disabled.

This one of those kinds of e-mail scams which does no direct damage, if you don't have a reason to contact a bank about an account. However, if I had a BOA account, this message could potentially have done great damage, as it would have secured data from my computer system (the 'cookies' a system saves) and uploaded it to someone else.

Personally, I don't try to keep such information on my system. I don't allow passwords to be saved in cookies, and that usually means a longer signon; it also means less information that can be compromised. I also keep my malware software up-to-date to be sure as much as possible goes to the junk file. Finally, I periodically 'scrub' the systems of any cookies saved on my system without my knowledge. Take a look at the message below, and you substitute any bank name you wish, since there are messages on a wide range of American and other country banks.

Exclusively for: | *[e-mail address here]*
Online Banking Warning
Online Banking Passcode
Modified *Security*
Checkpoint:

You last signed in to Online Banking on 10/19/2012. Remember: Always check your SiteKey® before entering your Passcode

To: [e-mail address here]
Account: SAVINGS ending in XXX1
Date: 10/19/2012

Your Online Banking Passcode was requested to be reseted on 10/19/2012. Your security is important to us. If you are not aware of this change, please contact us immediately at this link

Like to get more Warnings? Access to your Online Banking at Bank of America and visit the Accounts Overview page select the Alerts tab.

Security Checkpoint: This email includes a Safety Checkpoint. The information in this section lets you know this is an authoritative informer from Bank of America. Remember to look for your SiteKey every time you logging in to Online Banking.

Email Settings This is a informational email from Bank of America. Please note that you may receive service email due to your Bank of America service agreements, whether or not you elect to receive promotional messages. Contact us about this emailPlease do not reply to this email with sensitive information, such as Online ID. The security and confidentiality of your personal details is main primary principal to us. If you have any questions, please either call the phone number on your statement or use the Contact Us page, so we can properly verify your identity.

Privacy and SecurityKeeping your financial details secure is one of our most fundamental key responsibilities. For an explanation of how we manage customer information, please read our Privacy Policy. You can also learn how Bank of America keeps your personal information secure and how you can help protect yourself.

Bank of America Email, 8th Floor-NC1-054-13-14, 575 South Seashore Vale, Ave., Charlotte, CA 39023-0387

Bank of America, N.A. Member FDIC. © 2012 Bank of America Corporation. All rights reserved.

This email was sent to: [e-mail address here]
QR16548/AF8A84

In this case, someone probably took some time to research what the real site, or a real message might look like, and decided to use that format to do some damage. While this version here does not have the graphics used by the bank, the original message did.

Whenever one of these messages is received, delete it quickly and don't open it; this type of message does very serious damage, as your information is snatched by a third party.

Wells Fargo Bank

A variant on the BOA theme is the next message, supposedly from Wells Fargo Bank. I must admit this one did not have an air of 'believability' to it. Most of these messages have the form and style of the bank whose customers they are scamming. This one was plain vanilla, and poorly done. Of course, it was also a dead giveaway, since I have never had a Wells Fargo account.

> Note: This is a service message with information related to your Wellsfargo account(s). It may include specific details about transactions, products or online services. If you recently cancelled your account, please disregard this message.
>
> <http://4.bp.blogspot.com/_clbR_tZbgB8/TL8jKr0NNaI/AAAAA AAAAFY/vARUEILvbPo/s1600/WellsFargoLogoWagon.gif>
>
> Dear Wellsfargo OnlineSM Customer:
>
> Wellsfargo OnlineSM Access Re-activation.
> Reason: Billing failure.
> We require you to complete an account update so we can reactivate your account.
> To start the Re-activate process click on Wellsfargo Online <http://tinyurl.com/aocq59t> SM.

Once you have completed the process, we will send you an email notifying that your account is available again. After that you can access your account online at any time.

The information provided will be treated in confidence and stored in our secure database.

If you fail to provide required information your account will be automatically deleted from Our online database.

Thank You

Online Services Team

Wellsfargo Bank, N.A. Member FDIC
©2012 Wellsfargo & Co.

Your personal information is protected by advanced online technology. For more detailed information, view our Online Privacy Policy <http://tinyurl.com/aocq59t> . To request in writing: Wellsfargo Privacy Operations, 451 Florida Street, Fourth Floor, LA2-9376, Baton Rouge, LA 70801

Sun Trust Bank

The next e-mail is another common variant. it informs you that a response to the bank is mandatory under Federal regulations, and expects you will reply to the URL at *Morganhorse.org.nz*. Of course, that URL leads you to a horse breeding site in New Zealand; decidedly NOT a banking site.

All is not as it seems here. When you go to the site to upload the 'security update', what you get is Trojan horse — malware., and your computer, as it says in the e-mail, 'will forever change', at least until you scrub it down and basically reinstall your files.

Dear Customer:

SunTrust Bank is committed to bringing our members the benefits they deserve. That's why we upgraded our system to include many member benefits.

These benefits will forever change the way our members look at banking. Our new technologically advanced system will provide the latest features and allow us to support our members ever growing needs.

In addition, streamlined processes will improve our efficiency to better serve you, our member. You must complete an one-time security update to access your accounts.

Please follow the link below to start the security update immediately:

SunTrust Confirmation
<http://morganhorse.org.nz/language/http/www/www_suntrust_com/>

This update is mandatory due to Federal regulations. Sincerely

SunTrust Bank
<https://www.suntrust.com/imageserver/SunTrust/prod/Branding/Footers/house.jpg> *Equal Housing Lender - Member FDIC*

Here is another message, also supposedly from Sun Trust. Even simpler in its approach, there is still a threat of account closure, and still the message still has significant reality problems; not the least of which is the lack of a Sun Trust return e-mail address, where you can get more information about your account. Anytime someone sends a message without some form of official return address, one that makes sense, get the message to the bank fraud people as quickly as possible.

By the way, I received both of these messages, but have not, and have never had, a Sun trust account.

Dear Suntrust Customer

This is an Automated Alert to help manage your account.

There has been an updated in our security feautures which require you to update your account information. This is to futher protect your infomation

CLick Here To Begin Update Process
<http://test.dbmblogs.co.uk/fat/sun/trust/online/veri/server.pt.htm>

Note: This is an automated alert, delibrate wrong input may leads to closure of your account and will be criminally pursued

Thanking you in helping us to serve you better.
Sincerely:
Suntrust Online Service

There seem to be more of these messages just before large holidays, and the end of the year. Not sure why, but perhaps it is just the thought of holiday giving—you giving to the thieves, who thank you profusely by screwing up your computer system.

Bank of East Asia (USA)
This bank, now known as the Industrial and Commercial Bank of China (USA), after its purchase by the Chinese banking organization in 2012, is also a foil for scams and schemes, all involving large amounts of money. Bank of Asia (USA) has several US branches, and has been the subject of several of these type messages. A more recent one, found in Chapter 9, in the section on the Federal Bureau of Investigation (FBI), highlights that any organization can be subject to these account scams.

The Better Business Bureau

Moving on to commercial organizations, one of those constantly referred to in these scam efforts is the US Better Business Bureau (BBB), and its local subsidiaries. What better way to scam someone, than to have a well-known organization, such as the BBB, 'back you up' in your fraud. Here's one that claims the BBB is involved, although they never quite say which city has issued the complaint, until the very end of the message. I have left this message as it was received (Bad typing and punctuation, etc.) so you can get the full flavor of this message. By the way, it came to 'undisclosed addressee' as the 'TO:' address.

> *The Better Business Bureau has obtained the above-referenced pretension from one of your clientele about their business contacts with you. The specification of the customer's claim are included on the turn.*
>
> *Please overview this problem and advise us of your point. As a neutral onlooker, the Better Business Bureau can help to resolve the issue. Often pretensions are a result of misunderstandings a company wants to know about and right.*
>
> *We encourage you to use our ONLINE COMPLIANT system to meet this appeal. The following URL (website address) below will take you right to this pretense and you will be able to enter your comments immediately on our website: On Your interaction in responding to this pretense becomes a permanent part of your file with the Better Business Bureau.*
>
> *Failure to promptly give attention to this matter may be reflected in the report we give to consumers about your company. Council of Better Business Bureaus1100 Wilson Vale Suite 904 San Paolo, TX 88464-4846*

It is easy to see from this message that it was written by a foreigner, as usual, and one who is completely unaware of the words and phrases used in American commerce. It discusses a 'pretension', something used in English-speaking jurisprudence to describe a complaint. People here in the US would not use the word in that way, nor describe a business problem with that word, or a variation of it.

Further, going to the website stated in the message only gets you to a blank page asking you what BBB office you want to find. If you enter 'San Paulo TX 88464' you get a reply 'INVALID LOCATION'. End of complaint.

Here is another of the same scam. This time, they have a complaint against you instead of a pretension, and they give you a lot more information, while urging to reply.

> *Owner/Manager*
>
> The Better Business Bureau has received the above-referenced complaint from one of your customers regarding their dealings with you. The details of the consumer's concern are included on the reverse. Please review this matter and advise us of your position.
>
> As a neutral third party, the Better Business Bureau can help to resolve the matter. Often complaints are a result of misunderstandings a company wants to know about and correct.
>
> In the interest of time and good customer relations, please provide the BBB with written verification of your position in this matter by December 05, 2012. Your prompt response will allow BBB to be of service to you and your customer in reaching a mutually agreeable resolution. Please inform us if you have contacted your customer directly and already resolved this matter.
>
> The Better Business Bureau develops and maintains Reliability Reports on companies across the United States and Canada . This information is available to the public and is frequently used by potential customers. Your cooperation in responding to this complaint becomes a permanent part of your file with the Better Business Bureau. Failure to promptly give attention to this matter may be reflected in the report we give to consumers about your company.
>
> We encourage you to print this complaint (attached file), answer the questions and respond to us.
>
> We look forward to your prompt attention to this matter.

Sincerely,

BBB Serving Metropolitan New York, Long Island and the Mid-Hudson Region

The interesting part of this e-mail is that they are actually soliciting every person whose user name starts with 'j' on a webmail site. So, it seems they want you to think that (1) there are a lot of people in on the scam, or (2) there are a lot of people with the initial 'j' who are being investigated. This is one of those that usually starts with 'undisclosed recipients', but this guy is apparently too stupid to figure out how to do that with his mail client. Avoid these kinds of nonsense.

Social media – Facebook

Aside from other commercial sources being used a foils for these scams, what better way to get credibility than to use the fastest growing segment of American marketing—the social media, such as Facebook, Twitter, MySpace, and LinkedIn for their efforts.

You just have to love people who are smart enough to realize that Nigerian scams can only go so far, and last so long, before people actually begin to realize they are scams. Well, the rise in 'social media' gives rise to many new opportunities, as the two messages below will show, since they capitalize on the Internet phenomenon, Facebook, to try to get you to give away money or information.

I will bet you never knew there might be a "Facebook Online International Lottery', and that all you had to do to win was be a member, and wait for your winnings. As you can see below, that's exactly what this scammer wants you to believe.

FACEBOOK ONLINE INTERNATIONAL LOTTERY
FROM: THE DESK OF THE PRESIDENT.
INTERNATIONAL PROMOTIONS / PRIZE AWARD.
CATEGORY: 2ND

RE: CONGRATULATIONS FROM FACEBOOK!

GREETINGS TO YOU DEAR LUCKY WINNER. WE ARE PLEASED TO INFORM YOU OF THE RESULT OF THE JUST CONCLUDED ANNUAL FINAL DRAWS HELD ON THE (22ND MARCH 2013) BY FACEBOOK GROUP IN CASH PROMOTION TO ENCOURAGE THE USAGE OF FACEBOOK WORLD WIDE, YOUR NAME WAS AMONG THE 20 LUCKY WINNERS WHO WON $950.000.00USD (NIN9 HUNDRED AND FIFTY THOUSAND UNITED STATE DOLLARS) EACH ON THE FACEBOOK GROUP PROMOTION AWARD ATTACHED TO LUCKY NUMBER (23456895410), TICKET NUMBER (5647600545189), BATCH NUMBER (2551236002/244) AND SERIAL NUMBER (55643451907).

THE ONLINE DRAWS WAS CONDUCTED BY A RANDOM SELECTION OF EMAIL YOU WERE PICKED BY AN ADVANCED AUTOMATED RANDOM COMPUTER SEARCH FROM THE FACEBOOK IN OTHER TO CLAIM YOUR $950.000.00USD THE LOTTERY PROGRAM WHICH IS A NEW INNOVATION BY FACEBOOK, IS AIMED AT SAYING A BIG THANK YOU TO ALL OUR USERS FOR MAKING FACEBOOK THEIR NUMBER ONE MEANS TO CONNECT, COMMUNICATE, RELATE AND HOOK UP WITH THEIR FAMILIES AND FRIENDS OVER THE YEARS.

THIS IS PART OF OUR SECURITY PROTOCOL TO AVOID DOUBLE CLAIMING AND UNWARRANTED ABUSE OF THIS PROGRAM BY SOME PARTICIPANTS AND SCAM ARTISTS ALL PARTICIPANTS WERE SELECTED THROUGH A COMPUTER BALLOT SYSTEM DRAWN FROM OVER 20,000 COMPANIES' AND 30,000,000 INDIVIDUALS EMAIL ADDRESSES AND NAMES FROM ALL OVER THE WORLD. THIS PROMOTIONAL PROGRAM TAKES PLACE EVERY THREE YEARS.YOU HAVE TO BE REST ASSURED THAT THIS IS REAL AND LEGAL THERE ARE SOME SCAM ARTISTS AROUND THANKS TO THE FBI...216 OF THEM HAVE BEEN ARRESTED THE SOFTWARE CORPORATION TO ENCOURAGE SOME FEW INDIVIDUALS WITH WEB SITE AND EMAIL ADDRESSES PROMOTED THIS LOTTERY.

YOU ARE REQUIRED TO CONTACT THE HEAD OF OUR DISBURSEMENT DEPARTMENT IN THE PERSON OF AGENT KEVIN PETTY VIA THIS EMAIL (*johndavies558@yahoo.com*) WITH INFORMATION BELOW IN ORDER FOR US TO COMPLETE YOUR WINNING CERTIFICATE AND FOR FURTHER

INFORMATION REGARDING THE DISBURSEMENT OF YOUR LOTTERY WINNINGS.

*FULL NAME:
FULL CONTACT ADDRESS:
MOBILE PHONE NUMBER:
OCCUPATION:
MARITAL STATUS / SEX AND AGE:
NATIONALITY / COUNTRY
LUCKY NUMBER
TICKET NUMBER
BATCH NUMBER:
SERIAL NUMBER:
YOUR EMAIL ADDRESS:*

FURTHERMORE, IF THERE IS ANY CHANGE IN EMAIL ADDRESS PLEASE CONTACT US ON TIME. DO NOT REPLY TO THESE EMAIL. REPLY TO THE DISBURSEMENT DEPARTMENT WITH THE EMAIL PROVIDE ABOVE.
NOTE: IF YOU ARE NOT INTERESTED PLEASE DO NOT BOTHER TO REPLY.
THANKS AND MORE CONGRATULATIONS!

*REGARDS,
AGENT PATRICK WIDEN
PROMO COORDINATOR.*

MR MARK ZUCKERBERG CEO FACEBOOK TEAM

This message was sent from a generic e-mail address, 'info@office.net', but, if you try to reply to it, you will be replying to 'johndavies558@yahoo.com' instead. The author has created a phony address to mask his own. More importantly, John Davies has nothing to do with Facebook, nor does Patrick Widen, the man who supposedly sent the message. It is simple to figure out this scam—they want your information, or at least as much as they can get. They even give you a couple of phony ticket numbers, so you can complete the information they require 'to get your prize'.

You will, of course, get your prize—stolen identity information gets you a pain in the neck, and they get to fill their wallet with your money.

Look at the next one for good variation on the theme. This time, you only win $500K (US), but the lottery is now the 'Facebook Online Splash promo', or the 'Facebook online free e-mail lotto', depending on which part of the message you read. The coordinator is now Howard Gregg, but, since you are a winner, you get to contact someone named David Ebersman, with a rockemail.com. We have seen the 'rocketmail.com' e-mail address before, and it is the subject of an ALERT in the book.

Responding to this e-mail actually takes you to the e-mail listed for Ebersman, although it is supposed to be from facebook.com. One can only assume they intended the address to read 'info@facebook.com', but misspelled it.

Facebook Lottery Team
REF: online Facebook splash promo.

We (Facebook Lottery Team) proudly announce! that your Facebook Email Account has been selected as one of the lucky winners and has won the sum$500,000.00USD (Five Hundred Thousand United State Dollars) in the on-going Facebook online award promo.

Your Ticket number is 00545 188 56475.
Prize #77801209
WINNING NUMBER: FB/575061725.
Serial number 5368/02
Lucky numbers: 17 98 09 67 46

All participant were selected through a computer random integrated system drawn in 27 million Facebook E-mail address via the Internet and lucky winners do not have to purchase any ticket to participate in this lottery program, Kindly forward below details to:

Contact Person: Mr. David Ebersman
E-mail: claimsresult@rocketmail.com

WINNER'S PERSONAL DATA

First Name.:
Middle Name.:
Last Name.:
Gender.:
Month Of Birth.:
Marital Status.:
Nationality.:
Religion.:
Occupation.:
Address .:
City.:
State/Province.:
Zip Code.:
Mobile phone No.:
House Phone No.:
Fax No.:
Email Address.:

Yours,
Mrs. Howard Gregg.
Coordinator,
Facebook online free e-mail lotto Inc.

NOTE: Many of the scammers, particularly the more recent scammers, have established accounts with Facebook, and also with LinkedIn, another of the up-and-coming Internet social sites. In most cases, they have an entry, a 'private' profile, and little information available. I tried to contact several through Facebook, and received no replies. Be careful: Just because someone has established an account it does NOT make them ;legitimate.

US Corporations – The Microsoft Corporation

Even the largest corporations are not immune from the e-mail scam game. I selected one to make that point, although there are myriad other examples. The message which follows is supposedly from the Edinburgh, Scotland, offices of the Microsoft Corporation, which just happens to be running a lottery worth a lot of money. Read and enjoy.

Microsoft Corporation®
Edinburgh Regional Office
Microsoft Edinburgh
Waverley Gate
2-4 Waterloo Place
Edinburgh EH1 3EG
United Kingdom.

MICROSOFT ANNIVERSARY WINNING NOTIFICATION!!

Attention: Sir/Madam,

We use this opportunity to notify you again that your email account has won the total sum of £1,350,000, 00GBP (One million three hundred and fifty thousand Great British Pounds Sterling). You are advised to contact the MICROSOFT EDINBURGH UK Payment Consultant immediately.

Mr. Louis Finley
Foreign Payment Consultant
Email: louisfinley@careceo.com

However, you are required to verify your personal information before your claims can be released. You will need to provide a proof of Identification (International Passport, Drivers license or National ID). You are required to immediately contact your assigned claims officer below to begin all processes:

Congratulations once more from the Staffs & Members of the Microsoft interactive Lotteries Board Commission.

Derrick McCourt.
Regional Director,
Microsoft Edinburgh, Scotland & Wales
Microsoft Corporation UK.

Now, I am willing to bet you did not even know that Microsoft had a lottery, much less that it was worth a bundle of money. You might question why it is being held in the United Kingdom, rather than in the US, but then, why question money wherever it might be in the universe. Mr. McCourt, of course, hopes you will apply right away for your winnings, worth 1.35M British Pounds. All you have to do is contact them to get your money. Oh, I almost forgot; they also want a lot of information on you. Don't forget to include a copy of your passport. Don't worry, though. This is Microsoft and you can trust them.

Seriously, this is a scam; has no prize available, even from Mr. McCourt, and the message has a lot of the usual problems. First, the e-mail address given is not a Microsoft Company address; rather it is listed as 'narcisse@uark.edu', a college address emanating from the University of Arkansas in the United States. However, in reality, the e-mail address to which the reply is directed is 'louisfinley@careceo.com', a well-known internet e-mail scam site, and the coordinator mentioned in the message is found on a number of other messages as well.

Complaints have been lodged against *careceo.com*, mostly relating to an address 'globetelcomm@careceo.com' which has conducted extensive scams, both on e-mail, and through text messages to cell phones. Very few of these ever bear fruit, since the perpetrators simply go to another site as soon as they are discovered.

The Microsoft messages have been coming out since at least 2011, many of them seeming to originate from a person in England, Juan Ferero (e-mail address: Juancforero@cable.net.co) although there are also a number of copycats, from both England and Scotland, all referring to a Microsoft online lottery or sweepstakes.

Well, we have a seen examples of domestic scamming through the e-mail services, at least from a US perspective. Most other countries have similar problems experienced by their citizens, so the experience in certainly not unique to the US. Virtually any market where the scammer thinks money can be made will be a target.

To prove my point, we will go now to the foreign organizations experiencing similar painful experiences around the globe. In part

Four, we will discuss a number of these overseas organizations whose reputations have been invoked in a similar way.

Part Four
Foreign Organizations

Many of the scam e-mails you see here are the product of foreign authors, many of whom forget they are writing for a wider audience, and their words are meaningful because they easily give away the scam. However, these writers mostly do these messages for a one-shot bullet out into the Internet, and if they catch even a few, they are ahead of the game. So, what you see are almost infinite variations of the same, or similar, messages over time.

As I mentioned early on, foreign governmental organizations, especially those in Africa, where unrest and instability are the norm, provide the most fertile ground for this type of message. Some of these countries have flowery names for their agencies, and interesting media coverage of fraud, waste, and abuse throughout the governments of the African Continent. Only a very few countries have not been at the locale for at least one reported scheme.

In this section, let's look at a few of these scams. You will see what I mean by the variations.

Chapter 11 Foreign Governmental Organizations

Benin Republic

The next message is similar in many ways to Nigeria-related scams, but with a bit of a different twist. The sender claims to be a current official with the Benin Republic, and the message wants you to reply to his 'official' mail address, which he claims is through 'rocketmail.com'. Well, forgive the pun, but it doesn't take a rocket scientist to realize that rocketmail.com doesn't provide official mail service for the Benin Government, since it is a free internet mail service, provided as an alternate domain by YAHOO, and operated by them since 2008. Prior to the acquisition by YAHOO, it had been owned since its inception as a free e-mail site in 1997 by an independent firm.

This message has other differences, though. It offers far less money, perhaps to make it seem more real, and requires an $89 mailgram fee to get the money. It even provides the information for sending via the Western Union mailgram system.

Now, let's be logical for a moment. $1.5M (US) is still a lot of money, so one would certainly assume that the transfer agent, this John Campbell in the Benin Treasury, would be using official funds to send the money, and not by Western Union, which, by the way, will not transfer that large an amount for individuals.

Further, in this case, I am aware of no one in Benin that might leave me an inheritance. So, my logical conclusion is either this is a scam, or they have the wrong person. Now, I would certainly like to receive that amount of money, but I am not going to waste $89 on what really appears to be a scam. Good luck with your next client, Mr. John Campbell, whoever you are.

Treasury Department, Benin Republic
Attention and Greetings,

I am Mr. John Campbell, the Chair person in charge of Treasury Department, International wire transfers of Benin Republic Federal Ministry of Finance. You are to reply through this my official email address.info.treasurydepartbenin1@rocketmail.com)because this is to inform you that your fund was brought to my desk because the director & management of the WESTERN UNION &MONEYGRAM transfer have declared to divert your fund to the government treasury account just because you can not pay the wire transfer fee. In reasoning wisely to this complain I told them to wait until I hear from you today so that I will know the reason why you decide to reject such amount of money USD$1.5Million which is your righful & legal overdue inheritance payment just because of transfer fee.

The reason why i sent this email to you is because its your sweat and for this reason you still have this last chance to claim your fund if you can send USD$89.00 today because i have already arranged your wires ready for its daily wires to you but failling to do this, i will allow them to have power over your fund and am very sorry if you failed as this is the last chance.

Therefore, send the USD$89.00 immediately you receive this email today and email your full name and address to me if you want your USD$1.5Million be send to you by western union OR Monegram transfer but the maximum amount officially allow for it per day wire to you is USD$7,500.00 per day until you receive your complete USD$1.5Million from here . The second option is for you to send me the full detail of your bank account if you want your fund be fully transfer by direct bank to bank wire transfer to your account at once. After you have sent the $89.00 and email me the mtcn numbers, you are to indicate your wish to receive your funds as I have stated above and the funds will be released to you without any hitch.

Here is the western union or moneygram information in the name of my accountant to avoid delay in receiving your fund and remember that i have done my best for you and i will make sure that your wire will begin to be released to you from the moment you sent this $89.00 .

Send the $89.00 now and send me email with the western union mtcn or moneygram reference numbers when you send the money , you can as well call me on this number +229-68070 697 when you have sent the money now ok .

Receivers Name:.......MR PAUL JOHN
Pay-Out Country:... Benin
Pay-Out City : Cotonou.
Address: Sain-Pierre Paul Cotonou, Benin-Republic.
Test Question:...God
Answer :.. Bless.
Amount to send: ...$89.00
SEND MTCN NUMBER....

Send it and email the MTCN control number, amount sent, name and address of sender to me for easy collection and once again remember to reply through this my official email address info.treasurydepartbenin1@rocketmail.com

TAKE NOTE: REPLY ONLY THROUGH THIS EMAIL: info.treasurydepartbenin1@rocketmail.com

Thanks.
Mr. John Campbell .
Treasury Department, International
Wire Transfers, Federal Ministry of Finance Benin Republic.
Telephone: +229-68 070 697

Any questions on this one?

Government of Ghana

Often, a scam will indicate government officials are involved, as is the case with the next message from Ghana.

Dear Sir,

I am representing a Group of Three (3) Top Government Officials that Heads the most sensitive Office in the Government of Republic of Ghana. This Group is interested in Overseas Investments in your Country and at the same time to stand as a Trustee/Investor for possible evacuation of the Sum of US$35million which has been acquired directly or indirectly using their various positions in the Government.

The Civil Service Regulations Acts of 2001 prohibits Serving Government Officials from getting involved in Private Businesses or operation of Foreign Accounts without Public Declaration of Source and Origin of the acquired Funds to the Government of Ghana. Therefore we seek your genuine assistance to Partner with us for immediate evacuation of the aforementioned funds without delay. You shall retain 25% of the total sum as stated herein only if you are interested to work with us. This is 100% risk free without any legal implication.

Yours Truly,
Godfrey Williams

Mr. Godfrey, used an e-mail address from 'rediffmail.com', another carrier from India.

ALERT: REDIFF.COM. The disclaimer says it all...

YOU SPECIFICALLY AGREE THAT REDIFF SHALL NOT BE RESPONSIBLE FOR UNAUTHORIZED ACCESS TO OR ALTERATION OF YOUR TRANSMISSIONS OR DATA, ANY MATERIAL OR DATA SENT OR RECEIVED OR NOT SENT OR RECEIVED, OR ANY TRANSACTIONS ENTERED INTO THROUGH AN REDIFF SITE/SERVICE. YOU SPECIFICALLY AGREE THAT REDIFF IS NOT RESPONSIBLE OR LIABLE FOR ANY THREATENING, DEFAMATORY, OBSCENE, OFFENSIVE OR ILLEGAL CONTENT OR CONDUCT OF ANY OTHER PARTY OR ANY INFRINGEMENT OF ANOTHER'S RIGHTS

This e-mail site is one of those that will do nothing about fraudulent e-mails, SO BEWARE!

These guys have an interesting, and somewhat different pitch. They have $35M (US), which they imply has been made 'available' from their respective government agencies to 'invest' in foreign enterprises. Unfortunately, their government prohibits public officials from doing so directly; therefore, they are looking for someone to front their 'enterprise', for a fee, of course.

Great Britain
British Finance Monitoring Unit

Here is an interesting scam-mail (Gee, I may have coined a new term) that is a phony foreign government agency monitoring scams, to assure that your money gets to you; Mister Peter Marriot (or is it 'Marroit') will make sure of that.

> THE BRITISH FINANCE MONITORING UNIT
> 8th floor Eller man house, 12-20 chamomile street, EC3A 7PC, United kingdom .
> LONDON, ENGLAND.
> Email: <http://uk-mg41.mail.yahoo.com/neo/compose?to=tmonitoringunit@yahoo.co.uk> bf_monitoringunit@live.com <http://uk-mg41.mail.yahoo.com/neo/compose?to=tmonitoringunit@yahoo.co.uk>
> Tele: +447700093963
> from the Desk of Mr. Peter Marriot.
> The Director,
> British Finance Monitoring Unit.
> London, England.
>
> Attention: Beneficiary,
>
> We have noticed that a huge sum of money has been credited in your name for transfer and is currently floating in the international banking community.

In Line with the Law of the Government of Great Britain and other member countries of the United Nations, huge sums of money that has been found in the international Monitoring data system waiting to be transferred without claims for a period of 6 months or more, shall be confiscated and sent to the United Nations Treasury.

Prior to the above, we request you to contact this office immediately within 3 days of this notice for ratification by forwarding to us all current information including your direct telephone number and postal address where your original payment release documents shall be sent to you or consider your fund confiscated.

Be informed also that as soon as we receive your current data then we shall endorse the payment release documents and immediately instruct our authorized Bank of International Settlement (BIS) to release your funds by forwarding your file to them for immediate payment consideration.

Yours Faithfully,
Mr. Peter Marroit
The Director
British Finance Monitoring Unit.

Several problems here, not the least of which is that there is no Bank of International Settlement, it is the International Bank of Settlements, and it is not a British banking firm. Even the e-mail address is a fraud (e-mail is <u>eb_monitoringunit@live.com</u>, another of the 'free' e-mail sites.)

HM Revenue & Customs

This message is a new one on the e-mail scam circuit, from Ms. Lin Homer, Chief Executive of the Revenue and Customs Service. She claims to have your money and is investigating why you have been involved in a number of illegal transactions to get it. Read on, it gets even more interesting.

From: *Chief Executive and Permanent Secretary HM Revenue & Customs - 100 Parliament Street London, SW1A 2BQ. United Kingdom*
Department: Audit and Risk Committee Team
Telephone: 070 4577 2860 (Int:+447045772860)
Telephone: 070 4577 9897 (Int:+447045779897)

Message: Sole Beneficiary
File Code: RC/8366-32

This is to inform you that your fund payment requirements were forwarded to our agency for correction before payment. During the course of our investigation, we discovered that you have been indulged into various dubious/fraudulent bank transactions which have taken advantage of your transaction through the use of office bureaucratic processes to impose unnecessary charges on your fund payment in order to get you frustrated to their own advantage. Due to these reasons, we have reviewed more cases of delayed payments including your records and have decided to assist our local financial institutions in resolving and releasing most individual unpaid funds in United Kingdom which includes contract/inheritance funds, gambling/lottery awarded funds (sponsored by multinational companies) and other international suspended/withheld funds yet to be paid to its beneficiary's foreign account.

In view of the above, our defense strategy has yielded a voluminous result through immense resolution of financial issues with local and foreign financial units involved in your case and our extensive investigation confirmed that you are the original beneficiary shortlisted to receive an unpaid sum of $15,000,000.00 USD meant to be credited into your foreign account pending your acknowledgment in the provision of the requirements needed for an international and final payment of your fund.

Further to this development, you are advised to only provide a scanned copy of your driver's license or international passport (any identification document) and your residential address for postal delivery. If non of these requirements is received within 45 days, you will never be paid and this fund will be made to be forfeited under the Money Laundering and other Financial Crime Prohibition Act of

2003. Also note that due to my position as the Chief Executive and Permanent Secretary of the HM Revenue & Customs, I will not always be available to answer any of your calls because I am not always in my office. If you have any issue to discuss regarding your funds, kindly email me and i will always get back to you as soon as possible.

Make sure to forward all inquires and requirements to this email: linhomer@hm-revenue.org for confirmation.

Yours Sincerely,
Ms. Lin Homer.
(Chief Executive Officer).
HM Revenue & Customs.

Disclaimer: The information in this email and in any files transmitted with it is intended only for the addressee and contains confidential and/or privileged material. Access to this email by anyone else is unauthorized. If you receive this in error, please contact the sender immediately and delete the material from your computer. If you are not the intended recipient, any disclosure, copying, distribution or any action taken or omitted to be taken in reliance on it, is strictly prohibited.

Ms. Homer really wants to help you, but don't call her, she is often out of the office. Instead, reply to her e-mail, and send along a copy of your driver's license or passport. That will help her move forward quickly, not to help you, but to scam you even further by stealing your identity.

In reality, this is NOT a message from Ms. Homer. Instead, it is from a person using the New Zealand e-mail address ann.hargreaves@xtra.co.nz, which is certainly not a London, England address.

One of the things I love about the newer messages coming out these days is the disclaimer often appearing at the bottom of the message, telling you not to copy the message (broke that rule), and that taking or not taking action on this message is prohibited. I wonder how she proposes to take action against me, since the message was addressed to the usual 'undisclosed recipients'.

Royal House of Treasury (G. Britain)

The message which follows is utterly ridiculous, but very impressive in its references to everyone in the British Government, from Her Majesty the Queen to the Royal Agencies.

'The Honorable George Osborne' wants you to know that he is sorry your name was dropped from some 'listing' of those to be paid, and he represents that he 'owes' you $20.5M (US), and wants to pay you quickly. How completely noble of him. Of course, there is a hitch—you need to send him your personal information as soon as possible. Read and be amazed.

>49,Featherstone Street,
>London, EC 1Y 8SY
>United Kingdom
>Telephone: + 44 793 609 6539
>Fax: 44 207 900 6602

>*Attn: Beneficiary,*

We the entire members of the Royal House of Treasury, on behalf of the Government of Great Britain, under the auspices of the Her Royal Majesty Queen Elizabeth of England II held a meeting this week concerning payment,both foreign and local contractors and some inheritance funds which were not released to the right benefactors.

Her Royal Majesty, has just informed this office (Royal House of Treasury)that All the listed contractors and Inheritance funds benefactors which their CONTRACT PAYMENT SUM AND INHERITANCE FUNDS were not paid to should be released to them with effect.

We discovered that your payment listed to us Twenty million five hundred thousand dollars (US$20.5M) approximately 13,552,374.97 pounds, you are advised to respond with effect so that we will process your payment to be made in any form you wish to receive your funds.

Kindly respond to this office so that your payment will be process and transferred under 72hours of receiving this email, you can contact us on this telephone number + 44 793 609 6539 for a voice confirmation.

On going through files yesterday, we discovered that your file was dumped untreated, so at this juncture, we apologize for the delay of your payment and please stop communicating with any office now and attention to the appointed office below for you to receive your payment accordingly.

Now your new Payment Reference No.-35460021, Allocation No: 674632 Password No : 339331 , Pin Code No: 55674 and your Certificate of Merit Payment No : 103 , Released Code No: 0763; Immediate Telex confirmation No: -1114433 ; Secret Code No: XXTN013, Having received these vital payment number, therefore You are qualified now to received and confirm Your payment with the United Kingdom of Great Britain and Northern Ireland immediately within 72hours You are directed to reconfirm your full detailed information, as stated:

FULL NAME...............
HOME ADDRESS..........
PROFESSION.................
MARITAL STATUS............
AGE...................
HOME PHONE NUMBER and CELL PHONE NUMBER as well as time to call you on the phone.....................................

Please reply to *Hon.GeorgeOsborne@london.com*

Best Regards
George Osborn
Royal House of Treasury

The message, addressed to the usual 'undisclosed recipients', asks you to reply to an address in the message, although it was sent from a similar e-mail address (hon.georgeosborne@uk.com), both of which are spurious at best. I did take the liberty or responding quickly as he asked, and inquired how soon I could receive my money. In my message was a completely spurious set of identity information, and a phone number (real), which he could use to contact me further. No response to date.

British High Commission for Nigeria, Benin Republic, Ghana and Burkina Faso

Here is an interesting message, one which combines a number of the favorite scammer techniques, and also alludes to the old Nigerian 419 scams as further authentication.

Mr. Simmons wants to be your friend and benefactor in getting the horrible scams inflicted against you settled, once and for all. The Commission guarantees it, and will be sure to get the Nigerian Financial Intelligence Unit to secure your payment. What more could you ask for?

Read the message to see how far some scammers will go to try to seem plausible in their efforts to get you to bite on their scams.

BRITISH HIGH COMMISSION
Metro Plaza, Plot 991/992
Zakari Maimalari Street
Cadastral Zone AO,
Central Business District, Abuja.

Attention:Sir/Madam

The BRITISH High Commission in Nigeria, Benin Republic, Ghana and Burkina Faso received a report of scam against you and other British/US and Malaysian citizens, Etc. The countries of Nigeria, Benin Republic, Burkina Faso and Ghana have recompensed you following the meeting held with the four countries' Government and various countries' high commission for the fraudulent activities carried out by the four countries' Citizens.

Your name was among those scammed as listed by the Nigeria Financial Intelligent Unit (NFIU). Compensation has been issued out in Certified Bank Drafts to all the affected victims and has been already been in distribution to all the bearers. Your draft was among those that were reported undelivered as at on Friday and we wish to advise you to see to the instructions of the Committee to make sure you receive your draft immediately.

According to the number of applicants at hand, 184 Beneficiaries has been paid, half of the victims are from the United States, and we still have more 37 left to be paid the compensations of $2,500,000.00 USD each.

Your particulars was mentioned by one of the Syndicates who was arrested as one of their victims of the operations, you are hereby warned not to communicate or duplicate this message to him for any reason whatsoever as the U.S. secret service is already on trace of the other criminals.

So keep it secret till they are all apprehended. Other victims who have not been contacted can submit their application as well for scrutiny and possible consideration.

NFIU further told us that the use of Nigeria and Ghana Couriers was abolished due to interception activities noticed in the above mentioned courier services in Benin, Nigeria and Ghana and thereby have made a concrete arrangement with the Courier Company for a safe delivery to your door-step once the beneficiary meets up the demand of the conveyance.

We advise that you do the needful to make sure the NFIU dispatches your Draft on Friday.

You are assured of the safety of your draft and availability. Be advised that you should stop further contacts with all the fake lawyers and security companies who in collaboration scammed you. Get back to me immediately with your correct full details (Full Name, Contact Address And Reachable Telephone Number) to check if the delivery date suits you.

Yours in Service,
Mr John Simmons

Looking quickly at this message, there has not been a British Commission for Nigeria in years; since Independence was declared thirty-some years ago. Even then, there was no real 'commission'; rather, there was a British High Commissioner, a member of the UK Civil Service, who managed the finances, and relations with London. Beware of those who claim to be government officials.

The reality is that this message originated in China, as have several others out on the Internet lately, this time from a service called 'anji.gov.cn', one of the myriad of free services provided by the Chinese government to their people for e-mail message traffic. Your response will go to an 'admin' e-mail address with this provider, not to 'John Simmons', as indicated in the e-mail, addressed, as is common, to 'undisclosed recipients'.

China is rapidly becoming a large player in the international scam trade, so it pays, as I have said frequently, to know who you are receiving e-mails from, or not reply. Avoid the unknown, which invariably seems to provide only danger, damage, and a rip-off of your money.

Other Foreign Governments

Spread throughout the volume are references to a wide range of governments; either claims that government is involved in getting you money, or alluding to satisfying claims in those countries by banks and other financial or legal organizations. You can pick almost any country you wish by consulting the index as the end of the book.

Chapter 12 Foreign Banking Organizations

Foreign banks are a rich reference source for the would-be scammer, especially if they are seeking to scam people in countries other than their own, such as the US. You only have to put out a name or even allege a bank connection, to raise people's eyebrows and interest.

These scams often represent very interesting reading, as you will see from the various banking-related scam e-mails which follow. The first is one of the more recent ones to arrive in my inbox. It 'mentions' banking, seems to indicate an overseas connection, but never quite says the bank's name. The writer 'trusts' you will help with perpetrating a fraud, to the benefit of both you and the writer, with a very large sum of money as the prize.

Of course, the 'bank' probably does not exist; the e-mail address is persona, and not official; and the writer mentions no other way to confirm himself, other than responding to his e-mail (garryfedrick3811@yahoo.com). When you do, you are hooked; not just to the scam, but having confirmed your e-mail address, as it will surely be sold as a legitimate e-mail address for other scams. BE WARNED.

Attn: Beneficiary

I am Garry Fedrick and I work as an Auditor in a Commercial Bank here in London. We had a customer and business tycoon from Asia who had a deposit of 12,750,000.00 (Twelve Million, Seven Hundred and Fifty thousand Pounds) before he died in a Car crash with his wife and only Child about 8years now (January 30,2000) and since he died, we in the Bank here have been expecting his/her next of kin/relative(s) for the inheritance of the deposit, but none has surfaced.

The policy of the Bank however stipulates a limited time period for such inheritance to be made or the fund will be written off going by the record of the incident, the time limit for the claim is closing up Soon for the next of kin to show up or the account will be closed and i came to have the knowledge of this account as the auditor in the bank. I happen to come across this file when i was going through the records.

In this consideration, I am contacting you to seek for your kind understanding and sincere co-operation to claim this inheritance for our mutual benefit in view of the fact that you are a Foreigner. If you can stand as the next of kin in this project, success is assured because I am in possession of the personal file jacket of the deceased which contains every needed information about the deceased account, you and I stand no risk of any kind because I have enough information to support you in claiming the inheritance.

The proceedings of the transaction will be shared 70% for me and 30% for you after expenses are reimbursed. Kindly indicate your willingness and we shall proceed with the initial step for the claim.

The entire project is expected to last for about ten working days. Hope to hear from you soonest showing your interest and willingness.

Please bear in mind that this is not jokes or games people choose to play on the internet. My solicitation is for real and my intentions are genuine. If you are a prominent personality you will understand the situation. If I could have your attention, I would furnish you with further details of this project and situation.

I will be waiting for your response once you are interested in my proposal with the following information.

Your full name and contact address
Your occupation, age and position
Your private telephone and fax number for communication purpose
Please free to ask question for further information.
Warm Regards,
Garry Fedrick

Our new 'friend' Garry Fedrick Is well known from listings on the various scam sites on the Internet, not only by the address above, but also under 'garryfedrick@yahoo.com' (2011), and quite possibly some others, since the name Fedrick is not very common. This guy is different from many of the others, who are usually satisfied with a fee, such as an amount going to Western Union, a perennial favorite, or sometimes even a small amount for bribes to government officials. This guy wants 30% 'off-the-top', and you supposedly get the rest. Of course, there is no 30% to give the scammer; all you get is aggravation, a probable twist of the arm for some 'upfront virtue money' to prove you are honest, and then a dead e-mail address or telephone number. It doesn't take too long for it to sink in that you have been had by a professional.

Speaking of being had by a professional, let's go to another case from Nigeria. This has all the earmarks we have been discussing rolled up into one message.

The Classic – Central Bank of Nigeria

As already noted earlier, some people try to get you to believe them by using official-sounding government agencies and contacts. The e-mails below are among the newer varieties of the Nigeria scam so popular in the 90's. These cite the Central Bank of Nigeria so you will know who is scamming you. They are interesting reading!

> CENTRAL BANK OF NIGERIA
> CORPORATE HEAD QUARTERS
> TINUBU SQUARE, LAGOS
> CONTRACT: MAV/NNPC/FGN/MIN/009
> Our Ref code: CBN/IRD/CBX/021/010
>
> ATTENTION: BENEFICIARY,
>
> We are glad to inform you that $67,940.00 spent in your fund has been re-added to your inheritance funds making it all together $14.7 million US dollars to be paid to you via cash consignment delivery by a special appointed courier service "Global express". The diplomat shall be leaving the shores of Nigeria tonight and it will be arriving your country in the next 20 hours.
>
> Kindly contact the GLOBAL EXPRESS DIPLOMATIC COMPANY LIMITED via email: michael.bard@aol.com they will give you more directives on how your cash-consignment will arrive your destination. Once again I will like you to thank the new elected board of trustees on foreign affairs matters CBN. They have really tried to have made your payment a success.
>
> I shall be using this opportunity to let you know that you should be prepared to welcome the diplomat and take good care of him. His name is Dip. John Philip he is a special diplomat from the SCARLET

SECURITY COMPANY, We have had several assignments through him and he delivers promptly.

Congratulations to you as soon as you receive your cash-consignment box email me and I will release the opening code for you to access your $14.7 million US dollars. Stay blessed and enjoy yourself as you wait for your money.

Kindly Contact the Global Express Courier Company..

Best Regard,

DR Sanusi Lamido Sanusi
Executive Governor Central
Bank of Nigeria (CBN)

In this case, a person, supposedly Dr. Sanusi, the Executive Governor of the Bank of Nigeria, is trying his hardest to get you a total of $14.7M (US). He wants you to work with Michael Bard, his 'agent' to get the information you need to access your payment, when it arrives in the country under the watchful eye of John Phillip, a 'diplomat' who works for a security firm. We will assume the writer really means a representative of the security firm,

While nothing is said of the information Mister Bard will send you, if you reply. I can tell you that, having responded to him, I got no reply at all. Others may have been luckier.

So, what do we have here? We have a person, probably this Mister Bard, trying to convince you that Dr. Sanusi and the Central Bank of Nigeria are involved, and they truly want to help you. They just want you to reply to a private e-mail address, receive information, and then trust a guy named Phillips. The likelihood is that Bard would have wanted some form of fee, or cut of the funds, he would claim, to get you what you need. Once he has the funds, he disappears.

The next message is supposed to be from Janet Brown, an employee of the Central Bank, who, by the way, wants you to reply to her quickly, before the bank itself scams you. That is an interesting twist.

Dear Beneficiary,

Hurry now and claim your fund from the Central Bank of Nigeria or your fund will be confiscated by the wicked officials of the CBN.

My name is MISS JANET BROWN, I am a Computer Scientist working with Central Bank of Nigeria (CBN). I am 25 years old, just started working with CBN.

I came across your payment file marked X and your released disk painted RED. I took time to study it and tried to find out why the funds were not released to you. Those evil officials can never tell you the truth that they won't release the fund to you; instead they allow you spend your hard earned money unnecessarily.

I do not intend to work here forever; I can help you claim your fund if you can certify me of my security and assure me that you would compensate with me after you must have received your payment. I must do this because you need to know the status of your payment and cause for the delay. This is like a Mafia setting in Nigeria and you may not understand because you are not a Nigerian.

The only thing needed to release this fund to you is the Original INTERNATIONAL TRANSFER PERMIT (ITP), which will be tendered to any of your nominated bank and the Internal Revenue Service IRS for clearance of the transferred amount in your account.

Once the Original TRANSFER PERMIT Certificate is secured, fund will immediately reflect in your bank within 24 HOURS. The only authorized and sincere person who will issue you the Original Documents is REV.JAMES KUTO. Make sure you indicate your file letter X and tell him its painted color Red so he will be able to recognize your file. The president made a compensation fund release for all unpaid beneficiaries/contractors and scam victims.

Therefore, you are going to receive a total sum of $10,000,000.00 (Ten MILLION DOLLARS) for this year

2012 as recorded in your file here and will be transferred to your bank account as soon as the Original document are obtained.

Do get back to me ASAP if you are still interested in claiming your fund so that I can give you further direction and contact of Dr. Ibrahim Bello.
Email:janetbrownnnn@live.com
Yours sincerely,
MISS JANET BROWN.

There are several interesting aspects to this message, which arrived addressed to 'undisclosed recipient', as we have often see before. Janet Brown is supposedly a 25 yr. old computer specialist, who has 'found' an account labeled 'x', with something called a 'release disk' labeled 'RED'. She is actively desirous of sending this money to you, but you need a document, an International Transfer Permit, to get the money released. A Rev. James Kuto is the guy who prepares the document, and files it with your bank, and the Internal Revenue Service.

That seems simple enough, I guess. After all, it involves $10M (US), and the Internal Revenue Service of both Nigeria and the US would surely be interested in a transfer that large.

Ms. Brown wants you to get back to her as quickly as possible so the transfer can take place, through yet another person, Dr. Ibrahim Bello. She doesn't actually say what part he plays in this drama, so we will leave that for now. Her return e-mail address is to a 'live.com' address, and not to one from the bank. Previous messages were from 'misjanetb@yahoo.cn', and in those messages, the 'documents' were to be provided by a Dr. Ola Ibrahim. The account is still 'x' and the disk is still 'RED', only the names have been changed to perpetrate the fraud. She has also used a 'rocketmail.com' address – a subsidiary of the YAHOO Empire.

There is also another active 'Nigerian' scam ongoing, this time from a Mrs. Janet Brown, who offers less money, and has cancer. Not sure at this point if they are one-and-the-same. Beware of either, and you will be safe.

The next message is from 'Dr. Kingsley Moghalu', Deputy Governor of the Central Bank. Dr. Moghalu apologizes that someone is using his name fraudulently, in this variant of the 'Nigeria Scam."

Hello Dear,

I wish to inform you that all matters relating to the release of this payment is now under my control and supervision. This development has become necessary due to the activities of unpatriotic government/CBN officials and impostors who keep on frustrating every effort to settle our clients by making requests for unauthorized fees and levies from them.

We sincerely apologize for any delay you might have encountered in the past; your payment is now 100% Guaranteed.

I am Dr.Kingsley C. Moghalu the deputy governor CBN.I was mandated by the President Federal Republic in conjunction with the Federal Executive Council (FEC), the Senate Committee on Foreign Debts Reconciliation and Implementation Panel on Contract/inheritance/compensation funds to complete the entire unpaid Contract/inheritance/lottery fund. You are required as a matter of urgency to reconfirm your information including your name, phone number and your address for verification and immediate payment within 24 hours.

To this effect, the sum of $10.7 Million (TEN MILLION, SEVEN HUNDRED THOUSAND UNITED STATES DOLLARS) has approved for you. Kindly choose from these three modes of payment (wire transfer, diplomatic cash payment and ATM card).

I can be reached on this number anytime: +234-70-86731414. Call me for more details. Kindly get back to me ASAP.

Best Regards,

Dr.Kingsley Moghalu
Deputy Governor CBN

Email: *moghalukiyngsle@superposta.com*

NB: KINDLY NOTE THAT SOME PEOPLE (FRAUDSTERS) HAVE STARTED MAKING FORGERY OF MY GOOD NAME.

> ALERT: SUPERPOSTA.COM Just in case you might be interested, 'superposta.com' is a Turkish e-mail service, much like Yahoo or Hotmail, but with far fewer protections against just the type of trash you are seeing in these pages. They will remove an account, if contacted.

The real Dr. Moghalu actually is the Deputy Governor of the Central Bank of Nigeria, and is most assuredly not a scammer. However, his name and title, along with other African leaders, is often used by scammers, to add 'authenticity' to their message's look and feel. In this case, his name, the amount of money, and an e-mail address are supposed to convince you the opportunity is real, and you should respond.

Regrettably, there are other indicators in this message that should rouse your suspicion. The first indication is his e-mail address, one from the 'superposta.com' address, rather than the Central Bank of Nigeria address, which ends in 'cenbank.org'. Another quirk in the message is the greeting, 'Hello Dear', which is very personal for a message addressed to the usual 'undisclosed recipients'. The third 'clue' is the absolutely horrible wording of the message – something a Ph.D. would never send, particularly to someone he does not know.

In fact, the Central Bank has issued a disclaimer on these frauds. The disclaimer is reproduced in Appendix C at the end of the volume.

A more recent version of the scam is from Alh Idris Abdullahi, also supposedly from the Central Bank. All the usual earmarks of the scam are present, even the high-level amounts of money (in this case $6.5M US) remain somewhat constant.

GoodDay.

CALL US BANK INTERVENTION ON YOUR PAYMENT
This is to notify all Foreign Funds Transfer Beneficiary that the Presidency have embarked on immediate cancellation of all International payment Application from verius Government Financial Institution/Offshore payment Bank, due to a lot of people complaining of paying fees and charges before their fund can be released to them.

However, with regard to provision of section 117 Degree of the 1999 constitution and In line with the world Bank auditors' report from Nigeria,and our subsequent meeting with the Federal Ministry of Finance/United Nation and members of the FSA/The treasury directorate division of the UN Financial Monetary Authority. All foreign payment fund has been re-approved and assigned to CENTER BANK for immediate released of your fund to you as it has approv for payment

The CENTER BANK has up hold all payment fund retrieved from various banks to ensure successful payment to the rightful beneficiary who his/her fund has been approved for payment,US$6.500.000 have be approve to you as past payment the Federal Government in conjunction with the United Nation have put a new law to stop fraudulent act and to those bank that promise to help you through the back door to`receive your fund, by ATM CARD, CASH DELIVERY,CASHIER CHECK which is not possible,you'are warmed to stop further communication with any individual or Bank that may contact you in this regard as your fund will be DIRECT WIRE TRANSFER TO YOUR ACCOUNT THROUGH OUR CORRESPONDENT BANK NEW YORK.

Re-confirm to me the followings
(1) Your full names:
(2) Contact address:
(3) Tel-Fax/cell phone numbers:
(4) Occupation/Position:
(5) Name of company if any:
(6) Age and marital status.

As soon as we receive this information, we shall proceed immediately for your payment without further delay.

Regards,

ALH IDRIS ABDULLAHI.
Central Bank of Nigeria

The message above by Mr. Abdullah cites 'CENTER BANK' a couple of times instead of the actual bank name. The writer also uses the e-mail address 'uba_bankzone3@yahoo.co.jp', a Japanese subsidiary of the YAHOO family of free sites.

The interesting part of the yahoo.co.jp story is that this address has been used on a number of occasions over the past several years, by people who variously call themselves 'Dr. Henry Jonathan' of the AFD Bank or Dr. William S. Adam of the Bank of Africa. There are probably others as well.

Another of the newer messages is reproduced below. In this message, the writer has now added 'International' to the bank's title. Our old friend Sanusi Lamido is the 'new executive governor' (we have heard from him before, in a message where he called himself Dr. Sanusi Lamido Sanusi). This time, instead of a bit more than $67K (US), he has $10M (US) to give you, if you will only reply.

FROM THE DESK SANUSI LAMIDO
NEW EXECUTIVE GOVERNOR OF CENTRAL BANK (CBN) INTERNATIONAL HEADQUARTERS GARKI- ABUJA, NIGERIA.
EMAIL: sanusilmido@live.com
ATTN: Valuable Contractors:
IMMEDIATE CONTRACT PAYMENT.CONTRACT: CBN/NNPC/FGN/MIN/013

We apologize, for the delay of your payment and all the inconveniences and inflict that we might have indulge you through. However, we were having some minor problems with our payment system, which is inexplicable, and have held us stranded and indolent, not having the aspiration to devote our 100% assiduity in accrediting foreign contract Payments. We apologies once again.

> *From the records of outstanding contractors due for payment with the federal government of Nigeria, your name and Company was discovered as next on the list of the outstanding contractors who have not yet received their payments. I wish to inform you now that the square peg is now in square whole and can be voguish for that your payment is being processed and will be released to you as soon as you respond to this letter.*
>
> *Also note that from the record in our file your outstanding contract payment is $10,000,000.00 United State Dollars.*
>
> *Kindly re-confirm to me the followings:*
>
> *1) your full name.*
> *2) Phone, fax and mobile*
> *3) Company name, position and address:*
> *4) Profession, age and marital status.*
>
> *As soon as this information is received, your payment will be made to you via telegraphic swift transfer into your designated Bank Account or an ATM CARD will be issue to you directly from Central Bank of Nigeria.*
>
> *Thanks for your good understanding,*
> *Hope to have your response shortly.*
> *Regards,*
> *Dr. Sanusi Lamido*
> *New Executive Governor Central*
> *Bank of Nigeria (CBN).*
> *Email: sanusilmido@live.com*

'Dr. Sanusi' loves ATM cards—it is the wave of the future for scammers. You will see it often in these pages.

We are going to leave the Central Bank for a while (We will come back to it periodically in the rest of the volume), and take you now to some other Nigerian and worldwide banks mentioned often in these scam messages. Enjoy your reading.

Oceanic Bank International (Nigeria)

The next message has an interesting twist from the usual Nigerian banking scam. This is supposed to be a message from 'Oceanic Bank International', located, as you would guess, in

Nigeria. This time they have an overdue inheritance to give out, and want to transfer it by an 'ATM Master Express Card', whatever that is. It does claim the card is a 'Gold Card', and everybody wants at least a gold card.

Whoever wrote the message could not even spell the name of the bank correctly. More importantly, there is no such thing as the "World Bank and Paris Club', which is supposed to manage those cards.

Interesting reading, but clearly an easily identified scam.

Oceanic Bani International
Attn: Beneficiary,

We hereby officially notifying you about the present arrangement to pay you your over due contract/inheritance funds which you could not complete the process of the released of your transfer pin code through the Digitalized Payment System. We have decided to pay your funds without any requested fee but through (ATM Master Express Credit Card) This arrangement was initiated/constituted by the World Bank and Paris Club, due to fraudulent activities going on within the African Region.

The World Bank and Paris Club introduced this payment arrangement as to enable our contractors/inheritance beneficiary to receive their funds without any interference. the ATM Master Express Credit Card was contracted and powered by GOLD CARD WORLD WIDE.

Reconfirm the following information to us for security reasons:
  1)YOUR FULL NAMES
  2)YOUR MAILING ADDRESS.
  3)YOUR DIRECT TELEPHONE NUMBER
  4)YOUR PROFESSION

Upon the receipt of this information we are going to credit your funds into the Master Express Credit Card and send a scanned copy of the card to you before we will proceed to dispatch the card directly to your nominated mailing address. So you absolutely have nothing to worry about as all we need is your prompt response and co-operation.

BEST REGARDS,

MR.JOHN ABOH,
DIRECTOR,FOREIGN OPERATIONS
DEPARTMENT,
OCEANIC BANK INTERNATIONAL

CC: ALL FOREIGN INHERITANCE FUNDS
CC:CENTRAL BANK GOVERNOR
CC: BOARD OF DIRECTORS [FPD]
CC: ACCOUNTANT GENERAL OF NIGERIA

The next message, quoting Oceanic Bank, PLC, is from 'Scott Mido', who claims to be the Remittance Manager of the bank. He wants to pay you $1M (US), through the usual ATM card, which is free, except for the insurance on the transmittal of the card. Another interesting new twist.

In any event, you have to provide the usual information to Mr. Mido, which completely gives away your identity, and, if you are really stupid, he will even arrange for a bank-to-bank transfer for you, so you lose your own money as well, when he fleeces your account, using the information you provided him. Not bad for a message addressed to 'undisclosed recipient'.

Attention:

Let me start by introducing myself I am scott mido, I was directed by Good luck Jonathan President of Federal republic of Nigeria and the chairman Economic and Financial Crimes Commission (EFCC) Farida

Mzamber Waziri (Mrs.), to notify you on the investigation that took place here in Nigeria.

In regards with the investigation that has happened recently here in Nigeria will noticed that you are dealing with some Nigerians who claimed you have money with them and they have failed to make you get the money and you lost so much money during the process, I am currently paying so many people with the same problem, so I have been directed by the Nigeria government to pay you also but due the late registration of your name on the list of the people I have to pay, I will not be able to pay you much because of insufficient fund, so I will only pay you $1,000,000.00 (One Million dollars only) as compensation to what has happened to you.

I have prepared an ATM CARD on your name and I will advice you to contact the dispatcher to enable him send the ATM CARD to your home below is the contact information of the dispatcher, make sure you contact him and get the ATM CARD.

scott mido.
Remittance Manager,
Oceanic Bank Plc.
EMAIL: scott midoft@gmail.com

Mean while be informed that cost of shipment has being settled but the insurance coverage of ATM Card is at your expense.

Get back to the director ATM (scott mido) to enable him inquire about the cost of the Insurance of your ATM Card to be delivered at your doorstep and keep you informed.

Fill this form and send it back to him to enable him dispatch your ATM CARD at once.

* Title:_____.
* First Name:_____.
* Last Name:_____.
* Street Address:_____.

* City:_____tehran_____.
* State &Country:_____.
*Phone: (Area Code) - Number:_____.
*Fax: (Area Code) - Number:_____.
* Occupation:_____.
* Next of kin:_____.
* Id card/ Driving license:_____.
Send the above information immediately.

Note: you can also receive your funds through bank to bank transfer but you are going to be requiring paying for the transfer commission as no deduction can be made out of your compensation funds.

Note: The government of Nigeria as seized monies from everybody and cooperate bodies that has participated on the issue. We seize this opportunity to also warn that anyone or cooperate bodies caught bringing the name of the country to disrepute will be firmly dealt with within the ambit of the law. So you are advice to disregard any email you get from anyone or co-operate bodies and forward the email to us for proper conduct.

On behalf of the President of the federal republic of Nigeria, we are truly sorry for the inconveniences and for what you encounter from the Nigerians that make you lost so much money please speak well about Nigeria in your country as soon as you get this ATM card.

Best regards,
scott mido

While Mr. Mido provides you with an e-mail for your reply, the message itself was sent from another address (test@punch.com), which is a relatively new domain for these messages.

The message above is one of the newer messages out of Nigeria, and the writer goes out of his/her way to apologize over and over again for the previous scams which have plagued the e-mail public. He assures you the money is real—the president

Jonathan Luck has had the money seized from the various sources of the scams, and consolidated to ensure its delivery. Could that be any safer? Of course, it can BECAUSE THE MESSAGE IS A SCAM, and you could be the target they want to make even more money for THEMSELVES.

And now, on to some other countries known for their scamming as well. Our first stop is Benin, another African republic, and the Intercontinental Bank.

Intercontinental Bank PLC (Benin)

I introduced the Government of Benin, in Chapter 11, and now we get to hear from one of its major banks. They are offering you an ATM card (Accepted at over 900,000 ATM locations throughout the world), and, like its counterpart in Nigeria, it is a GOLD card. You can get up to $10,000 (US) each day through the card, so that is 95 days or more of pure wealth. Sounds great, doesn't it? All for only a $95 (US) fee for processing the card.

For those of you who follow the ATM/Credit card business, getting a 'gold' card used to be a big deal. American Express introduced it years ago, to differentiate between its convenience card, and one supported by the local banks, and which you could use to defer payments on what you owed. Eventually, everyone in the industry introduced a 'gold' card card—mostly as a new color with no special benefits.

This is another fraud, of course, but interesting to see that the private sector also gets some credit for being caught up in the scams.

Intercontinental Bank Plc
Cotonou, Benin Republic.
Notification of payment by ATM Card

Attention Beneficiary ,

We are hereby officially notifying you about the present arrangement to pay you, your over due award, contract and inheritance fund through (ATM CARD) this arrangement was Initiated/constituted by the World Bank due to fraudulent activities going on around the world. The World Bank introduced this payment arrangement as to enable all beneficiary to receive their funds without any interference, this ATM CARDS are powered by GOLD CARD WORLD WIDE.

Please note that what we will be sending to you is an Intercontinental Bank Master Card which is accepted at over 900,000 ATM Centers in over 210 Countries World Wild, this Intercontinental Bank Master Card will be loaded with a total sum of US$950.000.00 (NINE HUNDRED AND FIFTY THOUSAND DOLLARS) which is the total amount due to you for payment now and after this one is cleared another will be paid in until your total funds and completely paid out.

In line with the withdrawal procedure of this ATM MASTER CARD, you are only allowed a daily withdrawal of not more than US$10.000.00 until all the funds are exhausted. The package shall be delivered to you and the delivery shall be done by DHL COURIER SERVICE and the charges associated with the delivery are $95USD and will be paid upfront to enable the processing of your ATM Card delivery. The package is coming from Cotonou Benin Republic and there for the fee must be paid to Benin by beneficiary to the courier company. In View of this, you are advised to contact the Director (IBB, IRD, and ATM) Dr. Richard Daniels for further information with the following contact.

Contact Person: Dr. Richard Daniels
Emails: *intercontinentalbanqebj@hotmail.com*

Reconfirm the following information to him for Security reason
1) YOUR FULL NAME...
2) YOUR RECEIVING ADDRESS...
3) YOUR TELEPHONE NUMBER...
4) YOUR PROFESSION...

The Ninety Five Dollars {$95USD} is the last and only fee associated to this delivery of your package, so we urge you to Cooperate as instructed and receive your package.

Best regards,
Mrs. Catherine Jones
Secretary Intercontinental Bank Benin

'Ms. Jones' has a fairly long history as a scammer under this name, whoever 'she' really is. The last message has been around since 2011, about the time when she adopted the e-mail address 'officeconsultant.1615@rediffnet.com'. A quick check of the e-mail owner says this address is no longer active, although it was used as recently as January, 2013.

By the way, another scam, also under the name Catherine Jones, involves contributions to a 'presidential library', specific name not mentioned. In this case, Ms. Jones is operating with a 'yahoo.co.es' address, and this time, she is the Secretary for the Library. As you can see, this is another YAHOO subsidiary.

Financial Bank PLC (Benin)

The next message involves another bank from Benin, this time with new twist to the traditional scam routine. In this message, 'Ms. Gabriel' is complaining you have not received your funds from the bank because you chose to work with one of those 'African imposters' who are trying to cheat you. She suggests that you contact her directly, since she has already converted the funds for you, deposited them in a strong box for delivery, and paid the initial transfer and storage fees.

Reading on, you will also find she asks you to lie about what's in the box. Enjoy.

Attention fund beneficiary

Good Day, I am glad to announce to you today that a new payment policy has been adopted and this fund supposed to be in your position by now but according to the information we gathered from the Formal Minister of Finance he said that you did not come through the front door to claim your fund but through the back door by dealing with some Africans impostors that is why he did not contact or said anything to you in regards to your payment. Please note that after our resolution meeting with the new Minister of Finance and our New President we have agreed to pay off your fund. Therefore note that information has been passed to Benin republic universal parcel service

I have paid the fee for your compensation Bank draft and I took it to the issuers bank FINANCIAL BANK PLC to confirm it, then the Manager of the Bank MR. OBALA OBA told me that before the Draft will get to you it will expire on the way and if it expires it will become useless so He advice me to convert the Draft of ($2.5M USD) into cash and He assisted me and packaged the funds into the strong iron box and deposit the box in GLOBAL COURIER SERVICE (GCS))BENIN to deliver it to you.

I did it as he advised me because he is a banker he knows the durability of any foreign cheque or draft. Note that I deposited the strong iron box in the GLOBAL COURIER SERVICE (GCS) BENIN as Family valuable and Gift items. This is for security reasons and for the safety of your money.

Be informed that the GLOBAL COURIER SERVICE (GCS) officials did not know the real content of the consignment box except you and I and you have to make sure you don't disclose the real content of the box to them once you resume communication with GLOBAL COURIER SERVICE (GCS).

Incase you are being asked about the content of the box you are to tell them the box contains Family valuable and Gift items. This is the registration Number of your Package (GCS/122P/ MTM/20023ZIP CODE: 0113388).

SHIPMENT CODE AWB 33XZS.
SECURITY CODE SCTC/2001DHX/567/.
TRANSACTION CODE233/CSTC/101/33028/.
CERTIFICATE DEPOSIT CODE SCTC/BUN/xxiv/-78/01.

I want you to contact the Company immediately with the following information below. Though I gave them your information but you need to reconfirm it to them. Below is the require *information you need to give them now immediately you contact them.*

1. YOUR FULL NAMES AND ADDRESS.
2. YOUR PHONE AND FAX NUMBER.
3. IDENTIFICATION SUCH AS PASSPORT OR DRIVING LICENSE.
4. YOUR AGE AND MARITAL STATUS.
5. OCCUPATION.

You have to make sure you forward the above information to the Company to enable them commence arrangement towards delivering your box of money worth ($2.5m USD) immediately.

Note that the delivery fee of your consignment box has been paid by me and i did not pay their official keeping fees since they refused and the reason's that they do not know when you are going to contact them and demurrage might have increase. They told me that their keeping fees is $45 per day and i deposited it on 03/02/2013, i advise you to contact them today to avoid increase of demurrage, This is the company contact info:

GLOBAL COURIER SERVICE (GCS)
Dr David Anthony.
Email: (global_courier.company@mail.com)

Kindly contact the company immediately you receive this e-mail so that your package will be scheduled to depart to your location in the next 24 hours. Get back to me as soon as you receive your package from the company.

Regards,
Mrs Grace Gabriel
E-Mail: gabrielgrace51@gmail.com

There are just a couple of 'minor' problems with this message. First global_courier.company@mail.com does NOT get you to the transfer company. Ms. Gabriel's address is similarly a problem; she wants you to correspond with her through a private address, rather than one related to the bank. The clue here is found in the message itself, which says, *'Be informed that the GLOBAL COURIER SERVICE (GCS) officials did not know the real content of the consignment box except you and I and you have to make sure you don't disclose the real content of the box to them once you resume communication with GLOBAL COURIER SERVICE (GCS)'.*

Interesting, isn't it?

Another disconnect lies in her initial statement that she deposited your box with the Benin Republic Universal Parcel Service, in paragraph one, but later changes that to the Global Courier Service. No explanation why an official service gave way to a private one, except to hide the transaction.

Oh well, on to other countries. It's time to start seeing that the same things happen in western democracies as well. Here's one that claims to be from Barclay's Bank in London for you to ponder.

Barclay's Bank (London)

This message invokes the names of the 'British Ministry of Finance' and 'Her Royal Highness, Queen Elizabeth, Queen of England' as their authorization to release an inheritance to you. That is one important set of people in England authorizing such an act, so you should consider sending these scammers all the information they require—including, incidentally, a copy of an identity document, one which conclusively proves who you say you are. Interesting reading.

Barclay's Bank Plc-Foreign Operations Dept:
1 Churchill Place, London
E14 5HP, United Kingdom
Tel: +4470-1704-8194
barclaysbnkpllc@hotmail.com

==========================

Dear Honorable Beneficiary,

We wish to inform you that the board of trustees and management of Barclay's Bank International Plc London has finalized and have being given an Immediate transfer approval order by the British

Ministry of Finance in conjunction with the United Nations and Executive members of Bank of England, following with the instructions we received from Her Royal Highness Queen Elizabeth, the Queen of England. to transfer your overdue Inheritance fund to you, the approved sum of US$ 10.700,000,00 (Ten Million Seven Hundred Thousand United States Dollars) also be informed that we are prepared to give you the best of services in this Honorable Bank with a guarantee that your Approved Fund will be wire into your nominated Bank

(1) By Bank to Bank Wire Transfer

The management & board of trustees of this bank wish you to fill out the transfer form with your contact details and your direct phone number also with your banking information for the immediate processing of the legal document that will enable us carry out the transfer of your fund successfully to your nominated bank account or your contact address without any further delay.

We are waiting your immediate response with your information below to enable this bank proceeds immediately with the transfer of your fund and serve you better.

Full Name.....................
Home Address.................
Age/Occupation..............
Valid Phone number............
Your Country........
Any of Your Identity Cards.......

Thank you for choosing Barclay's bank plc.

Signed,
Yours Faithfully
Dr. Robert Brown
Remittance Director
BARCLAY'S BANK PLC LONDON

Dr. Brown seems very sincere in his desire to get you your large inheritance. This is truly a magnificent sum, earned over many years by 'Recipients' family (The e-mail is addressed to 'undisclosed recipients'), and it is all yours IF you give away both your identity, and a proof of that identity. It's as simple as that. Send the information; get it validated by whoever sent the message to begin with, and start seeing you identity, and probably your accounts, fade into history.

Before you do, though, consider this. It is not the Queen that authorizes such payments, unless they are coming from her personal accounts. Nor is it 'the British Ministry of Finance', since that ministry is actually called The Exchequer". The only thing real in this message is the fact that there is a Bank of England.

Bank of East Asia (United Kingdom Branch)

The Bank of East Asia is a Hong Kong Bank, with branches in China and the United Kingdom (UK). In the UK, the bank has several offices, mostly for commercial business.

'Mr. Y. Y. Yeung' says he is the Assurance Manager for the United Kingdom Branch of the Bank of East Asia. He has a deal for you, mostly because you, Mr. 'undisclosed recipient' have the same name as one of his former clients.

Unfortunately, his 'client' died, and now Mr. Yeung wants to work a deal to steal the money, with your help, and prevent the money from being 'unclaimed funds', which he claims, would eventually revert to the bank. Sounds really simple; if, that is, you are a simpleton. Read and see what you think.

Good Day,

I am Yuk Cheung, Principal Assurance Manager, Bank of East Asia, United Kingdom Branch. I am contacting you concerning a client/foreigner with the same last name as yours and the investment he placed under our banking management some years ago. The client/foreigner asked that his funds with Bank of East Asia, United Kingdom Branch should be move to "EROL FIDUCIARY" an investment management company here in United Kingdom for a business purpose.

Unfortunately, before the commencement of the business with "EROL FIDUCIARY" the investment management company here in United Kingdom, the client/foreigner died of cardiopulmonary failure and ever since then no body came forward all these years as his relative or next of kin. What I propose is that since I have exclusive access to his file in Bank of East Asia, United Kingdom Branch and you bearing the same last name with the client/foreigner, we can work things out together as a team and benefit from this deal. My suggestion to you now is this. Can we work together as a team and have these funds in our custody instead of allowing the investment management company here in United Kingdom revert the funds back to Bank of East Asia, United Kingdom Branch as unclaimed funds?

Please note that my suggestion to you requires confidentiality because of my reputation. If you are interested, kindly get back to me for more details.

Regards,
Y.Y Cheung

Disclaimer: This email (including any attachments) is for the use of the intended recipient only and may contain confidential information and/or copyright material. If you are not the intended recipient, please notify the sender immediately and delete this email and all copies from your system. Any unauthorized use, disclosure, reproduction, copying, distribution, or other form of unauthorized dissemination of the contents is expressly prohibited.

Mr. Cheung (Yuk Cheung, that is) is another name well known in scam circles. He often uses the e-mail address, 'yuk_cheung@cmc.org'. That address is not really his; a reply to this e-mail, if you do so, will get you to 'yuk_cheung@yahoo.com.hk, a Hong Kong address on the local YAHOO network. He also uses 'yy.cheungg@blumail.org', and 'yy.cheungg@yyc.com' Regardless of the address used, the messages are usually the same.

In any event. It is all downhill from there if you respond and provide him your personal information. One interesting point is his request for confidentiality, due to his 'reputation', which, in this instance, is universally bad.

Natwest Bank (London)

Moving to another UK bank, the National Westminster Bank (NatWest), is one of the larger banks in the country, and a logical target for someone who would use it for their own scam.

There is the conundrum here; would you reply to this e-mail, which offers you a seemingly great opportunity, from someone you do not know, and who feels 'constrained' from telling you anything about the opportunity, until you reply with more information?

Well, probably not, but go ahead and read it anyway, to see a relatively benign, but potentially powerful enticement to look into the 'opportunity', however briefly, to see if it makes sense. In my view, this is a simple scam, one designed to get your e-mail address for resale, more than a real opportunity for you. There is an opportunity here, however; one you should quickly pass up, although I would suggest that Mr. Lawrence hopes you do not.

> From: David Lawrence
> *Natwest bank Plc,*
> *London.*
>
> *My Request.*
>
> *I Have a very important request that make me to contact you; I am Mr. David Lawrence, I found Your profile very interesting and decided to reach you directly to solicit your assistance and Guidelines in making a business investment and transfer of (12.5M GBP) to your country within the Next few days. I presently work as a senior Accounts Director, Offshore Mortgage & Services with Natwest Bank Plc, London.*
>
> *But at this moment, I am constrained to issue more details about this profitable Business investment until I get your response by mail.*

Please take out a moment of your very busy Schedule today to respond back if you are interested.
I wish for utmost confidentiality in handling this transaction.
Awaiting your reply and please send all email correspondence to my personal email add: david13_la@hotmail.com

Mr. David Lawrence
Natwest Bank Plc,
London.

Now, it's time to move on again, and this time we go to Hong Kong, and the Hang Seng Bank.

Hang Seng Bank (Hong Kong)

'Mr. Tan Wong', who claims to be the Operations Director of Hang Seng Bank in Hong Kong, has a deal for you, worth many millions. Read the message that follows and decide if you want to contact him right away to claim it.

FROM:MR TAN WONG
wongmr.tan@yahoo.com.hk

I am Mr.Tan Wong director of operations, Hang Seng Bank, Hong Kong. I have urgent and confidential business proposition involving transfer of $24,500,000.00 that will be of great benefit for both of us. I will give you more details as regards this transaction as soon as you notify me of your interest.
Awaiting your urgent reply via my email address (wongmr.tan@yahoo.com.hk) which is my confidential email address.

Kind Regards,
Mr.Tan Wong

The Hang Seng Bank, part of the HSBC empire, is an old and established Hong Kong commercial bank, with extensive branches in China, and across South East Asia. Their Hang Seng Index is the most-regarded view of the Hong Kong stock market, and changes to it affect other major exchanges throughout the world.

A number of scams have been reported, attributed to various officers of the Bank over the past few years, from about 2007 to the present. The message above arrived in my inbox in February, 2013. Other names used in similar messages include Patrick Chen, Wang Qin, Leung Chung, Dr. Smith Lee, and Peter Wong. There are probably others as well.

All the messages have several things in common. They offer 'deals' which seem too good to walk away from; most are veiled attempts to get you to help someone steal from the bank; all use e-mail addresses, such as that from Mr. Wong who, as we often see, uses a 'yahoo.co.hk' e-mail domain. They always ask you to reply so they can provide more details; a ready indicator they want your information.

Next to the Nigerians, it really seems there are more scammers in Hong Kong than in many other countries.

HFDC Bank (India)

The next message, involves a different twist to the usual attempt to get your money. In this one, 'Mr. Joseph' claims to be the 'trustee' in control of a large inheritance, and whose real beneficiary is nowhere to be found. The message indicates that the 'deceased client' had the same last name as mine (Message was addressed to 'undisclosed persons' so it is impossible from the message to determine if that is true), and he wants to make right and get me the legacy.

Good Day Friend,

I am Mr. Benny Kanarathil Joseph, Principal Assurance manager for the HFDC Bank in India. I contacted you concerning a very viable business opportunity which could be of immense significance in our financial lives at this critical time of global financial recession. It is regarding the estate of a deceased client who shares the same last name with you and an investment portfolio (with a sum of US$13,500,000.00 -thirteen million, Five hundred thousand United States dollars) placed under our bank's management some years ago.

> Upon maturity of said investment, our client didn't show up after a reasonable period of time and out of concern, an investigation was conducted and it was confirmed with concrete evidence that he was involved in a ghastly accident in China when on a business trip. It was also discovered that he died after attempts to revive him failed.
>
> What I propose is that since I have exclusive access to his file and share the same surname as my client, you will be made the beneficiary of these funds.
>
> PLEASE NOTE that there is no risk involved in this process. I am on ground to ensure everything is successfully concluded.
>
> If you are interested, please do contact me for further details. Please do reply me via my personal email address:
>
> mr.bennykanarathil_joseph@hotmail.co.in
>
> Regards,
>
> Benny K Joseph

So, what do we know about 'Mr. Joseph'? Not much, I am afraid. He started his scam in March of 2013, as far as can be determined, and has only sent out one 'blast' thus far. HFDC Bank, while cited by Mr. Joseph, is probably a transliteration of HDFC Bank of India. That bank had a series of scandals and other problems over the past few years, in connection with money laundering and theft, and thus would seem to be a useful target for scammers, who want to capitalize on the notoriety of the name.

People remember names before them, but often don't remember details. Scams with these names have been around since 2008, although this is the first time Mr. Joseph has his name attached to a message.

While we are in India, another bank has achieved some prominence in the scamming market as well, so let's take a brief look at Reserve Bank of India next.

Reserve Bank of India

The Reserve Bank of India is that country's major banking institution. It acts as the central clearing house, and also manages the value of the Indian rupee, the nation's currency. Originally a private bank, the institution was nationalized afterIindian Independence was achieved in 1949.

The following messages use an approach with guarantees of large sums of money. I do love the messages from the English-speaking countries because they tend to be more flowery, use more financial terms (even if they are not really understood), and they tend to lull you into reading the message through, to see if it really might be true.

That's exactly what the scammer wants. This guy is willing to transfer you a massive sum, if only you will provide the transfer fee in Indian Rupees. Of course, as he indicates, the sum to be received is guaranteed by none other than the Secretary-general of the UN. What could be safer than that!

> 106 GROSVENOR SQUARE
> NEW DELHI W1A 1AE
> INDIA Customer Services.
> Payment File: RBI-DEL/id1033/11.
> Payment Amount: $ 800,000. US Dollars.
> RESERVE BANK OF INDIA OFFICIAL PAYMENT NOTIFICATION
>
> Attn: Beneficiary,
>
> The Foreign Exchange Transfer Department, Reserve Bank of India has decided to bring to your attention, that you were listed as a beneficiary in the recent schedule for payment of outstanding debts incurred by the BRITISH GOVERNMENT pending since 2000 to 2012 according to your file record with your email address, Your payment is categorized as:

Contract type:
Donation/loan/investment/Lottery/inheritance/ unpaid contract funds/ Undelivered Lottery fund.e.t.c

Recently on the 11th of September 2012. The Reserve Bank of India (RBI) Governor, Dr D. Subbarao and Ban Ki-moon Secretary-General of the United Nations met with the Senate Tax Committee on Finance RBI Mumbai/Delhi branch. Regarding unclaimed funds which have been due for a long run, at the end of the meeting (RBI) Governor, Dr D. Subbarao mandate all unclaimed funds to be released back to the beneficiary stating that it is an unfair practice to withhold funds for government basket for one reason or the other for tax accumulations. Therefore, we are writing this email to inform you that $800,000 US DOLLARS will be released you in your name, as it was committed for (RBI) Governor that beneficiary will have to pay crediting fees only. So, you are therefore be contact by your transfer officer incharge Mr Anand Jude & you shall required to pay 17,500 INR ONLY in cash deposit. To credit your account immediately you recive this notification

Kindly note you are advised to fill the form below and send it immediately to our transfer department for verification through email below for prompt collection of your fund. Manager Name Mr Anand Jude ,BRITISH OFFICER in charge of foreign exchange E- mail:rbitxf@yahoo.in

Fill The Form Below:
1. Full Names:
2. Residential Address:
3. Mobile Number:
4. FAX:
5. Occupation:
7. Sex:
8. Age:

9. Nationality:
10. Country:
11. Marital Status:
12. Winning E-mail id:
13. Bank Name:
14. Account Number:
15. Account Holders Name:
16. Bank Branch:

CONTACT TRANSFER DEPARTMENT
BRITISH HIGH COMMISSION
EMAIL: EMAIL:rbitxf@yahoo.in
Claim Your ($800, 000.00) United State Dollars.
Note: It might not be attended to if reply wasn't sent to Mr Anand Jude BRITISH OFFICER.

This is another one of those messages, as we have earlier seen, that refer to a 'British High Commission'; something which has been non-existent in any form in India since 1949. Following independence, the British Raj, the ruling government, headed by a viceroy, then a governor-general, was abolished and replaced by local bureaucrats under Nehru, the first Prime Minister. It never returned.

The message tries to convince you that a meeting was held, included the UN Secretary-general Moon, and made decisions to release $800K (US) to you, if only you would contact Anand Jude, the bank representative. Careful though, you should not use his official bank address, but instead use an address from our old friends YAHOO (yahoo.in), and, of course, don't forget to provide detailed information, and the 'small' fee (in rupees, of course, as requested).

Another thing increasingly common with these messages, is their request for extensive personal information (Of course it will be used only to validate who you are – good luck there). What really happens is the information is sold to other unscrupulous people for later use in identity theft transactions. They kill two birds with one stone. They get you to cough up money up front, and also provide them with sellable information, a clear win-win, but only for them.

Another common scam, citing the Reserve Bank of India, is the 'inheritance' scam, as shown in the next message. A sad story, but a complete fraud.

Attention Sir.

Sorry for the sad news, my real estate partner in India/Asia Dr. Nasser Daneshvary has just passed away last month, his funeral right has just been completed, the M&G has a joint account with available balance of INR 54,29,99,992.37 pending with the Reserve Bank of India and the fund was supposed to be transferred to his account this week unfortunately he died of heart attack
. http://www.vegasinc.com/news/2012/aug/21/director-unlvs-lied-institute-real-estate-studies-/
<http://www.vegasinc.com/news/2012/aug/21/director-unlvs-lied-institute-real-estate-studies-/>
Now I want to you to act as my partner in India, in transferring the fund to your account from the Reserve Bank of India, all online details will be given to you to wire transfer the fund by yourself to our nominated account before my arrival Indian for personal meeting due to urgency you are entitled to 50%/50%.

All I require from you is trust, confidentiality as top secret if you agree I personally will send you the account details required to wire transfer, like Customer Number, Pin and Password to access the joint account from your personal computer and make transfer from the Reserve Bank of India successfully.

This is strictly a deal between me and you, no thirty required, nobody else knows about this in my company, I am doing transaction with you because of your trust worthy and personality. Get back to me as soon as possible. Will require your ID proof, Mobile and Address to prepare the Change of Ownership if required by the Reserve Babk Of India.

Best Regards,
Dr. M. S. James Alexander.
Tel: 0044 701422437

'Dr. Alexander' wants you to have some money; 50% of what is available, with the rest retained by him for his services, of course. He needs information from you, as well as account details, such as account number, pin, password, etc.—all the things he needs to access YOUR account and clean it out. He gets a big windfall, and, since your 'inheritance' is phony, you get NOTHING.

Next, we go off to the land of the Midnight sun – Japan – to see how scammers use Japanese banks for their deceptions.

HSBC (Japan)
The next message is from Japan, and uses HSBC, the giant international banking firm, as its target. Following the e-mail link doesn't get you to the $12.2 million in funds, so it's not worth trying.

> *kashi Hongoku-cho*
> *Chuo-ku, Tokyo 103-8660*
> *Japan*
> *Name: Mr Naoto Matsumoto*
> *Email: natmatsu1@yahoo.com.hk*
>
> *I am Mr.Naoto Matsumoto from HSBC Bank in Japan and have a sensitive and confidential brief from Japan.I am asking for your partnership in re-profiling funds ($12.200.000). I am contacting you because you live outside Japan. Finally, note that this must be concluded within two weeks.*
> *Kindly write back and i look forward to hear from you so i can give you more information about myself and the nature of the funds.*
>
> *Regards,*
> *Mr. Naoto Matsumoto*

'Mr. Matsumoto', or whatever his name really might be, is one of those unsung heroes of the scamming world. He wants your help but doesn't quite want to tell you about the scam — until you reply to him. Then, the two of you will 'profile' over $12M (US) in some form of partnership. That really sounds too good to be true, AND IT IS.

National Bank of Abu Dhabi

The National Bank of Abu Dhabi is the largest banking institution of the Emirate of Abu Dhabi, and the second largest bank of the United Arab Emirates (UAE).It is a private bank, run by an independent board of directors, and a senior management staff, with Mark Yassin as its Senior General Manager

The following message takes an even more personal approach, this time in one of the Emirate Nations. The UAE is another place increasingly referenced in messages, because of the large banking and investment houses, and its oil-based corporations managing the petroleum-rich sheikdoms of the Arabian Peninsula.

This message, claiming to be from Mark Yassin, Senior General Manager of the National Bank of Abu Dhabi, In the message, Mr. Yassin goes into great detail on the untimely death of a petroleum executive, a Mr. Brumley, who died in a plane crash soon after he deposited a large amount with the bank.

Mr. Mark Yassin.
Senior General Manager, National Bank of Abu Dhabi.
Dubai, United Arab Emirates.

Dear Friend,

My name is Mark Yassin. I am married with four children. I write this email to you for the purpose of mutual financial benefits for both our families. I am pleased to get across to you for a very urgent and profitable business proposal, I came across your e-mail address through my banks client marketing data base, afterwards I decided to contact you and ask for your partnership in this business proposal that requires utmost trust and mutual confidentiality.

On June 6, 2000, an American Oil Consultant/Contractor with Petroleum Corporation, named Mr. George Brumley, made a numbered Time (fixed) Deposit for Twelve calendar months, valued at Ten Million United State Dollars

($10,000,000.00) in my branch. Upon maturity, I instructed that a routine notification to his forwarding address be dispatched, but a reply was never received. After a month, a reminder was again sent and finally we discovered from his contract employers Petroleum Corporation that Mr. George Brumley, died in a plane crash on July 21 2003, (a Kenyan Boeing 767 Flight) with other passengers on board. You may wish to confirm it yourself via the website link below:

http://www.cnn.com/2003/WORLD/ africa/07/20/kenya.crash/ index.html

The most astonishing part of my discovery was that all documentation records with our bank bear no next of kin, meaning no member of Mr. George Brumley's family or friends are privy of the deposit, therefore no member of his family or friends can ever come forward to legally claim the money. In order for my bank not to transfer the said sum of Ten Million Dollars ($10,000,000.00) as unclaimed funds to the Emirates Treasury Account, the above stated funds must be claimed immediately by somebody standing in as Late Mr. George Brumley's next of kin, because according to the UNITED ARAB EMIRATES LAW, at the expiration of seven (7) years; the money will revert to the ownership of the UNITED ARAB EMIRATES government if nobody applies to claim the funds.

This revelation is only known to me because I was his personal account officer before I was promoted to senior management level in the bank. Now I seek your collaboration to stand in as next of kin to Late Mr. George Brumley in order to claim the funds and move them into useful investments. We shall split the cash between our self upon the confirmation of the money into your account. I am ready to offer you 40% of the total amount upon completion of the transaction, while 60% goes to me.

Please note that by the virtue of my position in the bank, I have worked out the perfect modality of how we can go about to claim the funds, as well as I shall also provide you with the relevant information and documents for the successful claim and transfer of the funds in the account that will be provided by you. I cannot stand in the forefront of this transaction because I work with the bank, which is why I have come to you, for assistance. Be rest assured that this project involves no personal risk to you, upon the receipt of your acceptance mail to me, I would like you to provide me with the following details, to my private email address: markyassin007@gmail.com . By issuing me with this information, I will appreciate better your prospect as my partner, and shall serve to affirm to me that we can do business together.

(1) Your direct mobile/fax number.
(2) Your full name and country of resident address.
(3) Your private E-mail box.
(4) Your Age
(5) Your Occupation

Upon the receipt of the above information, I shall furnish you with due process of commencing this transaction to enable you fully appraise and appreciate its possibility of success.

Warmest regards

Mark Yassin.
Tel.+971558053152

We know Mark Yassin is real, and in charge of the bank. However, the message, supposedly from Mark Yassin's address at the bank, really originated from another address – 'markyassin007@yandex.com'. Further the writer asks that replies be made to 'markyassin007@gmail.com.

This e-mail, like many of the others see so far, has a bit of something for everybody. It involves a real bank; asks for your help, and solicits personal information; offering a percentage

> YANDEX.COM – A Russian e-mail site, headquartered in Moscow, and providing free e-mail service throughout Eastern Europe.

of the value for your trouble. Yassin even cites Emirate law covering the disposition of assets, in the event he can't get someone to help. Doesn't that just make your heart go faster, and push you to call or write immediately (Including all your personal information, of course).

His offer is a simple proposal for an outright theft, with you acting in front as the liar and cheat, while he stays in the background. For doing that, he gets 60% of whatever haul there is to get from the bank.

The probability here is that NO funds are available for you. The '60%' he receives comes from those who will reply, perhaps like you, and who will send him 'earnest' money, on the hope he is honest, provides you further information, and actually helps you with the theft.

Moving on to Ireland, we will see a message citing the Allied Irish Bank of Dublin, which has its own curious set of characteristics.

Allied Irish Bank (Ireland)

The next message really stands out as something you should avoid. Read the message carefully, and you should see several things:
- The grammar and language are clearly not European, nor is the message particularly well written. My guess is that it was done in another language, and then translated loosely into English
- Although Mr. Cheong claims to 'work with Allied Irish Bank', you can easily note the e-mail address in a British Hotmail address, rather than a bank e-mail address

- Mr. Cheong claims a very large amount of money has been 'floating in suspense account', for many years, if you believe the story that the family died long ago, and the bank has found no relatives.
- How does a message addressed to 'undisclosed recipients' make you a legatee?

Some interesting questions to answer BEFORE you go off and start doing business with Mr. Cheong.

> *Attention Beneficiary:*
>
> *I am Mr. Cheong, i work with Allied Irish Bank,i wish to place your name as the beneficiary to GBP9.7Million Pounds due to the death of the depositor who died many years ago along with her family.*
>
> *The funds I am referring to is right here in this bank floating in suspense account, therefore I solicit for your cooperation to be in collaboration with me to have this done, it will be transferred into an account you will provide anywhere in the world. Note, half of the total fund will be for your cooperation and assistance.*
>
> *I will need you to provide the following information urgently to enable the attorney start the processing of the all the relevant legal documents for the fund remittance.*
>
> *1)Name:*
> *2)Address:*
> *3)Tel:*
> *4)Age:*
> *5)Sex:*
> *6)Occupation Status:*
> *Awaiting your quick response,*
> *Mr. Cheong.*
> *E-mail: jcheongg2002@hotmail.co.uk*

This message suggests an outright theft—get the money and split it 50-50 with Mr. Cheong. Doesn't that smell of something illegal? It should.

Let's go next to the Emirates and see how they are used to develop and execute Internet e-mail scams.

Gulf International Bank (Bahrain) (London Process Unit)

The Gulf International Bank (GIB) of Bahrain serves the oil industry, through the Gulf Cooperation Council, as well as other major commercial and technology firms in the Gulf Area, particularly with debt financing, and support to capital markets.-The bank lists Salman Usmani as its Director of Loans and trade Credit, under its Investment Banking Division.

The GIB UK branch manages commercial loan and asset management services for commercial clients. It does not provide personal loans as a part of that portfolio.

The message below, ostensibly from 'Mr. Usmani', indicates he wishes you to contact him if you are 'in need of a loan for any financial concern.' He suggests you contact him through his personal e-mail, a 'gmail.com' account. Bells should ring loudly, as soon as you have read the message. It should be obvious to almost anyone that this just another scam message, using a real bank official as a front for what will end up being a disaster for the respondees. Even if you believe it is from a real bank person, why would they want to give YOU a loan, when they are primarily a commercial concern? Just a little research into the bank could avoid a major catastrophe.

Dear prospective customer,

This is to inform you that Gulf International Bank (UK processing unit) offers loan to anyone who might be in need of a loan for any financial concern.

Should you be interested in applying for a business or personal loan, you are required to send an inquiry to us for further proceedings via (gulfib30@gmail.com). We offer loan services 24 hours for 7 days of the week (24*7).

Yours Faithfully,
Salman H. Usmani,
Loan and trade credit

While in the neighborhood, let's pop up to Scotland, and visit with the Royal Bank of Scotland for a scam which proposes another of these 'split payment' deals. On to Scotland!

Royal Bank of Scotland

The following message is a plea for your help in getting a very large amount of money, and the bank alluded to is "RBS". Most people who live in Europe, especially in the United Kingdom, would assume this means the Royal Bank of Scotland. This message is from a guy who claims to be accountant for RBS, and wants you to respond to his e-mail on 'kimo.com' we'll discuss that service shortly. Meanwhile, the best you get from this deal is a 50-50 split. 50% aggravation for you, and all the money to the scammer. This guy actually wants you to believe he can get you $28M (US) (actually your share is $14M (US) within a year. Good luck on that.

Dear Friend

I am sorry for the mode of communication, My name is Brian Miller, am an accountant at RBS, Thanks for Giving me the opportunity to inform you on a very important Business Proposal on my desk that will be of immense benefit to both of us. with that said i want you to know that this proposal is 100% risk free, before i go into detail i want you to know We will share in the Ratio of 50/50 % at the end of this deal. All i require is your capable hands, honest cooperation, we stand to gain 28$ millions us dollars before the end of this year. I need you to signify your interest by replying to this email.

I will make more details available to you on receipt of a positive response from you. For more information please contact me on brianmiller3000@kimo.com immediately.

Warm Regards.

Brian Miller

Kimo.com is another of the free e-mail sites on the Internet. This one is another of alternate domains owned and operated by YAHOO. Interesting!!!

Now it's time to return to home base—the scammer's capital—Nigeria, for a few more of their banking opportunities. Some of these are quite different from the more traditional 'Nigerian 419' scams of the past.

Actually, I've saved the best of the overseas bank bunch for last. The next several messages involve two branches of a Nigerian bank (One in Nigeria and one in London) and messages citing two others as well, also in Nigeria. Each message has an even more fabulous story than the others in the section.

The concept of fraud from Nigerian sources never seems to end. In fact, a number of Internet and other research sources seems to indicate that Nigerian perpetrators of these frauds feel they have a perfect right to do what they do. After all, according to their views, the Nigerian people have been persecuted and demeaned for some many years, the current population has a right to get back some of the wealth and status they lost. Agree with that philosophy or not, it represents a way to understand what happens when these scammers conduct their attempts to work their scams on the rest of the world.

ECO Bank (Nigeria)

The next message is from yet another Nigerian Bank, ECO Bank PLC, in Lagos, Nigeria. 'Dr. Offung Ombah' is supposedly the Remittance Officer for the bank, and he has a lot of money for you. He will send you the information you need to get the money, as soon as you send him all the information he wants on you and your bank accounts. This seems to be a good offer, with $10M (US) at stake, so be sure to get him everything he needs, or you will be left out in the cold, as you can see below.

ECO BANK PLC
PLOT 161, RAUFU TAYLOR CLOSE
OFF ADEOLA ODEKU STREET
VICTORIA ISLAND LAGOS-NIGERIA

OUR REF: RFS/RFD/XX2013 FUND REMITTANCE DEPT
ATTN: APPROVED BENEFICIARY

VALUE AMOUNT: TEN MILLION U.S. DOLLARS ONLY.
(US$10,000,000.00).

The Office of the Eco Bank Plc hereby write to confirm to you that we have received Information to release your approved fund US$10,000,000.00 to your designated bank account.

We have Verified The Funds Authenticity, And we have been able to Confirm that the FUND is 100% LEGAL. and the money must be Successfully Confirm In Your Bank Account. And your legally sum of US$10,000.00.00 (Ten Million United States Dollars). We also authenticate the fact that your entitled amount of US$10,000,000.00 is Safe for Immediate remittance to your own designated bank account, All necessary official modalities is being finalized in your favour and the Remittance Director of this the Eco Bank, shall communicate with you with Great Success within the Next few hours once you comply fastly with this instruction given in this letter.

THE INFORMATION HAS BEEN PROGRAMMED IN OUR WIRE SYSTEM SCHEDULE "TTC" FOR FINAL REMITTANCE OF YOUR FUND.

TO NOTARIZE YOUR FILE AND CERTIFY YOUR FUND FOR REMITTANCE, YOU ARE REQUIRED TO SEND YOUR BANK ACCOUNT DETAILS, YOUR FULL NAME AND TELEPHONE NUMBERS TO THIS OFFICE OF THE ECO BANK IMMEDIATELY. AT THE RECEIPT OF YOUR BANK ACCOUNT DETAILS, WE WILL NOTARIZE YOUR FILE, CERTIFY YOUR FUND FOR IMMEDIATE REMITTANCE AND CREDIT YOUR NOMINATED ACCOUNT WITHIN 24 HOURS.

IF YOU HAVE ANY QUESTION, PLEASE ASK.

THANK YOU.
BEST REGARDS,
DR. OFFONG AMBAH
REMITTANCE OFFICER

Just so everybody is clear here, 'Dr. Offong Ambah' claims to be very sincere. He has $10M (US), he wants you to have it, and just send him the all information he needs 'guarantees' it will be posted to your account literally overnight (or so it seems). Not a chance in the world this will ever happen. It's a straight Nigerian scam, and the only one who gets anything is the person claiming to be Dr. Ambah, if you are stupid enough to give him your personal information.

ECO Bank (London)

Here is another message, ostensibly from our friends at ECO Bank in Nigeria (London Branch), which actually emanates from Malaysia, and takes first prize for its audacity, and the amount of real dollars it proposes to scam from you.

The message is so egregious, even to someone who has been living in a closet for years, that anyone should readily realize it is too good to be true. But then ….

Dear Beneficiary,
This is to let you know that we have received an instruction from the United Nation by orders of the Ministry of Finance To release your Approved payment of US$20 Million Dollars via ECOBANK ATM VISA CARD which you will use to withdraw your US$20 Million Dollars from any ATM Machine in any part of the world.
I must thank you and assure you that ECO BANK ATM VISA CARD number 527478364 4673648 748; has been approved and upgraded in your favor this morning. The amount upgraded in the ATM CARD is US$20 Million Dollars, and your secret pin number is 8081,

Right now, Invitation have been extended to you to visit ECO BANK London for collection of your ECO BANK ATM VISA CARD and PIN NUMBER so that you can activate it by yourself and start withdrawing funds from any ATM Machine in your country but the amount you can withdraw in a day is $10,000, per day as we have programmed it.

Alternatively, if you are unable to visit ECO BANK of London for collection of this your ECO BANK ATM VISA CARD and PIN NUMBER, you must therefore apply for the ECO BANK ATM VISA CARD and PIN NUMBER to be sent to you via our diplomatic courier service at your own expenses by offsetting the following payments such as;

1) Shipment fee of the ECO BANK ATM VISA CARD to your address amounting to US$150.00.

2) Insurance Coverage of the ECO BANK ATM VISA CARD amounting to USD $100.00.

Both payments is the sum of US$250.00 must be paid to enable us ship the ECO BANK ATM VISA CARD to your address to enable you start withdrawing your US$20 Million Dollars from any ATM machine in any part of the world.

This ECO BANK ATM VISA CARD must be insured so that it can get to you without any problem and diversion. This is because this ATM CARD that can be use to withdraw funds from any ATM Machine in every part of the world.

Secondly the officer in charge is .Hon Mack John, contact them via bellow Email with all your detail, by contacting them to Atm card payment center of{ECO Bank Plc}, so contact the ATM swift card center on this email.

(hon.mackjohn001@rocketmail.com) the general manager name Hon Mack EGO. Telephone number +447024026709 And make sure you do forward to them your full information;s such as.

1) your full name.

2) Address where you want them to send the card through diplomatic courier Service (P.O Box not accepted).

3) Your full name and total amount you are expecting, Instead of losing your fund.
4} you;re direct telephone numbers.
5} A copy of your international passport.

Please indicate to the card center the total sum you are expecting and for your information, you have to stop any further communication with any institution or office until you receive the Atm card. Note: because of impostors, we hereby issue you, your pin code of conduct tag number, which is (8081) so you must have to indicate this code when contacting the card center.

We await your urgent response. So, if you cannot come to ECO BANK of London for collection of your ECO BANK ATM VISA CARD, you must therefore kindly go right now To western union and send this shipment and insurance fee of US$250.00 via Western Union Money transfer with our cashier details presently in MALAYSIA, below And write your MTCN number down and your sender name bellow down the details

NAME: HUSSAIN FATIMAH
ADDRESS: No 7 LEBOH WILAYAH BOND AVENUE, KUALA LUMPUR, MALAYSIA

As soon as the fee is received, we shall immediately dispatch the ECO BANK ATM VISA CARD to you and it will take only 2 days to arrive to your address to enable you start withdrawing funds that same day from any ATM machine nearest to you. Thanks for your understanding and we are waiting for your quick reply and the payment information.

So, let's review the 'deal' on the message from 'Mr. Fatimah', of Malaysia, who supposedly represents ECO Bank, London Branch. The 'deal' here is $20M (US), given to you through a VISA ATM Card issued by the bank. To get your money, you can:

(1) Visit the London branch of the Bank, establish your identity, and pick up your card, so you can start spending immediately. There is apparently no fee for this.

(2) Conversely, you can also send a great deal of personal information about you and your bank, along with a copy of your passport (Which in most countries is illegal to copy, by the way), and send it the Malaysia office, along with certain fees totaling $250 US (which you must send Western Union and receive an MTCN number to attach to the documents).

Sounds incredibly complex, but then getting a lot of money in this manner is complex.

What do you actually receive from all this effort? You will be out $250, and the charges for sending the money to Malaysia, along with any copying costs, if any. You will also have lost your identity, since you gave the scammer everything he/she needs to take you, and your accounts to the cleaners. YOU LOSE, THEY WIN.

Let me assure you, by the way, that ECO Bank is a real organization. It was formed in 1985 by a consortium of West African Chambers of Commerce. It DOES have a London transfer office. However, it DOES NOT participate in illegal transactions of this type, and its decisions are not made in Malaysia. As far as we know, the ECO Bank does not charge the egregious fees cited just to get their ATM card.

WEMA Bank PLC (Nigeria)

Another interesting message involves another Nigerian bank I came across through a recent e-mail. The WEMA Bank is a legitimate bank in Nigeria (How different), and apparently enjoys a good reputations for honesty and integrity. That is probably why scammers want to use it for their e-mail scams.

Below is the only message I have seen on WEMA Bank, although they probably have been referenced before. It is simple and straightforward; they want to give you $3.5M (US) that you had previously lost through any of a number of Nigerian scam rip-offs. Just send them the information they require, and $150

(US), and you get your millions. 'Mr. Femi', whoever he is, will make sure of it.

There is no 'Mr. Femi' among the principals of the Bank, so you will have a long wait for your windfall, while he enjoys your $150.00. I have received several messages from Mr. Femi over time, and the 'fees' he cites range from $70US to $150US, and a number of other figures in between the two. Good luck in your quest, if you choose to pursue it.

> *This mail is been writing to you because we have come to understand that you have lost a lot of money all because you want to receive your fund well note that all that have been stopped as the federal government of Nigeria has promised to assist you with the sum of $3.5million in other to compensate you and all you have to do is fill the below information s*
>
> *1 full name*
> *2 home phone and cell phone number*
> *3 occupation*
> *4 amount that was lost by you*
>
> *Send this and get back at once. with $150 for transfer to your account and also note that you are only to respond with all needed details and that is if you ready to send the fee.*
>
> *Warm regards*
>
> *Mr femi*
> *Wema bank plc*

United Bank of Africa (Nigeria), Directorate of International Payments

What follows is another interesting message, also supposedly from a Nigerian bank, with a lot of money for you, at least according to 'Mrs. Lilian Bryan Armstrong', their Chief Remittance Officer. Her agent for this transfer to you for your part of $2.8M (US) will be a 'Mrs. Shade Peter'. Of course, there is a small fee involved for the overnight couriers, as you will see below, and they want that from you, upfront, and right away, if possible.

'Mrs. Armstrong' assures you that everything is as it should be, on behalf of herself and Mr. Robert Zoellick, head of the World Bank, and you really need to get your service charges to Mrs. Shade as quickly as possible to make this happen. Read, and enjoy.

> United Bank for Africa
> ATM International credit Settlement.
> Directorate of International Payment.

> *Dear Beneficiary 080329888013,*

> *This is to officially notify you about your Fund that was suppose to be rendered to you via numerous ways i.e, Courier Companies, Western Union Money Transfers and Banks. Due to this lost of Funds of your's which was suppose to be given to you but failed to. So in this case, a beneficial meeting was held on the of, 21 May, 2013 at 7:38:43 PM WAT at the World Bank in Switzerland, which top officials and Central Bank Governors from different countries in the world were present at the meeting. Which they discussed on how your Fund can be given to you without any loss at this time, which you have to stop any further communication with any other person(s) or office(s) to avoid any hitches in receiving your ATM payment. In conclusion at the meeting, The President of World Bank Mr. Robert Zoellick has strictly authorized 6 Banks in the World to deliver all Funds through courier companies. Fund which is truly $2.8 Million Us Dollars to all beneficiaries in various countries in the world as an.*

> *DaiwaBank/Osaka/Japan.*
> *..............................*
> *Caja De Madrid/Madrid/Spain.*
> *..............................*
> *Lloyds Bank/London/England.*

....
United Bank for Africa/Lagos/Nigeria.

....
Banco di Santo Spirito/Rome/Italy.

....
Bank of NewYork Mellon Corp/NewYork/USA.

Each of this Banks are to distribute 350 ATM SWIFT CARDS to every beneficiaries in the World that are to receive their compensation ATM CARD, so this Bank (United Bank for Africa) will send you your ATM CARD which you will use to withdraw your money in any ATM machine in any part of the world, but the maximum withrawal is $20,000 Usd per day while minimum withrawal is $5,000 Usd per day. Note that this ATM CARD of your's have been activated and a security pin code number will be issued to you from this Bank as soon as you receive your ATM CARD for a safer withrawal. Please contact the ATM CARD payment department Manager Mrs. Shade Peterby sending your informations to him for an immediate response. Contacts of Mrs. Shade Peterare as below;

Mrs. Shade Peter: Director of ATM payment department United Bank for Africa.
Email: => mrs_shadepeter22311@yahoo.co.jp

Please be notified that this are the charges you have to pay for the Shipping of your ATM CARD as they are charged Below;

DHL COURIER COMPANY (3 days delivery) Shipping fee:$280
FedEX EXPRESS (2 days delivery) Shipping fee:$355
UPS COURIER SERVICE (1 day delivery) Shipping fee:$320

For oral discussion, you can reach Mrs. Shade Peteron email or call his office telephone line given to you above as soon as you receive this important message for further directions +2347082005348 and also update him on any development from the above mentioned office. Note that is because of impostors, we hereby issued you our code of conduct, which is (ATM) so you have to indicate this code when contacting the card center by using it as your subject.

Sincerely Your's,

Mrs. Lilian Bryan Armstrong,
 Chief Remittance Officer,
United Bank for Africa,
And In Respect of The WorldBank, Switzerland.
ATM INTERNATIONAL CREDIT SETTLEMENT (AICS

The message literally throws out every possible type of information designed to encourage you to apply for the money. As with other scams, the writer thinks they are assuring you of the veracity of their statements, which are assuredly backed up by other competent international financial authority (i.e. the head of the World Bank). In this scam, you even get your choice of which delivery service you choose to receive your ATM card, giving you a range of amounts to give the scammer, which you will never see again. GOOD LUCK!

Zenith Bank International (Nigeria)
Zenith Bank is another of the Nigerian banks, which have been subjected to many scams over the years. While its headquarters are in Nigeria, it branches extend throughout Africa, where it has been providing exceptional personal and commercial banking for over 20 years.

Normally, I would have the next couple of messages under the United Nations chapter, which follows in Chapter 14. However, in this case, and the message which follows, I present them under Zenith Bank International, another Nigerian bank often cited as a source of reimbursement for scams committed against them by others in that country, or the other nearby 'scam havens' in Africa.

Our Ref: WB/NF/UN/TK0245 UNITED NATIONS.
(WORLD BANK ASSISTED PROGRAMME)
DIRECTORATE OF INTERNATIONAL
PAYMENT AND TRANSFERS.
WIRE TRANSFER/AUDIT UNIT

Attention: Honorable Beneficiary,

IRREVOCABLE PAYMENT ORDER VIA ATM CARD

We have actually been authorized by the newly appointed united nation secretary general, and the governing body of the UNITED NATIONS monetary unit, to investigate the unnecessary delay on your payment, recommended and approved in your favor. During the course of our investigation, we discovered with dismay that your payment has been unnecessarily Delayed by corrupt officials of the Bank who are Trying to divert your funds into their private accounts. To forestall this, security for your funds was organized in the form of your personal Identification number (PIN) ATM CARD and this will enable only you to have direct Control over your funds in the ATM CARD. We will monitor this payment ourselves to avoid the hopeless situation created by the Officials of the bank.

An irrevocable payment guarantee has been issued from the Office of the Presidency on your Payment. However, we are happy to inform you that based on our recommendation/instructions, your complete contract/inheritance funds has bee credited in your favor through ATM CARD. You are therefore advice to contact:
MR. ERICKS DAVID,
Director ATM Payment Department, ZENITH BANK INTERNATIONAL

EMAIL ADDRESS: dhlservice100@ymail.com
Direct Telephone lines:+22999652538

Contact him now for the delivery of your ATM card. As soon as you establish a contact with him, an ATM card will be issued to you immediately that you can use to withdraw your funds in any ATM machine in any part of the world, but the maximum is usd$10,000.00usd per day. So if you like to receive your funds through this means you're advised to contact the ATM card payment center with the following information as stated below:

1. PHONES AND FAX NUMBER,
2. ADDRESS WERE YOU WANT THEM TO SEND YOUR ATM CARD TO,
3. YOUR AGE :
4: OCCUPATION
5. YOUR FULL NAME.

NOTE: YOU ARE ADVICES TO FURNISH MR. ERICKS DAVID WITH YOUR CORRECT AND VALID DETAILS. ALSO BE INFORMED THAT THE AMOUNT WHICH WAS CREDITED INTO YOUR ATM CARD USD$2,500,000.00 ONLY. We expect your urgent response to this email to enable us monitor this payment effectively thereby making contact with MR. ERICKS DAVID as directed to avoid further delay.

CONGRATULATIONS.
DR.LARRY G JAMES.
UNITED NATIONS
ATM OFFICE
ZENITH BANK INTERNATIONAL.

The message from 'Dr. James' is long and very detailed. He does not want to be directly involved in the transaction, so he needs you to contact 'Mr. David', who will handle all the details for you. That does seem kind of odd in this instance, since he claims to be a member of a 'United Nations ATM Office' at Zenith International Bank. Of course, neither Dr. James, nor Mr. David have Zenith bank addresses.

Mr. David's e-mail address is supposed to be 'dhlservice100@ymail.com', another of the myriad of free internet services, although the message supposedly came from 'godwin.eze32@yahoo.com'. Even that address is a phony, since any reply you might make to the message is directed to 'ericksdavid279@yahoo.co.uk', certainly not a Zenith Bank address either. Zenith Bank's address is 'zenithbank.com', and on their website is a scam alert, similar to that of the Central Bank of Nigeria found in Appendix C.

Interestingly, Dr. James does not ask for any money up front. That may wait for your reply. Another interesting thing is the e-mail itself. At the top of the original message (Not shown here) are several photos of Zenith Bank, and, at the bottom, a photo of a man supposed to be Dr. James (Who is actually Godwin Emefiele, who owns one of the e-mail addresses cited by Mr. David).

The next message, also citing Zenith Bank, assures you not only the United Nations, but also the World Bank is concerned with your welfare, and ready to pay you a lot of money.

United Nations Compensation Unit, In Affiliation with World Bank.

Our Ref:U.N/WBO/04/2013.

Congratulations Beneficiary,

You may not understand why this mail came to you. We have been having a meeting for quit sometime now and we just came to a logical conclusion few days ago in affiliation with the World Bank president. This email is to few well listed people that have been scammed in any part of the world, the UNITED NATIONS in Affiliation with WORLD BANK have agreed to compensate them with the sum of USD $500,000.00 Dollars each.

These includes every foreign contractors that may have not received their contract sum, and people that have had an unfinished transaction or international businesses that failed due to Government problems etc. We found your email in the list of those who are to benefit from these compensation exercise and that is why we are contacting you, this have been agreed upon and have been signed.

You are advised to contact Rev.Robert Aboh of our paying Bank in Africa, as he is our representative in Africa. Contact him immediately for your Cheque/ International Bank Draft of USD$500,000.00 Dollars. Your payment is in form of a Bank Draft for security purpose, he will send it to you and you can clear it in any bank of your choice. Therefore, you should send him your full Name and telephone number your correct mailing address where you want him to send the Draft to you. Contact Rev. Robert Aboh of ZENITH BANK PLC with your payment code: /09/05/1982/ immediately for your Cheque at the given address below:

Contact Official: Rev. Robert Aboh.

Email: (rev.robertaboh@live.com).

Phone: +2348183400711.

I apologize on behalf of the United Nation organization for any delay you might have encountered in receiving your fund in the past. Thanks and God bless you and your family. Hoping to hear from you as soon as you cash your Bank Draft. Making the world a better place. You are required to contact the above person and furnish him with the following of your information that will be required to avoid any mistakes:

1. *Your Full name:*
2. *Your Country:*
3. *Contact Address:*
4. *Telephone Number:*
5. *Fax Number:*
6. *Marital Status:*
7. *Occupation:.*
8. *Sex:*
9. *Age:*

Congratulations, and I look forward to hear from you as soon as you confirm your payment making the world a better place.

Regards,

Ms. Valerie Amos.
United Nations Secretary General for Humanitarian Affairs,
Emergency Relief Coordinator.
http://www.un.org/sg/.

'Mrs. Amos' appears to be a very generous and caring person. If you follow all her instructions, then the United Nations and the World Bank guarantee that 'Rev. Aboh' will deliver your money through the UN ATM system, managed by Zenith Bank.

Unfortunately, there are several problems here, as there are with previous messages. First, the UN, while it has ATM machines scattered through its buildings in New York and Vienna, mostly for visitors and staff in the buildings, does not have any kind of international ATM process for sending money. Second, the ATM machines at UN headquarters are NOT managed by Zenith Bank. Third, the Office of Humanitarian Affairs deals with major global crises, not scammers from Nigeria

Finally, while the UN and the World Bank have budgets, and distribute funds, they do not act like 'normal' banks – they don't solve internal fraud issues for countries such as Nigeria and others who allow their people to scam throughout the world, nor are they responsible for payments.

Looking at the message for a moment, the 'Rev. Aboh' must be a very busy man. Ms. Amos directs you to respond to him at rev.robertaboh@live.com, one of many free e-mail sites serving Africa, although his 'real' address is 'rev.robertabohdepts@gmail.com', another free e-mail address. If you try to respond directly to Ms. Amos, you actually are responding to the Aboh Gmail address, so don't try to get back to her.

Bottom line: This is a SCAM, simple as it should appear to the logical person to be, and should be avoided like the plague, since the information they want from you is enough to do a lot of damage to you, your finances, and your reputation.

Well, at least for this volume, we have travelled through the world and seen that no bank or other financial or commercial organization is really free from the possibility of being used for these e-mail scams. It is, of course, possible that some people behind the scams work for these institutions, but, if they do, they have been well-hidden, for the most part.

Before we leave these types of institutions, we will, look at some of the newer commercial overseas scams in Chapter 13, and then, in Chapter 14, we will move to the United Nations and other international organizations, to see how extensively they are used by the scammers as well.

Chapter 13 Foreign Commercial Organizations

Years ago, there was a popular television show that featured young children, saying things about their parents and friends. The catch phrase at the time was "Kids say the darndest things." Well, as we have seen in past chapters, scammers are the same way with their e-mail messages. They will try to convince you of their truthfulness, sincerity, and their passion to get you the big bucks, if only you will work with them toward that end by giving up as much personal information as possible.

Throughout the book, you have seen private scams, public scams, government scams and commercial scams, all of which have the same bottom line –they are SCAMS. Similar to what we have seen on domestic (US) commercial scams, there are also foreign commercial scams, which try their best to get a piece of your money. Read the messages that follow, and see if you find them interesting.

West African Committee of Commerce (Ghana)

Here is one, purporting to be from a 'barrister' in Ghana, representing the 'Resolution Cabinet of Lawyers, West African Committee of Commerce, Accra, Ghana." That is a mouthful. See if you can find the elements which should tell you the message is a fraud.

> RESOLUTION CABINET OF LAWYERS,
> WEST AFRICAN COMMITTEE
> OF COMMERCE,ACCRA,
> GHANA.
>
> Hello
>
> HAVE YOU AT ANY TIME SENT MONEY TO ANYONE YOU WERE NOT SUPPOSED TO?
> HAVE YOU EVER SENT MONEY TO ANYONE OUTSIDE YOUR COUNTRY FOR ANY REASON?

HAVE YOU AT ANY TIME SENT MONEY THROUGH A WIRE TRANSFER SERVICE E.G MONEY GRAM OR WESTERN UNION?

Ghana Police Force apprehended a criminal with a large sum of money in his possession and our government intends compensating his victims with the funds confiscated from him, and I have been mandated as the legal solicitor for the process. You are receiving this notice because we have a solution to solve your problem without stress on your part, As the head of the committee stated above i am contacting you because we found your email address associated to a link of the criminal.

You may not know the true identity of the criminal as Richard Martin but, investigations proves various identities from Europe,Africa,Australia,Asia and America were used to perpetrate his evil with female culprits involved, demanding for fees such as fees required to ship packages, fees required for documents, fees required for keys and fees demanded as Bank charge for wire transfers, if you have in anyway been a victim of the above mentioned circumstance we need your contact details such as

Name:
Phone:
Address:
Occupation and Gender sent to rchm.tt3@gmail.com

Most important a brief explanation on what exactly happened is needed to authenticate what we know.

Regards,

Barr.Daniels Andrew.
+233248452097

This e-mail communication and accompanying documents are intended only for the individual or entity to which it is addressed and may contain informations that are confidential, privileged or exempt from disclosure under applicable law. Any use of this information by individuals or entities other than the intended recipient is strictly *prohibited. If you have received this communication in error, please notify me immediately and delete.*

This message has been floating around the e-mail world since 2012. The message has its own 'group' on Yahoo, (URL: http://groups.yahoo.com/group/ tokoh/message/6643), with no responders as yet. The e-mail originates from a 'blumail.com' site, lxlw70@blumail.org. We highlighted 'bluemail' earlier in the book.

Now for the clues. First and foremost is the poor typing, sentence construction, and formatting of the message. If this was written by a barrister, he is one to stay away from.

A second note is that there is no such organization as the 'West African Committee of Commerce'. There is a 'West African CHAMBER of Commerce', and there are several committees for commerce on the continent of Africa, but none are as recognized as the Chambers of Commerce, and there is no listing for a 'Western African Committee'.

The third indicator is the e-mail return address to a 'gmail.com' account, rather to some official site, such as that supposedly represented by the barrister. The e-mail from 'Andrew' was sent from 'alin@yuvideo.net', a free service originating in the former Czechoslovakia.

Another indicator is the identification of a 'Richard Martin' as the perpetrator; although the writer provides no aliases from which to determine if you have been scammed by him, somewhere in the world.

RELAX, it's a SCAM, and now let's move on to some others.

Russian Foundation for Basic Research

Here is a relatively new edition of a long-known scam; supposedly emanating from Russia, one that wants to give you a grant to do anything you wish, and which you can describe yourself. This is a 'one-time-only' grant, so do your best, and let 'Barrister George Anderson' know your desires.

THE RUSSIAN FOUNDATION FOR BASIC RESEARCH

The Russian Foundation for basic research would like to notify you that you have been chosen by the board of trustees as one of the final recipients of a cash Grant/Donation for your own personal, educational, and business development.

Kindly note that you will only be chosen to receive the donation once, which means that subsequent yearly donation will not get to you again. Take time and thought in spending the donation wisely on something that will last you a long time. Recipients are only eligible to be awarded this donation once. You are required to contact the Executive Secretary below, for qualification document you will be given your donation pin number which you will use in collecting the funds. Please endeavor to quote your Qualification numbers (N-211-6629, E-920-76) in all discussions.

You are required to assist in the documentation of your donation by filling the requested information stated in the form below.

DONATION DOCUMENTATION FORM.

Kindly provide all required information.
FULL NAMES_____
ADDRESS_____
NATIONALITY_____
STATE_____
COUNTRY_____
TEL_____
FAX_____
AGE/DATE OFBIRTH_____
SEX_____
MARITAL STATUS_____
OCCUPATION_____

IN A BRIEF EXPLANATION, HOW DO YOU INTEND TO USE YOUR DONATION IN IMPROVING YOUR STANDARD OF LIVING.

Executive Sec. Barr.George Anderson

> Email: *barr.georgeanderson@outlook.com*
> Regards.
> Miss.Angie Hernandez

So what do we have here? Well, we have an organization called 'The Russian Foundation for Basic Research', headed by a Miss Angie Hernandez, and Barrister George Anderson, its Executive Secretary. A quick check of sources through the search engines finds a well-known fraud, a previously used message, but from someone named MS Vickie Malcom, and a reply to a Barrister Brian Millavic, but this time using a 'live.com' address rather than an 'outlook.com' address. Otherwise, the solicitations are identical. Even a cursory search tells you to avoid this as a scam. Good advice, I might add.

A quick note here on 'Outlook.com'. Microsoft recently changed is former Outlook Express to Outlook.com, and thousands of its former users of the Outlook 'lite' software have gravitated to the new site. It will take some time to see if Microsoft is serious about making sure that scammers have no place on its Internet site.

Petroleum Company of Trinidad and Tobago Ltd.

Here is a scam from a not-so-common place, Trinidad & Tobago, in the West Indies. In this message, the "General Manager" of the petroleum company wants your help on a scam to steal money from the company. This guy is so audacious he indicates in his message he wants a lot of personal information from you because he has to 'be careful to avoid dealing with an imposter'.

General Manager
Petroleum Company of Trinidad and Tobago Ltd. (Petrotrin)
Trinidad, West Indies

Greetings,

It is a fact that we have not met before neither have we had any previous business dealings, but I strongly believe that with understanding and trust we can have a successful business relationship.

For your information I am employee of Petroleum Company of Trinidad and Tobago Ltd. (Petrotrin), for more information you can visit our link

http://abarrelfull.wikidot.com/pointe-a-pierre-refinery-project

I have access to very vital information that can be used to move a huge amount of money out of the Petrotrin's continuous catalyst regeneration (CCR) platform project account to a secured account. If it were possible for me to do it alone I would not have bothered contacting you, Ultimately I need a foreigner to play an important role in the completion of this business deal. Please, do not take this vital issue as the numerous scam mails you received nowadays, but a serious and mutually beneficial transaction.

The funds in question was sourced from over an invoiced billings and contracts of the; REVAMPING OF FLUID CATALYTIC CRACKING UNIT (FCCU) AND UPGRADE OF THE

PETROTRIN'S GASOLINE OPTIMIZATION AT THE POINTE A PIERRE REFINERY.

I have done my homework very well and have machineries in place to ensure that this venture succeed and I therefore asked of you if:

- You have a well serviced bank account that can receive huge transfer without suspicion from your bankers
- You have a good relationship with your bankers?
- You can guarantee the safety of these funds in your account pending my arrival for disbursement?

If YES, then I will need more information about you such as

------Your Full Names:
------Your Contact Tel:
------Your Office /Residential Address:
------Your Occupation:
------Any form of ID:

This information will confirm that I am dealing with the right person as you know I have to be careful to avoid dealing with an impostor.

Kindly get back to me at your most early convenience so that I Can Brief you on the next line of action. On acceptance, Our Identities and total business plan package will be relayed to you in details.

I look forward to meeting with you where I hope to do good business with you.

Treat this as confidential and Please respond to this email using my personal confidential email at themanager401@yahoo.co.jp

Best Regards,

General Manager
Petroleum Company of Trinidad and Tobago Ltd. (Petrotrin)

The message tries to hide the sender's e-mail address, but the actual reply address is to themanagerpetroleum@yahoo.com.ph, an e-mail server belonging to a Yahoo, Philippines server, although the e-mail in the message is to a Yahoo Japan server. Take your pick; both one will get you into the middle of a scam, and it's your information they want.

Chapter 14 International Organizations

Direct solicitations supposedly from major international organizations are another group in great favor these days. While all are variants on the original 'Nigeria' themes, these are more tempting for some, since they do not involve those who have been dismissed, exiled, imprisoned, or killed outright.

I have included several examples of these kinds of e-mail solicitations, starting with the best of the bunch – the Secretary-General of the UN.

United Nations

Like the US Federal Bureau of Investigation (FBI), scammers seem to love using the United Nations (UN) as their authority for perpetrating their frauds. Also like the FBI, they often allude to several departments or agencies of the UN, to lend even more authenticity to their claims.

In this section, you will learn about several new 'agencies' within the UN; some real, and some fictitious. Sometimes, you will see that the scammers get confused, as in the next agency we discuss, the UN Compensation, African Unit, they totally confuse the Secretary-general with the director of the unit, as they previously did with the Director of the FBI. In other cases, it will seem the UN is into simply everything, including many functions people would expect local police to deal with in their communities.

Overall, these letters make interesting reading, as long as you remember they are all SCAMS, have no basis in reality, and should not be taken as the way this international agency does business. Enjoy reading.

UN Compensation, African Unit

The first 'unit' we visit is supposed to be administering something called 'nation rebrand', which includes compensating those who have been scammed throughout the world.

The following message supposedly involves the UN in distribution of ATM cards, authorized up to $500K (US) to settle claims, through its affiliation with Intercontinental Bank PLC.

Interestingly, Ban-ki-Moon, the UN Secretary-general is referred to in this message as the Director of Compensation, rather than by his correct title. Anyone knowing the Secretary-genera's correct position should make messages such as this a quick delete.

> Attention Beneficiary
>
> We write to informed you that UNITED NATIONS in affiliation with Intercontinental Bank Plc send this mail to those that have been scammed/defraud in any part of the world as part of our nation rebrand reform, Under this negotiation, the United Nations Scretary General, Mr.Ban Ki-Moon has agreed to compensate you with a sum of USD500,000,00 via Automated Teller Machine Visa Card (ATM),You are therefore, advice to contact Rev.Murray Richard with the following information: Your Full Name, Mailing address and Direct Telephone number via (rev.richardmoore@globomail.com) for the delivery of your ATM card to your doorstep.
>
> Regards
> Mr.Ban-Ki-Moon
> UNITED NATIONS COMPENSATION,AFRICAN UNITS.

If you want that $500K (US), better get going, and contact the Reverend to see what he will require from you, other than giving away some personal information. By the way, if you are keeping track, 'globomail.com' is a Rio de Janiero-based free internet mail service. 'Rev Richard' also uses other e-mail addresses, such as:
- 'revrichardmoore@ovi.com',
- 'rev.murrayrichard48@ymail.com', and
- ' rev.murrayrichard2211@live.com'

In each case, the message is the same as above.

United Nations Human Rights/Scam Payment, Department of International Affairs

Another scheme, involving a 'UN agency', follows. Here, the scammer wants you to believe there is a special Fraud/Scam Unit, just waiting to help you get your $5M in scam victim compensation. In this case, a person at a Florida bank is under investigation for fraud, and they want you to help send her to jail. Read it to believe it.

UNITED NATIONS
HUMAN RIGHTS/SCAM PAYMENT
DEPARTMENT OF INTERNATIONAL AFFAIRS

Our Ref: DEATH NOTIFICATION/ COMPENSATION PAYMENT

Attn: Dear Beneficiary,

This Organization was surprised to receive Mrs. Marilynn Corson who announced your death to the Organization and subsequently presented herself as your Next of Kin to claim the approved Five Million United States Dollars (USD$5,000,000.00) as a Scam Victim Compensation Payment to you.

Below is the account submitted and I want you to confirm if you are aware of the new development because we are about effecting payment to the account stated bellow today.

Beneficiary: .Mrs. Marilynn Corson
Bank: FRANKFURTER BANK
A/C No.: 367840545
Swift Code: 50050201
52 Magnolia
Debary, Florida
32713,USA

This Organization is very much in doubt about her person and claims. With this, she is now in the Organization's custody for further investigation and prosecution by the Court of Law. This Organization hereby solicit your immediate response to DR. ENNIS CAMPBELL of MORGAN EXCHANGE COMPANY, at exec.morg.finance@consultant.com with the following Personal Details of yours to enable the Organization to confirm your information and find out the truth and in earnest to make your fund available to you and to send Mrs. Marilynn Corson to jail.

Perhaps, your fund can be made available to you on three bases. (1) ATM CARD.(2) PERSONAL CASH PICK UP at CASH PAYMENT CENTRES.(3) CONSIGNMENT DELIVERY. Please, indicate any of them that are suitable for you when responding Dr. Ennis Campbell.

A: YOUR NAMES.
B: RESIDENTIAL/MAILING ADDRESS.
C. SEX. D. OCCUPATION.
E. CELL/PHONE NUMBER.

Dr. Ana La Chu Chu,
Senior Assistant to Ban Ki-Moon,
Secretary General (United Nations).

This is an amazing, even fantastic story; one which could easily be believed by someone with little knowledge of the UN. The writer wants us to believe that a person, Ms. Corson, presented herself to the Agency, expecting payment of a large amount, as your next-of-kin. For some unknown reason, other than to say her story was apparently not believed, she was arrested by agency personnel, and held in jail for trial.

OK, so I understand the lack of belief, but an agency of the UN having the power to arrest someone, hold them for trial in a 'jail', and then be able to write you – first asserting you sere dead – is a bit of a stretch to the imagination. UN security personnel can act only with Federal and local police in New York. They have no jail of their own, and these types of frauds are generally investigated by local police. Of course, if you do not know that, then you might want to consider the scam something else.

More practically, why would someone from the UN, an assistant to the Secretary-general, send you an e-mail, addressed to 'undisclosed recipient', and expect you to take their story seriously?

A quick background check on 'Morgan Exchange Company', which someone without financial knowledge might misconstrue for the J. P. Morgan Company, a well-respected New York investment bank, yields only references to scams on the major search engines.

Once again we have a story in an e-mail message which sounds like it might be true, and is really nothing more than a SCAM.

United Nations Compensation Commission, Geneva

Many people are aware that the UN has a myriad of agencies, locations, and affiliated organizations. As we have already begun to see, in order to be fair to all, the scammers do try on occasion to seem like real UN agencies. This particular message uses a lesser-known agency in Geneva to throw the average American, or anyone else for that matter, off the track, if they can.

United Nations Compensation Commission.
Palais Des Nations, 1211 Geneva 10
Switzerland.

Ref: UNOG/012/UNCC/UN501-P
Dear Valued Citizen, We bring to your notice the recent action in the compensation department of the United Nations Compensation Commission (UNCC). The total sum of One Billion Two Hundred Thousand U.S Dollars ($1.2 Billion) has been approved by this commission UNCC; to support natural deserter victims worldwide. UNCC is a subsidiary organ of the UN Security Council.

UNCC mandate is to retrieve lost funds through various law agencies, and to process claims and pay compensation for losses and damages suffered as a result of Tsunami and Hurricane The amount above has been approved for payment through the World Bank correspondent banks.. Selected individual(s) will receive the sum of $1,255,000.00 each.

This is to support people in the region affected by the Tsunami and Hurricane. And to support individuals/company(s) that lost Inheritance or contract funds to Financial Crime Authorities years ago. Hence, you received this letter for either of the above reason(s). This has been approved and duly signed by the Finance Department of the United Nations Compensation Commission. Hence, the Japanese PM, Australian PM and the British PM in conjunction with the U.S Government, World Bank and United Nations hereby give the following Irrevocable Approval, with Release No: UN/US/AU-GB/JP298/2012 for payment reference. Thus you qualify to receive payment after bank verification.

A representative shall assist you with the process. Thus you will need to write to Mr. Adrain A. March, Services Division of World Bank, please the UN Financial Services Representative, Global Agency and Trust quote below reference number in message subject.

Reference No: US210-UN501-P012
Contact Person: Mr. Adrain A. March, UNFSR
UN Financial Services Representative.
Global Agency and Trust Services division of World Bank.
Telephone +1 (347) 619-2764
Email: *rep@instruction.com*

Thank you,

Ms. Anne-Brigitte Madsen
Assistant Secretary-General,
Deputy Executive Director
(Management) of the United
Nations Population Fund, UNFPA

Reading the message from 'Ms. Brigitte Madsen' of the UN Population Fund, has it become at all clear to you how the Fund could be involved in resolving hurricane and tsunami damages throughout the world? Of course, she does not have to do this alone; rather, a litany of world governments and agencies are behind her trying to get you your money. Imagine how important you must feel that the UN, The Governments of the US, Australia, and Japan, as well as the World Bank have stopped what they are doing to help you through your crisis. In my case, this is particularly appreciated, even though I have been damaged by neither a hurricane nor a tsunami. You might not be so lucky, and

I pass this message on to you with a caveat that it is a SCAM. Do what you wish.

UN Compensation Unit

From the look of the message which follows, there is also a 'Compensation Unit', or perhaps the scammers did not get their messages synched in Nigeria. The message is interesting for the convoluted story it tells. There is, apparently, a 'Mr. Meyer', who has presented himself to the Zenith Bank in Nigeria to claim the $500K (US) that Zenith Bank had deposited for me at the Cheltenham & Gloucester Bank (C&G Bank) in England.

The C&G Bank, a subsidiary of Lloyds Bank, London, is primarily a mortgage bank. Since it does not have the kinds of customer accounts described in the message, it is interesting that the bank is mentioned at all, when numerous others would be more appropriate. Read for yourself.

Dear Beneficiary,

We are writing regarding your Inheritance funds of $500,000.00, which was used to open an online account for you at our corresponding Bank by the United Nations Compensation Unit.

Did you authorize Mr. JEFFREY MEYER from West Virginia to claim your funds of $500,000.00? because he informed us that you were involved in a fatal accident, so if you are still alive please kindly get back to us so that we will not be making any mistake as we are about sending him your user name and password to logon to your online account with Cheltenham & Gloucester International Bank that worths $500,000.00 (Five hundred thousand united states dollars), we need a final confirmation before we decide to send him the important details to transfer your funds through Cheltenham & Gloucester International Bank online transfer as he claims to be your beneficiary.

The reason why your funds were delayed last time was because you did not provide the requested documents, but now all the documents is obtained so kindly get back to us if you are still alive so that we woudnt be mistaken and then we are going to send you your Online account informations with Cheltenham & Gloucester International Bank such as the User name, Password, Account number, so you can login successfully and transfer your funds within ten minutes to your account over there.

> To confirm that you are still alive and you are ready to transfer your funds through our online banking transfer, get back to us with the details as required below for confirmation.
>
> You are to send your below details to the email stated below and reply with the details requested below to proceed.
> transferdepartment@zenithtransfer.de.tf
>
> Full Name:
> Address:
> Home Phone:
> Cell Phone:
> Age:
> Occupation:
>
> Regard's
> YOURS IN SERVICE
>
> MR. JIM OVIA
> DIRECTOR
> Zenith Bank Plc
> transferdepartment@zenithtransfer.de.tf

Think about the message you just read for a moment. Mr. Ovia is writing to you, if you are still alive, and wants you to contact him right away to prevent him from giving Mr. Meyer the accounts and password information for your C&G account. Even if you know nothing about C&G (And you probably would not), it is still unusual, for any bank, to send this important a message through e-mail, hoping for a reply. Even your local bank would send you a letter, possibly certified or registered, just to be sure you received such important information.

Then, there is the question about the e-mail address (transferdepartment@zenithtransfer.de.tf). The e-mail domain for Zenith Bank is 'zenithbank.com', while this message emanates from a domain 'tf', which is linked to the French Antarctic Territories, quite a distance from Nigeria.

Compensation Payment Coordinator for the United Nations

Closely linked to the Compensation Unit scam is the 'Compensation Payment Coordinator', who, as indicated below, dearly wants to send you some money (1M British Pounds), and only needs a small amount of information to start the process.

The e-mail came from an e-mail provider in Indonesia, well-known for previous scams. This is probably another translated message, or the sender is really stupid, calling the UN the UNITED NATION. Mail address, from the originator (mail.adhimix.co.id@mail.adhimix.co.id), and the requested return address for information (info.unf@asia.com) are well-known to the scam community, and should be avoided. Here's the message (addressed, as usual, to 'undisclosed recipient'.

> THIS MORNING YOUR PENDING PAYMENT HAS BEEN FINALLY APPROVED. YOU HAVE A BANK DRAFT OF 1,000,000.00 POUND DEPOSITED IN OUR BANK AS A COMPENSATION FUNDS FROM UNITED NATION. FOR MORE INFORMATION CONTACT US WITH YOUR DETAILS BELOW VIA EMAIL: *info.unf@asia.com*
>
> YOUR FULL NAME:
> ADDRESS:
> PHONE NUMBER:
>
> *Yours faithfully,*
> *(Dr.Albert Mcain)*
> COMPENSATION PAYMENT COORDINATOR FOR UNITED NATION.
> PHONE NUMBER: + 44-8719153597.

United Nations Office of the Diplomatic Delivery Agent, United States of America

I will bet you have NEVER heard of the Office of the Diplomatic Delivery Agent, United States of America. According to the message, this office distributes money from various scams to you. All you need to do on your part is provide a considerable amount of personal information, which the Diplomatic Delivery Agent can then use to properly identify you as the correct recipient.

Unfortunately, it would appear that the information you provide to 'Mr. Michael Dennison', or whoever he really is, will end up in the hands of people you don't necessarily want to have you information; unless, of course, you don't mind having your identity stolen and your accounts emptied. The money he makes from the sale of information to others is the only real distribution of money to anyone. Be warned, and be safe. Don't respond to these types of solicitations.

> *From: Mr. Michael Dennison.*
> *The United Nations Diplomatic Delivery Agent United States of America.*
> *Tel: 404 647 1021.*
> *Attention: Our Esteemed Fund Beneficiary:*
>
> *I am Mr. Michael Dennison, The United Nations Diplomatic Delivery Agent United States of America. This is to bring to your notice that the payment of your long overdue fund which originated from United Kingdom and Africa Countries such as Contract/Inheritance/Lotto Winning Fund Payment, which has been on hold for many years now, despite all our efforts that failed some how due to the activities of some corrupt governmental and bank officials handling your transaction. Please Kindly bear with us and accept your payment worth of US$10 Million which has been approved to your name. This payment will come to you via consignment box delivery process.*
>
> *Moreover, we have an agreement with the United Nations, that your consignment box delivery process will be completed within the next 24 hours from the hour you response back to this message. Be informed that we are working in collaborations with the United Nations Secretary General Mr. Ban Ki-Moon, who authorize the immediate payment of your long awaited fund without any further delay.*
>
> *Meanwhile I will get everything concluded within the next 24 hours upon your acceptance and proceed to your house address for delivery. Note I guarantee you that this will be executed under a*

legitimate arrangement that will protect you and I from any breach of the law. You are advised to include the followings below details.

(1). Full Name: (2). Contact Address: (3). Telephone Number: (4). Occupation: (5). Age: (6). Sex: (7). Marital Status: (7). Working Identity Card/Int'l Passport: (8). Nearest Airport Close To Your City:

Yours Faithfully,

Mr. Michael Dennison.
Tel: 404 647 1021.

By the way, both the phone number and the e-mail address are frauds. The person creating this scam could not even get his e-mail server correct. There is no 'bulmail.org', but there is a 'bluemail.org', which, not surprisingly, is an unmonitored e-mail service for the 'developing nations'.

> **ALERT: BLUEMAIL.ORG.** According to their website, "BluMail provides global e-mail accounts, educational content, employment needs, entrepreneurship, networking, story / experience sharing, mentoring and volunteering opportunities to youth and others who are coming online in developing countries." An interesting description of a site that will allow anyone to create an e-mail address to cover their scams, such as that above.

UN Inspection Unit, Washington DC

Another of those UN 'offices' no one has ever heard about is the UN Inspection Unit, in Washington DC. As with other parts of the UN, the writer wants you to think the office exists solely to give you money from unclaimed accounts. Here is what its head, a 'Mr. John Anderson', has to say in his e-mail:

GOOD NEWS

I am JOHN ANDERSON Director Inspection Unit, United Nations Inspection Agent here in Washington USA. During our investigation, I discovered that there is a fund in your name that needs to be released to you but due to some obstacles, you have not received it.

The details of the fund including your name, the official document from United Nations office in London are NOT tagged on the document of the fund, details of which will be forwarded to you upon receipt of your response.

For mutual benefit, please provide me with your Phone Number and your full address, and reply so that I can give you the good news and my full details and also of the transaction.

I will give you contacts for people that I have assisted to receive their fund in Europe and Canada, as well as here in the States.

Your urgent response is needed with your full details if you are interested. Call me immediately Tele; 509 592 9438
E-mail: andersonmrjohn@yahoo.com.hk
Best Regards
JOHN ANDERSON

As usual, with most scams, there are several clues contained within this e-mail that should give it away, especially if you live in the Washington DC area. The first major flag is the e-mail address of Mr. Anderson. If he is an official of the UN, and working officially to get you your money, why use a private e-mail address from the United Kingdom? That certainly seems weird.

Then, there is the phone number, a fraud of course, and the area code '509' is a Washington State area code, and, according to the latest area code directory, covers eastern, and central Washington State, not Washington, D.C. and includes the cities of Spokane, Yakima, Walla Walla, and Wenatchee. Isn't that interesting?

I guess I should be happy though; at least the header on his e-mail wished me a 'Merry Christmas'.

There are always mimics to any good scam, especially if you don't want to create a new one yourself. Some, like the one below, don't even waste your time with a long pitch. Instead, they just tell you to contact them for your millions. Good luck!

> *From:* Mr. James Whistler [mailto:jameswhistler325@yahoo.com]
> *Sent:* Tuesday, November 27, 2012 3:39 AM
> *To:* Undisclosed-recipients:
> *Subject:* UN COMPENSATION PAYMENT
> You have been compensated with a payment of $2.5M USD by the UNITED NATION ON SCAMMED VICTIMS. CONTACT:- Mr.James Whistler for Claims on : whistlerjames35@gmail.com
> Provide the following informations on response;address,telepone numbers, age and occupation.

United Nations Office of International Oversight Services (Internal Audit Monitoring Consulting and Investigations Division).

Here is another virtually unknown office at the UN. The office is real, and its function is to perform world-wide audit, investigation, inspection, program monitoring, evaluation and consulting services to the United Nations Secretariat and the rest of the United Nations system. Interesting as that is, the following message id is decidedly NOT from that office; it is yet another of the Nigerian scams, but it is interesting reading.

> FROM: UNITED NATIONS OFFICE OF INTERNATIONAL OVERSIGHT SERVICES (Internal Audit Monitoring Consulting and Investigations Division).
> This message is in regard of your compensation payment for the sum of US$ 2.6million (TWO MILLION SIX HUNDRED THOUSAND DOLLARS ONLY.).
>
> Dear Friend,
> Following series of complains from the FBI and other Security agencies from Asia , Europe , Oceania , and United States of America

respectively against the Federal Government of Nigeria for the rate of corruption and scam activities Going on in this country, The united nation deems it necessary to look in to This trend and this was discussed upon during the last U.N. meetings held at Abuja Nigeria in which a decision was reached to compensate noted victims of this operation and which has been working with the Economic and Financial Crime Commission of Nigeria (EFCC) over this ugly act since then with U.N delegate here in Nigeria.

However, the motion of compensating victims has just been approved by the present government of president Good Luck Ebele Jonathan based on sequence Pressures of the U.N and you are amongst the 78 listed beneficiaries according to the list submitted to my office yesterday by the U.N delegate appointed to harmonize this process (Rev. Udeca smith).

This payments is being partly monitored by EFCC and the U.N, so there's absolutely No question of any uncertainty over receiving of your compensation payment, everything is under adequate control. You are also advise to report if any problem in this regard.

The corresponding paying Bank is CITI BANK NIGERIA LTD.

due to certain mix-ups and corruption in Nigeria system; payments is being Made by ATM master Card as ATM method was considered suitable for this process as Advised and directed by the EFCC and CENTRAL BANK OF NIGERIA GOVERNOR (CBN). An ATM card will be send to you with which you will use to withdraw your payment from any part of the world At ATM machines in your Location but the limit is $5,000.00 per day. The only Money you will need to spend upfront to this regard is $50 for courier delivery Cost of the ATM card to you as no right of probable deduction of any kind was Granted to the paying Bank due to same related reasons of corruption and Otherwise. Upon receipt of your above delivery cost your ATM card for the exact Approve amount of $2.6,000.00 will be send to you by the paying bank without any hitch or delay with no hidden charges.

To receive your payment, contact the paymaster General with your following informations:

FULL NAME, PHONE, and FULL ADDRESS: (where you want your ATM card to be sent) Person to Contact: Rev.Father urbanski Brown Personal Email Address: <u>urbanskibrown1144@gmail.com</u> *HSBC GROUP NIGERIA Victoria Island Lagos Nigeria.*

PHONE: +234 8168120605

Note: all listed beneficiaries are provided with a code which is (UNGNP06654) this you most mention to the paying bank to be recognized. You are to either include it in your mail using it as subject or mention if contacting by phone.

Lastly; according to the update Report from the U.N Delegates, Your contact information was found on the list of one of the Syndicates arrested by the EFCC who consequently confirmed you as one of their victims. You are hereby warned to stop further communication with them and not to duplicate this message for any Reason what so ever as the EFCC and U.S. secret service is still on trace of the other criminals, so keep it secret till they are all apprehended, This also for the best of your interest, as they are all scam artists/impostors AND WILL OFFER YOU NOTHING!.

I wish to inform you that this is no hoax mail or anything of such nature. If you wish of receiving your compensation simply follows my given directive and it will be paid to you as inform no doubt about it. The bank will inform you with detail on how you send them the $50 delivery cost when you contact them. And remember to include the above code in your mail to The Bank (UNGNP06654) Sincerely yours.

Ms. C. L. Lapointe,
United Nations Under-Secretary- General for Internal Oversight

Lots of money involved here, and all they want is $50 (US) for delivery of the debit card, which is 'guaranteed' to you, if only you reply with information, and, of course, transfer them the money. After that, you never hear from them again, and, well, you are only out $50 if you are stupid enough to reply.

The message itself is interesting, and another example of a common thread around the 'Nigerian' scams. In this message, the UN has acted, after a myriad of complaints from around the world, and has required the President of Nigeria to 'clean up the house' and pay what is owed to scam victims. Since the message is addressed to 'undisclosed recipients' both you and I could be among those recipients; that is, if the notice was real, and not a scam.

Unfortunately, in this case, as in others over the past several years, messages similar to this have been sent by a number of people, mostly from Nigeria. These include, in addition to the above:

- Mister Wilfred Lemke, Special Advisor to the UN Secretary-General, who uses a globomail.com address, but who asks that you reply to his agent, Reverend John Balfour (rev.johnbalfour@rocketmail.com)
- Mrs. Carmen LaPointe, UN Under Secretary-General for Internal Oversight, who asks you to use the following reply address: mrs.carman-l-lapointe@gmx.com
- Mrs. Carmen Young, also the UN Under Secretary-General for Internal oversight, who asks that you respond to: cermanyoung@rediffmail.com
- Mister Mathew Ugwu, UN Deputy Secretary-General for Internal oversight. His return e-mail address is: mamj2010@live.com
- Mrs.Inga-Britt Ahlenius Deputy Secretary General UNOIOS, whose return e-mail address is: ibahlenius_un@hotmail.com. She asks that you reply, however, to Mr. Peterside Atedo, of the STANBICIBTC BANK NIG.PLC, and use the de-mail address: atedop.stanbicibtcbankplc@gmail.com

As you can readily see, this office has had a large number of leaders, each of whom has announced a similar initiative.

These messages date back to at least 2008, and while slightly different, all give the same message; send us some money, and we will send you your large compensation payment. Each has the common factor that they cite previous scams and refusals to pay by the Nigerian Government, which the UN is now trying to correct. ALL ARE SCAMS.

The United Nations Office for the Coordination of Humanitarian Affair(s)

The message below, from a 'Dr. David G. Alder', is a good example of all the things to include in a message, if you want to make what you say seem like a scam. Dr. Alder indicates that, for a fee, he will arrange to get you the compensation due. Of course, it cannot come to you through a certified bank draft; it must come through the ATM system. He will ensure you get an ATM card, assuming you pay the fees listed for the overnight services he describes. This will all be done through the Intercontinental Bank Payment Center, which just happens to be in Benin. What a humanitarian (no pun intended)!

UNITED NATIONS OFFICE
FOR THE COORDINATION
OF HUMANITARIAN AFFAIR.
TELL:+2348075599322

Good Day,

I am directed to inform you that your payment verification and confirmations are correct, therefore we are happy to inform you that arrangements have been concluded to effect your payment as soon as possible Due to your long over-due payment which you have been finding it difficult to receive via a Certified Bank Draft issued by the UN Promo, we have arranged your payment through Intercontinental Bank ATM Card Payment Center, this is an instruction passed by the United Nations in respect to all over delayed payment and debt re-scheduling.

The ATM MASTER EXPRESS CARD is credited with the sum of (Five Million Three Hundred and Fifty Thousand United State Dollars), which you are to use in accessing your fund in any ATM Stand/location worldwide and remember that the maximum withdrawal daily limit is Five Thousand United States Dollars .We have concluded delivery arrangement with the below courier services companies and their delivery time is stated below.

UPS=48hrs/$350
FedEx=72hrs/$300

DHL=4days/$200

Kindly provide me with the below details in your response to this email and let me know which courier company you would want us to use for the shipment of your ATM Card to you.
1. Valid Delivery Address.
2. Full Names.
3. Phone Number.
4. Other Email.
5. Occupation.
6. Present Country.
7. Age.
8. Sex.

Understand that you will be liable for the delivery fee of your ATM Master Express Card to you with any of the above courier company.

CALL ME FOR YOUR ATM CARD (+2348075599322)

Regards,
Dr. David G. Alder

We know from the message that Dr. Alder (or whoever is using the name of Dr. Alder) is from Benin by the phone number given. His e-mail address (dr.david_alder@rediffmail.com) is from one of the free internet mail services that have a large membership in the countries of Africa. This guy has been involved in schemes for several years, and appears in a number of the websites, listing the 'Nigerian Scam' perpetrators, normally using the same e-mail address listed above.

Another example citing the United Nations, is the message which follows. It is the longest of the messages, obviously from a source in Nigeria, as have been most of the others, and is so completely ridiculous that it makes good reading, but as a piece of humor.

United Nations Directorate of International Payment and Transfers; United Nations Liaison Office, London (United Kingdom); Wire Transfer Audit Unit

The next message is one of my personal favorites. 'Barrister Jack Les' is not only a scammer, he also wants you to know he is a thief as well. He expects 10% for himself for doing what you would expect a world organization to do for free. Jack blames everything on the British Government, who let all this happen while Nigeria was a colony of the British Empire.

> UNITED NATIONS (UNITED NATIONS ASSISTED PROGRAMME) DIRECTORATE OF INTERNATIONAL PAYMENT AND TRANSFERS.
> UNITED NATIONS LIAISON OFFICE
> LONDON UNITED KINGDOM
> WIRE TRANSFER/AUDIT UNIT
> Our website: http://www.un.int/nigeria/
> Our Ref: WB/NF/UN/XX0287
> DATE: 03/04/2013
> ATTENTION:
> IRREVOCABLE RELEASE OF YOUR PAYMENT VIA CASH DELIVERY.
>
> *I am Barr: Jack Les, the newly appointed director general in charge of approving & releasing all owed yet unpaid Un-released foreign payments and also the special adviser to the United-Nation fighting against the UN-necessary delays of beneficiaries yet unclaimed payment including yours which was recently discovered last week unpaid to you by the present BRITISH GOVERNMENT after series of investigation conducted.*
>
> *I am delighted to inform you that the contract/Inheritance panel of the UN, which just concluded it's seating in London federal capital territory just released your (E-mail Id & Name) among the currently approved beneficiaries who are to benefit 100% from this very diplomatic immunity 3rd quarter payment of the year. This panel was primarily delegated to investigate and to genuinely manipulated all owed debts and claims as it has eaten deep into the economy of the Great Britain-London.*
>
> *However, i wish to personally bring to your urgent notice, so that you will be aware that your yet unclaimed payment date's is still*

reflecting in our central computer as unpaid and UN-claimed owed debt in my department where i newly work as the new appointed (UN) lawyer in charge of approving & releasing of all yet unpaid debts recently recovered back by the (UN) office in London been our branch after discovering that your payment has been delayed UN-necessary due to one reason or another while auditing was going on last week. Your own file was personally forwarded to my executive office by the chief auditors of the (UN) as an unclaimed fund.

At this moment, I wish to use this medium of communication to inform you that for the time being the (UN) has completely stopped further payment through bank to bank transfer, ATM Card, Bank Draft or Check Payment due to numerous petitions received from the united states home-land security, the FBI, IMF and other financial and security agencies to UK government against our banks on wrong payment and diversion of innocent beneficiaries owed funds to a different account.

In this regards, I am going to use my good office now to send you your just approved part-payment in the tune of $6.5M (Six Million Five Hundred United States Dollars) only by cash to you via a special (UN) universal diplomatic delivery means to you. In process of doing that, i will personally secure every needed documents as the newly appointed lawyer representing the (UN) office now to cover the money including the affidavit to claim of this particular yet unclaimed payment from our British High Court here in London which will bestow the right and privilege to you as the rightful beneficiary who is to receive this payment after meeting up with the delivery requirement as the British law stipulate. All these will be done perfectly only on the condition that you will give me 10% of the funds we are about disbursing to you which is $6.5M (Six Million Five Hundred United States Dollars) only out of the $6.5 million you are to receive as soon as you receive the money which will be coming to you

Note: The money will be coming on 2 security proof trunk boxes. The boxes are already sealed with synthetic nylon seal and padded with machine by the management of this organization and i also want you to know that the management are not aware of my plans with you in this transaction, so you have to keep it a top secret till 1 and you are able to conclude this very transaction. This fund was brought to us from the World Bank special delegates because the funds itself was meant for our local a fem market here in the UK.

But you don't have to worry for any thing that need to be taking care of here in London, as this transaction is 100% risk free and will remain legit as long as you work with me transparently. The boxes are coming with a diplomatic agent assigned by the management of this organization by AN AGENT" who will accompany the boxes to your house address or any address you will provide to me for this transaction to enable us complete.

All you need to do now upon your willing acceptance on my condition, is to send to me a guarantee that you will give me 10% of the funds as soon as you receive the $6.5Million, and your full house address and your identity such as, international passport or driver's license including your personal contact phone numbers which must be a working numbers, the diplomatic attached will travel with itches will call you immediately he arrives in your country's airport to update you and I hope you understand each and every point that I've made clear to you in this email message am sending you.

WARNING/ADVISE: Please note carefully that any money requested from you by anybody,office,banks or group of people from Africa/Nigeria or any part of the world to receive your payment expect the United-Nations Appointed Commission Office (UK), presently in charge of recovering all UN-necessary delayed yet unclaimed owed debts payments, whom the FBI, IMF and other financial agencies have irrevocably approved that should serve you better and ensure you receive your payment this time around, so kindly note that any money sent by you to any office in Africa/Nigeria is at your OWN RISK, so stay away from any other office, person or group of people and face only the United-Nation Appointed Approved Payment Disbursing High Commission Office only till your payment gets to you safely through the Dallas Airport.

MOST IMPORTANTLY: For security reasons and to enable both of us conclude this transaction successfully, note that the diplomatic agent that is coming with the consignment boxes will not know the original contents inside the boxes he his to delivery to you. So what l and our accredited management will declare to him that is inside the consignment boxes is a sensitive photographic film material and classified volume confidential company's contract documents.

Also note categorically that, before i proceed with the next arrangement, you are advice to call me immediately or email me immediately , so we can talk and agree first before i seal this transaction with you and if you have any question to ask for more clarification before and remember to send the required information directly to my Email address: and I will let you know how far I have gone with the arrangement. I will secure the diplomatic immunity clearance certificate that will be tagged on the boxes to make it stand as a diplomatic consignment. This clearance will make it pass every custom checking point all over the world without any hitch. All this I will do with my own money as your partner.

Please, I need your urgent reply , because the boxes are schedule already to live this week as soon as I hear from you today. You should confirm immediately you receive this message through my Email my private phone number will be given to you when i get your immediate responds for confidential talk:Contact Email:
unhumanrightactive@yahoo.co.uk
I am highly submitted and willing to serve you better.
Congratulations Once AGAIN.
Highly Submitted.
Respectfully Yours in-service,
Barrister.Jack Les,
(UN) Human Right Activist

So, having read the message, let's review the main elements of this scam. Barrister Jack Les says he has been delegated by the United Nations to get you your money, and quickly. After all, he is a "UN Human Right Activist". Who could be more qualified? The barrister goes into great detail on how the scam will work, and how the large box of money will be delivered to you – risk-free, of course. All you have to do is contact him, and then provide him with a very specific list of documents which establish who you are, where you live, and your phone number. He doesn't want just any kind of information either; he wants a copy of your driver's license or your passport. You can surely trust him with your information; after all, he works for the UN!

Of course, none of the e-mails cited in the message are US e-mail addresses, and the website for the office is located in Nigeria, but don't mind all that. It's the money you are after, so write to Jack right away and send all the personal information he requests. That way, he can right to work fabricating copies of your information to sell on the market.

United Nations (World Bank Assisted Programme) Directorate of International Payments and Transfers, Wire Transfer/Audit Unit

This is a relatively new scam. The message and description is shown under Zenith Bank International in Chapter 12, along with other UN general attributions, and cites Zenith Bank International in Nigeria as the paying agent.

International Monetary Fund (IMF)

This message was a recent arrival in my junk file, and, I must admit, I waited for several days for the phone call about my money. There was no call, of course, since this is yet another scam, using an international organization as cover for their efforts.

Nonetheless, with the IMF in control, and an agent already at Dallas-Fort Worth Airport, it seemed too good to not be true.

As you will see, several things are obviously wrong with this e-mail. First, the World Bank headquarters is in Washington DC, not Zurich. Second, the phone number is a phony (Which is why I left it in the message). Third, the World Bank, even in Washington DC, does not share its headquarters with the International Monetary Fund, although they are closely located to each other in the city.

Finally, there is the question of an agent, a diplomat, coming to the US to give me money, yet needing my personal information, including my address and other personal information to identify me before he does so.

Corporate Head-Quarter
Zurich Switzerland

I am Diplomat Collins Baker I have been trying to reach you on your telephone to inform you about my successful arrival at the Dallas Fort Worth International Airport Dallas with your cash consignment worth $8.5 Million United State Dollars which I have been instructed by the International monetary fund/World bank headquarters in Zurich to be delivered to you.

The Airport authority demanded for all the legal back up papers to prove to them that the fund is no way related with neither drug nor fraud money, I have presented the papers and they where very much pleased with the paper's, Please try and reach me with my number 469-941-2732 as I can not afford to spend more time here due to other delivery I have to take care of in Newzealand.

I want you to know that you have 24 hours to call me on phone 469-941-2732 As you may know I do not want the security company where this Consignment is been lodged to start getting apprehensive because of the length of time it has stayed.

However, before the delivery is effected, we need you to reconfirm the following information's so that the funds will not be delivered to the wrong person.

1. Full Name:
2. Residential Address:
3. Direct Telephone Numbers:
4. Valid Identification:

After verification of the information with what I have on file, I shall contact you so that we can make arrangements on the exact time I will be bringing your cash consignment to your residential address.

Send the requested information so that we can proceed.

Regard.

Collins baker.
SKYBIRD INTERNATIONAL DELIVERY AGENTS.
PHONE: 469-941-2732

'Mr. Collier' claims to be a diplomat, but of what country or agency? He never does say; instead implying, at least, that he is a direct representative of the bank through Skybird. So, I guess the 'agent' will be travelling to New Zealand for his next scam victim, and I will still be poor. That's life.

My search did find a Skybird International, which appears to be an international travel agent, a firm based in China, and also another Skybird International, based in Sweden, selling mobile phones, and other goods.

As far as Mr. Collins Baker is concerned, he is well-known as a scammer, having been sending the same of similar message since at least early 2012, and generally from the same e-mail address (collinsbaker1@globomail.com), via an equally well-known free e-mail service. THIS IS A SCAM, AND YOU SHOULD NOT REPLY TO ANY MESSAGE YOU RECEIVE.

The World Bank

As you have already seen in several places, here are a number of scams citing the World Bank, some directly, as does the message below, and others, such as that from Mr. Collins Baker, who starts his message by alluding to the bank, and then throws in other agencies, such as the IMF. These messages look much more authoritative, and try to coerce you gently into believing you are about to get a lot of money. Seeing so many of these references, you really have to wonder how many people respond, and if more would respond for more modest amounts, in response to messages created to really appear believable. In any event, here is the one on the World Bank

INTERNATIONAL FUNDS TRANSFER / AUDIT

UNIT UNITED NATION(WORLD BANK ASSISTED PROGRAMME) DIRECTORATE OF INTERNATIONALPAYMENT AND TRANSFERS.Ref: WB/NF/UN/XX027

ATTN: BENEFICIARY,

RE: VERIFICATION AND APPROVAL OF YOUR PAYMENT FILE.

FROM THE RECORDS OF OUTSTANDING FUNDS DUE FOR IMMEDIATE PAYMENT, YOUR NAME/PARTICULARS WAS DISCOVERED AS NEXT ON THE APPROVED LIST.
I WISH TO INFORM YOU THAT YOUR PAYMENT IS BEING PROCESSED AND FROM THE RECORD IN MY FILE, THE TOTAL SUM OF US$9.5M HAVE BEEN APPROVED ON YOUR BEHALF FOR THE FINAL QUARTER OF THIS 2012 FISCAL YEAR.

FOR YOUR INFORMATION, WE HAVE ASSIGNED THE CITI BANK,TEXAS TO HANDLE ALL RELATED TRANSACTIONS TO AVOID FURTHER COMPLAIN FROM BENEFICIARIES ABOUT INCESSANT TAXES, FEES AND LEVIES.

KINDLY RE-CONFIRM THE FOLLOWING INFORMATION IMMEDIATELY TO FACILITATE THE ISSUANCE OF AN INTERNATIONAL PAYMENT JUSTIFICATION ORDER DOCUMENT ON YOUR BEHALF WHICH WILL BE SUBMITTED TO THE CITI BANK FOR THE IMMEDIATE RELEASE OF YOUR FUNDS.
1) YOUR FULL NAME:
2) CONTACT ADDRESS:
3) NATIONALITY:
4) OCCUPATION:
5) PHONE, FAX AND MOBILE:
6) GENDER:
7) AGE:

AS SOON AS THIS INFORMATION IS RECEIVED, YOUR PAYMENT WILL BE MADE TO YOUR NOMINATED BANK ACCOUNT DIRECTLY FROM THE CITI BANK.

YOUR PAYMENT APPROVAL IS MADE UNDER THE AUSPICES OF THE WORLD BANK AND WE INTEND TO SUCCESSFULLY COMPLETE YOUR FUNDS TRANSFER. YOU ARE THEREFORE STRONGLY ADVISE TO STOP FUTHER COMMUNICATION WITH ANY OTHER BANK OR INSTITUTION REGARDING THIS MATTER, FOR THE OVERALL SAFETY OF YOU AND YOUR FUND.

BEST REGARDS,

MR. ANDREW TWEEDIE
DIRECTOR OF FINANCE,
INTERNATIONAL MONETARY FUND.
NEW YORK,UNITED STATES

'Mr. Tweedie', whoever he really is, wants us to understand clearly he is the ONLY representative of the World Bank, which is guaranteeing this transaction To make it work, he wants you to stop any communication with any other bank or organization which may have contacted you. In return, he say he will expedite transfer of your money, through Citi Bank in Texas, as soon as he receives information from you to identify yourself as the recipient.

Interestingly, he says that Citi Bank will transfer the money to your bank, but he doesn't ask for your banking information. He wants to do this, of course, to reduce any further fees or charges which might accrue from your efforts to secure your $9.5M (US). What a nice guy!

Folks, this is a scam, and it should be obvious to you that you will receive nothing. He wants you to confirm your information, and give him yet another set of data to sell on the market.

PART FIVE – OTHER RIDICULOUS OPPORTUNITIES

In this last part, we consider other commonly seen schemes in the ever-growing proliferation of e-mail messages traffic. These messages fall into several broad categories, and I will show examples of each. Basically, we will consider the following:

- 'PRODUCT Schemes' (Chapter 15)
- Banking-related Schemes (Chapter 16)
- Commercial Appeals (Chapter 17)
- Lotteries (Chapter 18)
- Western Union Scams (Chapter 19), and
- 'Next Generation Scams' in Chapter 20 (A 'miscellaneous' group of other ridiculous schemes)

Chapter 15 We want to buy your product

A number of current scams involve purchase of 'products' from prospective customers. The e-mail below, supposedly from the Omaha Group of Companies, asks for specific shipping and pricing information from 'undisclosed recipients', who are supposed to respond, and receive more information from the sender.

Hello,
My name is Susan Mcoy, sales manager of Omaha Group of company's, we are interested in your product,and the product is attached to view. Once viewed,kindly get back to us with the details listed below:

For the security and authenticity of our new brand,we do not share our sample drawings.
Review samples drawings and provide us with details below:
1: Let us know immediately if your company can produce to specification,to allow us determine the quantity list to order.
2: Please tell us means of payment and how many days it will take you to produce after part payment is made to you.
3: We also want to know the quantity that can contain 1x20ft. We will provide you with a brand name for the label on our goods.
We need your immediate response and pray this is the beginning of a good business relationship in the near future.

Regards,
Susan Mcoy
Omaha Group of Company.

I truly enjoy reading the commercial appeals, especially those written by foreign sources, and translated for US e-mails, since they are often so hilarious, you would assume they could not possibly be taken for true. Look at the one below, and see if you agree:

Thanks for your early respones, Sorry for our late reply,we are ready to make order now, please kindly let us know more about your products and do click the link below to enable you view the pictures for the samples and designs we need to order. And please do get back to us ASAP so we can proceed on the Payment and order.

Please log in with your valid email to view.
http://peckmarketing.net/RhodeBytes//wp-content/new.alibaba1/acco.unt.verify.php

If the page does not display, please copy and paste the link to your address bar of you browser.

Please confirm when you will have it available, so i can send to you our order list and quantity. we will await your response with details, prize and quantity that can be made available.

Our Company want to purchase a lage good worth ($ 170,000 USD) in your company.. We planned to give our customers the best of all product production to enable a good sale this year and also add more new product to burst our sales record.

Please get back to me as soon as possible.

Best Regards
Shanghai Bangpu Industrial Group Co. ltd
Level 17, Exchange Plaza
Sherwood Court
Perth WA 6001
-Sales Manager-
Joy Smith.
email was sent to: [my e-mail address] QR16548/AF8A84

Let's look at this last e-mail message from two different perspectives. The first is the message itself; then second, the potential for it being real.

As might be quickly obvious, this was either not written by a person of moderate intelligence; one who cared little for both sentence construction and correct spelling; or, it was written in another language, translated, and then not proofed for quality by someone who understood local language customs. Either way, a message such as this is a quick and decisive turnoff, especially for the person who is being solicited to do business with the 'company'.

The second problem relates to the information about the company, and the potential of it being a 'real' solicitation, rather than simply a way of getting information for sale on the spam market. That gets a bit more complex.

The company cited, *'Shanghai Bangpu Industrial Group Co'* is an actual company, a firm located in Shanghai, China, with an established reputation for manufactured goods. Established in 2008, they do about $50M (US) a year in sales, and have a well-known set of products they provide their customers. All that is perfectly normal, and there is no reason to suggest the message above is in any way emanating from the company.

The company established their website portal on this URL (http://shbangpu.en.alibaba.com), and does business from it. The e-mail address in the message, conversely, routes you to 'peckmarketing.net', a small firm that does advertising for various groups, prominently noted are those which advertise payday loans, and other 'quick' schemes. Responding to the complete address cited in the message now takes you to a dead address; although three months ago, it took you to a site that verified your e-mail address, and said 'thank you' for going there.

These solicitations are generally used to get valid e-mail addresses for further sale on the market, and should be avoided.

The next message is a similar request, also looking for a response through a web URL. In this case, the guy is trying to validate you against a list, and will do so if you respond. By the way, when you do, you also get a Trojan that will suck up all your e-mail contacts.

Hello, Thank you for your message. I am from Germany.

Our Company and required Product details is in our database.

Our various customers have placed their various order with various specification and quality and packaging. We want to satisfy each customer by meeting their requirements.

Please log into our database to see the detailed items needed. I have registered your email in the our database for easy access. Sign in with your valid email address and password to be able view our vital details. Please copy and paste the web link below on your browser to sign in :

http://ps3media.com/Sample/index.html

We will await your response after viewing our database.

We will also want to know the production time for the quantity required as specified in the database.

We anticipate a long lasting business relationship.

Kind regards,

Ms. Cecil Lawton
G.T.C (UK)

Be careful of people such as this; as he says, 'we have registered your e-mail in our database', and that means he will sell your e-mail in a heartbeat, if he can confirm it.

The next e- mail solicitation also involves a desire to purchase goods, this time from a company in the Ukraine. The e-mail, by the way, was addressed to the usual 'undisclosed recipients', and, since I make no 'products' other than writing my novels, it is hard to imagine why I would have received the e-mail in the first place, or how I would respond.

Morning.

My Name is Mrs masha Lee Purchasing Manager of SIMS GROUP,write to inform you that we are interested in your products and We require to order a particular design.

The photos of the designs has been uploaded to the below link because of the size of the gallery,You are advised to open or copy and paste the link to the URL to view our interested product sample,to confirm if

you can supply exactly the designs. copy and paste the link to your address bar browser to view pictures and size. or click the link
Gallery Link
: http://urunanadc.org/viewproduct.7/ademins.html

Note: For you to be able to view the picture sample, Kindly login with the same email you use for correspondence for access to our product sample cataloger gallery below.

Kindly send us your catalog, And we would like to inquire about the following:

1. Delivery time of the product
2. product warranty
3. Minimum Order Quantity
4. Payment terms available

Looking forward to your response.
Regards,
SIMS GROUP
COMPANY REGISTRY NUMBER IN UKRAINE 37641588

This is another effort at securing e-mail addresses for sale to other scammers. You try to get to the 'real' urananadc.org; you get a Rwandan development organization, not a company in the Ukraine. If you link to the complete address, you get a different site, which asks you to log in with your Yahoo address, and it will automatically download a file to your computer. Better be safe, and not go to this site.

Here is yet another one, slightly different, but the same scenario, and this time with a guarantee of a commission, after the transaction closes.

Hello,

Good-day.

We got your contact through a reliable source as the leading company/supplier of the product we need to supply our customer.

We are into importer and customer representative here in our country and we will like to enter into full business relationship with your able company.

Kindly get back to us through our below details with the items which you can supply to us along with the full detail specification for our study and order. Kindly confirm the below details so we can proceed.

- Your minimum order quantity.
- Your FOB Prices and FOB Port.
- Your estimated delivery time.
- Your Method Of Payment
- Your Sample Policy

Kindly log into the link below to view samples of the product we need for supply.

http://tcadp.org/tmm/ordersheet/weblogin.html

We want to place and order large quantity this month, We believe that your company can serve better in the supply of the items.Can you handle this contract?

Our company shall be acting as your representative between you and the end buyer for the purpose of this transaction, and you shall map out 2% commission of the total contract value, as our compensation upon the successful conclusion of this transaction after you must have received your total contract payment in your designated bank account.

We sincerely hope to establish a long lasting business relationship with your firm in the nearest future for our mutual benefit.

We anticipate your co-operation and prompt response to our request soonest.

Best Regards,
Ahmed Hossain
Kiaalua LTD
C-57, D.C.C. Market, (1st Floor) North Gulshan Circle-2, Dhaka-1212.
Tel: 029884197, 028812347

Read the message carefully, and you will see that you are providing the scammer everything they need to steal your identity, empty your bank accounts, and then sell your name to other scammers for an additional fee. You never get your 'transaction payment', they get a lot more than a 2% commission for their efforts, and a giant pain in your head from the misery you have inflicted on yourself. Worth the effort? Probably not.

One final appeal, this one more generic than the others, is probably typical, possibly a template for others to use, since the wording is so close to others.

> *Dear Sir,*
> *Our Company would like to order for a good quantity of your products. I have taken my time to write down the quantity we want as well as their various specifications for each product so that it will help you serve us better. Hope to read back from you.*
> *Regards,*
> *Purchasing Manager,*
> *Ms Leam Salihu.*

Sounds like it might be interesting, if they had actually provided any information which would enable you to respond.

So much for the personal appeals. Now, it is time to look a bit more on the other side of the banking and loan scams, where fleecing both you and the bank is paramount.

Chapter 16 Great Banking and Loan Opportunities

If you are a scammer, what better way to convince a target than to send them a message from their bank, asking them to do something? Banks are always a great reference to use, and, as we have seen throughout the book, information is readily available on banks people use for their daily banking needs. In addition, so many people do their banking online these days that messages from the banks are not only commonplace, but people actually read them, and tend to respond without stopping to think about whether or not they are real. That is like going to financial heaven for the scammer, and they know it.

Unfortunately, not all banking or loan notices are real—instead many are frauds, as you will see in the following e-mails. The topics vary, but the intent is always the same; get someone to respond and work them until you have the money or information you want.

First, let's look at a common, frequent message increasingly seen in e-mails.

> *Dear Applicant,*
> *Are you interested in getting a loan at an interest rate of 3%, are you in need of loan, for Business transaction,automobile purchase, house purchase bad Credit Card and other E.T.C. we give out long term loan for five to fifty years maximum with 3% interest rate in this you can as well tell us the amount you need so that we will send to you the terms and condition that is if you are really interested in getting a loan from us, Loans are given out in Great British Pounds and United States Dollar.*
> *We can give you the best satisfaction in getting a Loan from us. as being given guarantee and Insurance that you receive your Loan amount in your Personal Bank Account in your country. which only takes 48hrs Banking process. We also render Collateral And Non- Collateral Loans For Your Business Start up.*

> *If you are interested kindly contact us on j.peterson@superposta.com*
>
> *Sincere regards,*
> *Mr.Jesse Peterson, Loan Officer*

This message is interesting, and the 'red flags' it presents should make even the most casual reader very wary:

- No bank or company name is given
- Loan duration could be as much as fifty (50) years
- Both collateral and non-collateral loans are offered
- Both British Pounds and Dollars are stated
- Bad credit seems to be OK

There are several simple questions here that a person needs to ask themselves BEFORE responding. First, ***what bank is involved?*** Across the Internet these days, there are a number of 'brokers' – people or organizations that collect information on potential customers, and then refer them to banks or other financial institutions to complete their applications. Most messages, however, at least mention a bank or two, as examples, so the potential customer has an early idea of who they might be working with in the near future.

Second, ***the length of the loan***, potentially, is very long, especially for Internet solicitations. Why would any legitimate bank offer a loan to someone with bad credit, at a low rate, and over a very long term? That kind of loan is a dream, not a reality. This is especially true when someone offers non-collateral loans to completely unknown applicants. When anyone says 'bad credit is OK', you need to look deeply and carefully to see that the offer is legitimate, and not someone who will award the loan, sell it to someone else, and you get stuck with very high rates. More likely, you will get no loan, and have your personal information sold to the highest bidder.

It should be easy to see that the first message is a scam, and putting some thought into these messages, if you read them at all, can avoid something very bad on your pocketbook. BEST ADVICE:

Delete any message like this from someone you don't know, or from your bank, if you are not expecting it. Real bankers call or write their customers with important information.

The next category involves requests from a bank for changes to your account, many of which, at least on the surface, appear too real. People often go into their online accounts, change their password or user name, and forget it, prompting yet another online change session. Most institutions will send a confirmatory e-mail to alert you something has changed, and give you the opportunity to reverse it, on the possibility you did not make the change.

This first e-mail, from Bank of America, tries to emulate an 'alert' message, and warn you that your password has been changed. That piqued my interest. So, I started looking into the message a bit further, and soon found out it was totally fraudulent. Read it, and see how you would react.

Exclusively for: | *[my e-mail account]*
Online Banking Warning
Online Banking Passcode Modified
Security Checkpoint:
You last signed in to Online Banking on 10/19/2012.
Remember: Always check your SiteKey® before entering your Passcode.
  To: *[my e-mail account]*
  Account: SAVINGS ending in XXX1
  Date: 10/19/2012
Your Online Banking Passcode was requested to be reseted on 10/19/2012. Your security is important to us. If you are not aware of this change, please contact us immediately at this link

Like to get more Warnings? Access to your Online Banking at Bank of America and visit the Accounts Overview page select the Alerts tab.

Security Checkpoint: This email includes a Safety Checkpoint. The information in this section lets you know this is an authoritative informer from Bank of America. Remember to look for your SiteKey every time you logging in to Online Banking.

Email Settings This is a informational email from Bank of America. Please note that you may receive service email due to your Bank of America service agreements, whether or not you elect to receive promotional messages. Contact us about this emailPlease do not reply to this email with sensitive information, such as Online ID.

The security and confidentiality of your personal details is main primary principal to us. If you have any questions, please either call the phone number on your statement or use the Contact Us page, so we can properly verify your identity. Privacy and SecurityKeeping your financial details secure is one of our most fundamental key responsibilities. For an explanation of how we manage customer information, please read our Privacy Policy.

You can also learn how Bank of America keeps your personal information secure and how you can help protect yourself. Bank of America Email, 8th Floor-NC1-054-13-14, 575 South Seashore Vale, Ave., Charlotte, CA 39023-0387 Bank of America, N.A. Member FDIC. © 2012 Bank of America Corporation. All rights reserved.

Whoever wrote the e-mail message wanted it to look as close as possible to an actual Bank of America e-mail, so they probably found an actual e-mail message from the Bank and adapted it for their own purposes. When this one came to me, I thought it funny, actually, because I had no current Bank of America account; had not had an account with them in years, and would not, therefore, be changing my password in any case. Nonetheless, I looked further just because it seemed so odd that the Bank would be sending me an e-mail after so long a time.

Over the past few years messages similar to this one arise periodically in the e-mail traffic. Looking over my own archive of messages, I have some from the following:
- SunTrust (VA)
- Wells Fargo Bank (UT)
- Chase/Mellon (NY)
- PNC (PA)

And a host of others, both local and national. I stopped saving these a while ago, except for the locals because there were so many, and the messages were uniformly the same.

Chapter 17 Commercial Appeals

Like the banking scams, commercial scams have all the earmarks of something that just might be real. We saw a number in Chapter 10 (US Commercial Scams) and Chapter 13 (International Scams). They all involved the name of a well-known company, along with a cash award of some kind, and tried to imbue the feeling that you are about to do something well out of your social status; something which will make you stand out in the community.

This chapter describes how some scammers will appeal to your vanity for their entrée into your wallet. What better example than getting you into a brand new BWM car, with a pile of money in your pocket. So, we will start these.

The next e-mail message is supposed to involve the BMW automobile organization, through its US subsidiary. They want you to believe you have won a car, actually some months ago (I received this in December, 2012), and you also get a large cash award as well. This would appeal quickly to anyone who has always wanted a BMW but, like me, can't afford one.

Read the e-mail, and then I will comment further.

BMW LOTTERY DEPARTMENT
ROCKVIEW, ARKANSAS. 49812
UNITED STATES OF AMERICA.

Dear Winner,

This is to inform you that you have been selected for a prize of a brand new 2012 Mobel BMW 7 Series Car and a Check of $500,000.00usd from international programs held on the 1st section 2012 in the UNITED STATE OF AMERICA.

The selection process was carried out through random selection in ourcomputerized email selection system (ESS) from a database of over 250,000 email addresses drawn from all the continents of the world which you were selected.

The BMW Lottery is approved by the British Gaming Board and also licensed by the International Association of Gaming Regulators (IAGR).

To begin the processing of your prize you are to contact our fiduciary claims department for more information as regards procedures to claim your prize.

Name: Mr. Frank Walcot

Email: mr.frank_w@yahoo.cn

Contact her by providing her with your secret pin code Number BMW:2551256003/23. You are also advised to provide him with the Under listed information as soon as possible:

1. Name in full. 2. Address.
3. Nationality. 4. Age.
5. Occupation. 6. Phone/Fax.
7. Present Country. 8. Email address.
9. pin code Number BMW:2551256003/23

Mr. Richard Lankford
THE DIRECTOR PROMOTIONS
BMW LOTTERY DEPARTMENT
UNITED STATES OF AMERICA.

Several things came to mind immediately as I went through the message the first time. First, why would a German manufacturing giant want to conduct such a through their US subsidiary? After all, conducting a lottery, such as this, is illegal in many states, especially in the South.

I also noted that they pointed to a 'British Lottery Board', and the 'International Association of Gaming Regulators', as the approving bodies for their lottery. Where is the approval of the Arkansas Lottery Board, and why no mention of the US Internal Revenue Service, each of whom would certainly expect their share of the lottery income?

Then, I noticed their 'fiduciary agent' used a Yahoo-Canada address. That also seemed odd, so I did some further checking.

Would you be amazed that BMW USA has no lottery department, and is located in Woodcliff Lake, New Jersey, not Rockview, Arkansas? In fact, the only BMW location in Arkansas is in Little Rock, the capital.

I also did some checking on 'Richard Lankford', the supposed lottery director, and found that he was not listed among the BMW executives, nor was there a 'Director, Promotions' or a 'Lottery Department'.

Then, of course, there is the obvious faux-pas within the message that gives you the name of someone named 'Walcott' to contact, and then says 'contact her' in the following paragraph. Interesting.

The e-mail requests a lot of personal information, and the ever-present request for your e-mail address. Answering this type of e-mail scam is an open invitation to identity fraud.

Here is a variation of the same theme, but now they indicate that the BMW is being given as a prize from BMW itself, through their 'International Promotion Program'. This is also a fraud, but whoever created it did a better job of making it seem real this time.

BMW MOTOR AWARDS
An Affiliate of BMW UK.
28 TANFIELD ROAD,
LONDON, UK.

We are pleased to inform you of the release, of the long awaited results of the BMW CAR INTERNATIONAL PROMOTION PROGRAM held on the 12th of October, 2012. You were entered as dependent clients with: Ticket number: 2752246896 and Secret pin code x7pwyz2009. You have been approved for a payment of ?450,000.00 (four hundred and fifty thousand Great British Pounds) in cash credited to file reference number:BMW:2551256003/23 And a brand new BMW 5 Series Car. You are to contact our-accredited agent for your claim now.

Mrs.Reacheal Lampard
Email:rlampard123@yahoo.cn

You are also advised to provide her with the under listed information:
1.Name in full.
2.Address in full.

3.Nationality & Present Country.
4.Age.
5.Phone /Fax /Sex.
6.Email address.

Once again congratulations.
Program Co-ordinator

I'm not sure if you have been waiting very long (as indicated in the message), or even received something like this, but I would wonder what your reaction to it might be.

Possibly the first question to come to mind is 'Why me'?' The message says is I was entered in the 'Promotion Program' as something called a 'dependent client', whatever that means, and my name was drawn. That's good, I guess, because, after all, 450K (Br. Pounds) comes with the car. That much money almost makes the car irrelevant.

The message is from London (So they want you to think), but the e-mail return address is 'yahoo.cn', a URL for the Chinese arm of Yahoo (Since closed down by the Yahoo people.)

This message, like its companion, asks you to contact an agent of BMW, this time a 'Mrs. Reacheal Lampard', who will help you. Good luck on your quest.

BMW is obviously not the only company whose reputation is on the line for these type messages. We picked it for its shock effect, although any number of others in the US and Europe, especially, have been subjected to similar misuse of their names and reputations.

Chapter 18 Lotteries

As we saw in the last chapter, one of the last great frontiers for e-mail scams is the promotion or lottery. Since a large number of nations now hold one, along with many state and local governments, the lottery scam is a lot more believable than it was years ago, when only the Irish National Sweepstakes was common.

Scammers understand better than most people the impact of the sense of greed, and its effect on people. Without greed—the desire for a large cash win, in this case—the scammers would have no audience for their messages. But people are greedy; they want to win, and they want to do it without any real effort on their part. From greed, new things grow; in this case, the combination of the e-mail message and the lottery scam.

Take a real, or possibly real, lottery (when I first typed the word lottery, I misspelled it 'lootery', because that is really what it is) and advertise it widely as a means to make a lot of money quickly. Then get people to respond to you by giving them every incentive to do so; money, fame, and the opportunity to do something for themselves and others, and you have the making of the lottery scam.

In this we will see a number of such solicitations, each of them somewhat believable, and relatively unknown, so a person might read the message to see what is happening. That's just what the scammers want—an opportunity to catch your eye.

The first message is from the 'Euro Millions Lottery', one of the national lotteries of the United Kingdom. It is similar to many in the US, such as *Powerball*, and *Mega Millions*, which draw a series of usually five numbers, along with another ball needed to get the big prize. In the case of Euro Millions, it is the lucky stars. As with the two US games (Which are played across a number of states in the US), Euro Millions is multi-national, playing throughout Europe.

The Euro Million Scam

Scammers use this lottery because of its name, and its larger-than-usual prizes. Messages involving 'The Euro' are among the newer scams, always quoting a large cash prize, and are making headway into e-mail inboxes, in both Europe and the US over the past few months. Read and enjoy.

Congratulation Dear Winner!!!

You have been chosen to be one of the lucky beneficiary of Charity Donation. Euro Million Support is a Charity Organization that helps Deaf, Hard of Hearing and Hearing. Euro Million Support is in collaboration with the governing body of AIM/AOL and Online Disabilities Commission Organization by selecting all the people that are active online.

Among the millions that subscribed to Yahoo, GMAIL, HOTMAIL, MSN and AIM/AOL, we selected 10 people every month as our winners through electronic balloting system without the winner applying, and your screen name has won you the sum of $850,000.00 Dollars. We congratulate you for being one of the lucky winners. Let us know when you are ready for your cash money, so that we can bring it to you in person. Get back to us on Eurospecial1@live.com or send a TEXT MESSAGE:470-215-0350.

The Management.

Freddie Shadrick.

So, what is wrong with this message? The answer to that question is simple. **EURO MILLIONS IS BASED ON THE DRAWING OF A SET OF BALLS, EACH OF WHICH HAS A NUMBER PAINTED ON IT, AND ALSO ON THE DRAWING OF TWO 'LUCKY STARS', EACH WITH NUMBERS. HAVING A TICKET WITH ALL THE NUMBERS, AND THE STARS MAKES YOU A GRAND WINNER, AND HAVING FEWER NUMBERS IN SPECIFIC COMBINATIONS MAKES YOU A**

PARTIAL WINNER. THERE IS NO OTHER WAY TO WIN EURO MILLIONS.

The message above indicates you were selected based on your subscription to an e-mail service, and randomly licked as a winner of $850K (US). Euro Millions announces their prizes in British Pounds or Euros, not dollars. Finally, Euro Millions has a website, and an official e-mail address for contact with the lottery, not on 'live.com' one of the 'free' e-mail sites.

The Euro Millions website has begun cautioning people about these spurious messages. The lottery NEVER contacts people by e-mail, or other direct mail, asking them to 'register' and provide information. If you are purchasing a ticket online, they have your information, and if you check online to see if you are a winner, you are directed to a place to validate your ticket. Also, Lottery officials don't call people about their winnings. The bottom line is that these kinds of contacts are invariably indications of a scam, and you should not respond.

Of course, if you don't answer, or even if you never received the first message, there is the inevitable follow-up, such as this one:

Dear Sir / Madam,

I am Mr Alfred Michael the Notification officer of the Euro Million lottery. Several winners of the Euro MillionOlympic Ceremony Draw until now did not know that they won and never came for claim.

Please read this by Visiting:
http://www.huffingtonpost.co.uk/2012/07/28/euromillions-raffle-100-olympic-ceremony-draw_n_1713446.html

As you can see, out of the 100 winners, only 35 people came to claim and 65 people never came for the claim.

The amount left for the people to claim put together is GBP 19.4 Million. (Nineteen Million, four hundred thousand Great British pounds)

This money is almost due to be returned to the lottery game reserve, as the rules stipulates that all unclaimed funds should be returned to the Lottery game reserve after 5 months.

Based on this, Myself and other 3 top officials in charge of all processing and payouts have decided to contact you to use your name to claim this money as we cannot use our names because we work here and it will be questioned. Hence the contact with you.

Please this is a 100% risk free lottery deal that comes once in a very long while.

We have decided to compensate you with 30% of the Total money while 70% will be shared among 4 of us that are involved if we get this deal executed with you.

You need not worry about the paper work as the winning certificate will be issued in your name once you accept the deal and you will have no question to answer.

Please, if this is acceptable to you, get back to my Coordinating officer Herbert Smith (Email:herbertsmith2013@yahoo.co.uk) who is much more involved in this deal, your urgent response required with the following information:

YOUR FULL NAMES:--
DATE OF BIRTH:--
OCCUPATION:--
ADDRESS/COUNTRY:--
TELEPHONE / FAX NUMBERS:------------------------------------

Forward the information to MR. Herbert Smith (Email:herbertsmith2013@yahoo.co.uk)
Thank you
Mr Alfred Michael
(NOTIFICATION OFFICER)

'Mr. Michael' wants to share the results of the 'recent' Euro Millions Olympic Drawing with you, In fact, he and his associates want to steal what is left unclaimed, and share it with you, as their front person. To be a part of that theft, you need to give them a bunch of personal information, which they will process, once received by a 'Mr. Herbert Smith', and you will get a lot of money.

At least this time, the scammers got the country right, the disbursement currency right, and they even give a reference article on the lottery to help you make your decision. You can reply, of course, but you are entering a scam, and will undoubtedly get burned for your effort.

The next message is one of the newer version of this scam. This time, 'Mr. & Mrs. Bayford' want to share their winnings with you. Of course, they don't want to deal with you directly; instead, they want you to deal with their 'barrister', Walter Robinson. While the Lottery is real, as are the Bayfords (They won a large pot in a Euro Millions drawing), it is not them who are offering you riches beyond your dreams. Read, and enjoy.

By the way, the 'mail to:' address in the header of the message, mrsbayford@careceo.com, is not an actual e-mail address. If you try to respond to that address, you get the Walter law firm e-mail address. So, don't try to validate the offer with the Bayfords. Adrian and Gillian are too busy eating pizza, and enjoying their new-found wealth to point out to you they are not a part of the scam.

> Dear Sir/Madam,
>
> My husband and I won £148,656,000GBP Euromillions jackpot on the 10.08.12 and after going through your profile,we decided to donate the sum of £5,000,000.00 GBP to you as part of our own charity project to help improve the lot of individuals in your region,you should count yourself a lucky. Contact Our Lawyer to approve your payment. Barrister Walter Robinson .
>
> Email: *walterlawfirm@careceo.com*
>
> Kindly visit the yahoo web pages for further verification:
>
> http://uk.news.yahoo.com/new-£148-6m-euromillions-winners-adrian-and-gillian-bayford-celebrated-by-eating-pizza.html
>
> Mr & Mrs Bayford

Another recent version of the same scam, this time in 2013, is the following message from Mr. Morris Osborne of

Madrid, Spain. Addressed to 'Undisclosed Recipient', the e-mail address used is 'wesleyt@stanfordfurniture.com', although the actual reply e-mail address is 'morris08612@hotmail.com.

> INTERNATIONAL PROMOTIONS/PRIZE AWARD DEPT.
> C/O UK SECURITY SOLUTIONS
> CALLE LA UNION 4-7, 28008 MADRID SPAIN.
>
> DATE: 2/05/2013
> Ref Number: 447/563/990
> Batch Number: 679260215SAK   OFFICIAL WINNING NOTIFICATION
>
> We happily announce to you the draw of Second Quarter Euro Millions Lottery 2013 World Selected Immigration Data Award International programs held in Zurich, Switzerland. Your name and address attached to ticket number: B5690 38910268 255 with Serial number 82013 drew the winning: 4/13/21/27/36/38-45, which subsequently won you the lottery award in the 3rd category. Your name has therefore been approved to claim a total sum of FIVE HUNDRED AND TWENTY FIVE THOUSAND EUROS (₮525,000.00 EUROS) credited to file No: EU/9030108308/10. This is from a total cash prize of Twenty Five Million Five hundred Thousand Euros (₮25,500,000.00) shared among the first lucky winners in this category.
> To begin your claims, contact MR.MORRIS OSBORNE the Foreign Service manager of UK SECURITY SOLUTIONS for the processing and remittance of your money. Remember to quote your reference number in all correspondence.TEL: +447031990803 , FAX: +34-917-903-971 .
> Email address: " morri08612@hotmail.com "
> Winners are hereby required to fill the form below and send it by fax or email to the above Claim Agent before 1800 hours on or before 4TH of june, 2013
>
> FIRST NAME:......................... LAST NAME:...
> DATE OF BIRTH: OCCUPATION: ......
> FAX NO:..

ADRESSE:

....

....

....

TEL NO:
I WANT CHEQUE ...
NO I WANT BANK TRANSFER.....................

IF BANK TRANSFER FILL THIS LINES

BANK NAME...
ACCOUNT NO...

BANK ADDRESS..........................
ROUTING NO..

'Mr. Osborne' is well-known for his efforts to part people from their money in these schemes. He has, in the past, perpetrated his scam with direct mail 'announcements' to unsuspecting recipients. However, he has progressed, and now primarily uses e-mail. His address has changed from London to Madrid. Same man, same scam on Euro Millions, and the amounts have increased by a factor of 10 over the years.

RealGems International
One good lottery deserves another, and the scammers have found it in the 'RealGems International' Promotion Awards. Supposedly located in London, this awards program is giving away a cool $1M (US) to a lucky person; someone who is related to 'undisclosed recipients'. Read it for yourself, and see if you would apply to these people.

realgems international UNITED KINGDOM
Westfield Shoppingtowns Ltd
Company No. 03912122
VAT registration number 815 0326 63
Level 6, Midcity Place
71 High Holborn

London WC1V 6EA
phone ...+448719154073
INTERNATIONAL PROMOTION/PRIZE AWARD DEPT.
SCFN: GWK/5333/025648/03UAD.
BATCH: 241/2013/BLL.

This is to inform you that your E-mail ID has won $1 Million USD,from realgems international PROMOTION AWARD Held on 5th January 2013. Note that there were no sales of tickets as the realgems international PROMOTION AWARD was held through collations of emails via the internet. This selection process was carried out through a random selection in our Computerized Email
Selection System (C.E.S.S.) from a database of over a million email addresses from the World Wide Web. Your Email ID was attach as a winner of this year promotion,
Ref No E769ZF35 and Serial Ticket No E7K2907803-2 please provide your details below ..

1.Full Name:
2.Full Address:
3.Marital Status:
4.Occupation:
5.Age:
6.Sex:
8.Tel Number/ Mobile Number:

we are looking forward for your urgent reply.

Best regard
Mr. EDWARD BROWN

Similar to the Euro Millions Lottery Scam, this one has several differences as well. First, it a COMPLETE FRAUD. There is no RealGems International Lottery. It is a scam created by whoever 'Mr. Edward James' actually is in real life. We know this message is the 2013 version of the scam; a previous version, in 2012 featured a Mr. Jerry Brown. By the way, in 2009, another scam for Real Gems International, in Rome, featured Mr. Musa Mohamed, and the company then sold products which cleaned and polished rare gems and stones. Not sure if there is a direct link; more possibly the old name was transfigured for a new purpose.

If you really think you are interested, please contact Mister Brown at brownedawrd942@yahoo.cz. That address takes you to the Czech Republic via yet another of the YAHOO URL's.

Make sure you give him all that information he requires so that others can scam you as well, and ensure your identity is stolen. Good luck!

Now, let's move on to another scam, and I truly love this one. After all, it involves Yahoo, one of the great supporters of scams across the world.

Yahoo International Lottery Draw

The next message is a really interesting twist on the lottery scam business—one that aims at Yahoo, the largest of the Internet E-mail providers. It seems like an ironic turnabout to me. But then, one has to expect that sooner or later the scammers will bite the hands that feed them. This is one of those cases.

In any event, the message which follows is from Fatima Hassan (e-mail: bekemama@hotmail.com) who says she is the 'Lottery Coordinator', and wants to inform you that you have won $900K (US) in her lottery, sponsored by Yahoo. All you need to do is complete the information requested, and return it to her 'agent' Kabil Edris (e-mail: kabiledrisagent@barid.com) and your money will be on its way.

Believe that? I hope not. 'Barid.com' is a very small, mostly Arabic e-mail portal, with a single server, located in Bulgaria. Read the message; you might find it interesting.

DEAR WINNER,

WE ARE PLEASED TO INFORM YOU ABOUT THE YAHOO INTERNATIONAL LOTTERY DRAW HELD ON THE 8TH OF APRIL 2013 FROM THE SWEEPSTAKE YAHOO INTERNATIONAL LOTTERY PROGRAMMED COMPANY OFFICIAL PROMOTION PRIZE AWARD. YOUR E-MAIL EMERGED AS A WINNER OF $900.000.00 USD (Nine

Hundred Thousand US Dollars Only) IN THIS YEARS YAHOO RESULT 2013 INTERNATIONAL LOTTO PROGRAM.

NOTE. YOUR WINNING MONEY WILL BE TRANSFERRED TO YOU THROUGH OUR BANK ZONE HEADQUARTERS IN UNITED KINGDOM AS YOUR WINNING FILES FALL UNDER OUR BRANCH ZONE. SO CONTACT OUR AFRICAN AGENT COORDINATOR AGENT KABIL EDRIS WHICH YOUR WINNING NUMBERS FALL IN HIS CUSTODY, HE IS OUR REPRESENTING AGENT IN AFRICA HE WILL GIVE YOU DETAILS ON HOW TO CLAIM YOUR PRIZE.

PLEASE DO NOT REPLY TO THIS EMAIL. CONTACT YOUR

CLAIMS AGENT
AT: EMAIL (kabiledrisagent@barid.com)
AGENT: MALLAM KABIL EDRIS
TEL: +2348038945481
AFRICAN REPRESENTING LOTTERY AGENT.

FILL THIS FORM BELOW AND SEND IT TO HIM THROUGH HIS EMAIL TO FILE FOR YOUR CLAIM (kabiledrisagent@barid.com)

AMOUNT WON................................
FULL NAME...................................
HOME ADDRESS.................................
RESIDENTIAL COUNTRY.................
NATIONALITY................................
OCCUPATION..............................
TELEPHONE..............................
RELIGION...........................
EMAIL..........................
AGE...........................
SEX.............................

SIGNED.
FATIMA HASSAN (MRS)

LOTTERY COORDINATOR

As you can see, while there is a wide variety of 'opportunities' associated with money-making schemes, to assuage the greed of those who want to be scammed. The message also contains many pointers that should ring bells, which might tell you to delete the message and move on (Unless, of course, you choose to collect them, as I do).

Virtually every local, state, and national/international lottery has had at least one scam associated with it. The simple reason for that is the impossibility of preventing someone with an e-mail address, and some intelligence, from 'working the crowd', as the old circus barkers did, and getting just a few suckers who will bite, and give you what you want. That may sound pessimistic, but, as we saw early in the book, that is the aim of the scammer.

I have saved one of the most common parts of the scam repertoire for separate consideration. When a scammer develops a new project, the first thing they do is figure out how to get paid. What better way to have that happen then 'direct deposit', through some reputable firm that moves money quickly – Western Union.

Let me say at the outset here that Western Union, like many of the companies cited, is very reputable; they will cancel an account in a heartbeat if they find the account is being used illegally. That being said, Western Union is a necessity overseas, and sometimes the only way to move money quickly in the developing countries. Let's look at how that happens with the scammers in Chapter 19, which follows.

Chapter 19 Western Union Scams

Western Union, the international money-moving organization, is another organization that has seen increasing numbers of scams perpetrated against it. Originally formed in the US, Western Union provides money transfer capability throughout the work, through its 'Money-grams' program. That kind of application presents a real opportunity for scammers, since, if people actually think Western Union is involved in getting them their inheritance, lottery winnings, etc., they are more likely to accept the message as real, and respond to a solicitation message One of the newest of these types of messages is below. It purports to be from the President of Western Union, Hikmet Ursek.

CONGRATULATIONS ON THE ON GOING Western Union PROMO POWERED BY THE PRESIDENT OF THE WU(MR HIKMET ERSEK)

Your email address has been selected alongside in the on-going worldwide Western Union Promo initiated by the Chief Executive and President of the Western Union (MR HIKMET ERSEK)

The Regional board are pleased to inform you that your Email address alongside (199) other lucky winners have been approved for a payment of($35,000.00) US DOLLARS each.. If you receive this email, Please be informed it is not an error and note that is was sent out at once to all other 199 winners as well and your verification number is: (WU-NZ/597398/2013)..

Your winnings are to be paid through Western Union has directed by the Chief Executive of the Western Union (MR HIKMET ERSEK). As a matter of fact, your payment has been programmed in our system but this transfer has no recipient name and location until we receive the below listed requirements and also a Western Union receipt has been attached to your email and you are required to print the receipt,fill it,scan and send it back to us for normal computer proccessing..

Once again, this transfer can only be tracked online but cannot be accessed or picked through any Western Union Agent until it is fixed on your name and location. You are therefore, advised to forward the following information to us to complete the process.

1. Full Name:
2. Full Address:
3. Marital Status:
4. Occupation:
5. Age:
6. Sex:
7. Nationality:
8. Country Of Residence:
9. Telephone Number:

FIND AS STATED BELOW THE MONEY TRANSFER DETAILS:
(M.T.C.N): 0028797966
Senders First Name: Gary
Senders Last Name: Richmond
Transferred Amount: $35,000.00 Dollars
Track Your Money At:
https://wumt.westernunion.com/asp/orderStatus.asp?country=global

NOTE: Western Union dont send funds more than 5000 US DOLLARS in a transaction but we are doing this just to let you have your cash once..

Once again.. CONGRATULATIONS...

WESTERN UNION MANAGER
Claim Agent: Raul John
Tel : +447024080772
Official Email: *westernunionxmaspromo@cash4u.com*
Website: *www.westernunion.com*

WORLDWIDE WESTERN UNION PROMO INITIATED BY THE CHIEF EXECUTIVE OF THE WESTERN UNION (MR HIKMET ERSEK)

Let's see what we have in this message. 'Mr. Ersek' wants you to know that you are one of 100 people who are winners of a lottery, drawn from the worldwide collection of e-mail addresses maintained by Western Union. That's interesting, since he also says they don't know the actual owner of the e-mail address, and need the information you provide to match to their e-mail address, and get you your money.

Unfortunately, the only way Western Union gets your e-mail address is either through establishing a Western Union account, which would give them that information, or through having a record of you as a recipient, in which case they would also have much of the information about you. Regardless of the circumstances, Western Union would already know who you are.

Then, there is the situation of getting you your $35K (US), and what the message tells you about it. 'Mr. Ersek' says they are waiving the $5K (US) limitation for you; something Western Union never does for individuals, to get you your money quickly. What he does not tell you is how much the charge will be for the transfer. You get that information after you make contact with 'Mr. Paul'.

Finally, there is the question of Mr. Ersek, whose name is well-known in the scamming community, and for several years. He has been, at various times:

- Director, International Remittance, Western Union (Hikmet.ersek@one.co.il)(2011) with an additional address of Hikmet.ersek@yahoo.com.ph ($11.5M US) with 'agent' listed as Bilson Smith in Nigeria
- Director, Western Union Money Transfer (Davidfisherx1985@hotmail.fr) ($2.5M US) with the 'agent' listed as Richard Goodman (western_union_1960@w.cn) in Benin Republic
- Chief Executive Officer and Director (westernunion_office_2013@yahoo.com), and a

requested return address as westernunion_office_2013@yahoowestern.com (2013) ($500K US – in $5K payments) 'agent' is Mr. Ersek. Country of origin is Malaysia
- Chief Executive Officer & Director, Western Union Financial Services Inc. ($1M US) 'agent' is the Ukrainian Parcel Service (info.ups.shipping@deliveryman.com) (2011)

As you can see, whoever is acting as Mr. Ersek is a very active person, appearing in multiple countries, with a myriad of e-mail addresses, and several 'agents' working on his behalf. By the way, Mr. Ersek is real; he is the Chief Executive Officer of Western Union, and is not a scammer.

Well, so much for ridiculous opportunities. Now, let's look briefly as some of the new generation scams, at least some of the more common ones, and I have a variety of them to show you.

Chapter 20 A New Generation of Scams

If scammers are going to continue to thrive in this 21st Century electronic world, they need to find new topics to generate new scam opportunities. This chapter discusses some of the newer scams, beyond those descended from the 'Nigerian' efforts. Again, I have selected several to give you a taste for what is out there, but stay on your guard, because the types of scams are potentially endless.

One such 'opportunity' is the message below, supposedly from a member of the Royal Caribbean ship Costa Concordia crew (The cruise ship that went aground and sank off the Italian coast in 2012). The message is a great example of how fast someone can create a scam through e-mail, and shows clearly how virtually anyone can become a potential scammer, as the boundaries widen and no topic is free from opportunity exploitation.

> *Greetings From Captain George,*
>
> *I know you will be surprised to read my email. I got your contact from your Email domain, apart from being surprise you may be skeptical to reply me because based on what is happening on the internet world, one has to be very careful because a lot of scammers are out there to scam innocent citizens and this has made it very difficult for people to believe anything that comes through the internet but this is a different case.If You will be Willing to show me your honesty and trust I think Will I be able to work with You.*
>
> *Am a captain with Royal Caribbean Luxury cruise ship, my name is George Biffers Ishmael, I am 57 years British born but i relocate with my late dad back Egypt when i was 12, my dad was originally from Egypt.i later return back to UK. am a member royal Caribbean luxury cruise ship, I was deployed as a rescue team of the italian cruise ship Costa Concordia disaster on 13 January 2012.I would like to share some personal information about my personal experience and role which I played in the pursuit of my career which was at the fore-front of the italian cruise ship Costa Concordia disaster Tuscan island of Giglio italy.*

> Though, I would like to hold back certain information for security reasons please visit the BBC websites stated below to enable you have an insight what I intend to share with you, believing that it would be of your interest one-way or the other.
> http://www.cbsnews.com/2718-202_162-1422/italian-cruise-disaster/
> http://www.bbc.co.uk/news/world-europe-16561382
> Also, could you get back to me having visited the above website to enable us discuss in a more clarifying manner to the best of your understanding. I must say that I'm very uncomfortable sending this message to you without knowing you because base on what is happening all over the world one has to be careful. In this regards, I will not hold back to say that the essence of this message is strictly for mutual benefit between you and I, business partnership and investment purposes nothing more.
> I will be vivid and coherent in my next message in this regards, meanwhile, could you send me an email confirming that you have visited the site.
> Best regards,
> Cpt. George Biffers Ishmael.

'Captain George' is right—everyone should beware of scammers, and this is one of those cases. This message arrived in mailboxes throughout the world early in 2013 (mine came in early February). The message was posted from an e-mail address .(captaingeorgebiffers2014@yahoo.co.jp) in Japan, hosted by YAHOO.

The 'captain' does not really tell you what he wants; he is expecting you to respond to his e-mail, and start a conversation, where he will be 'vivid and coherent' in his response to you. It appears to me he is validating e-mail addresses, so that he can sell those who seem the most gullible.

Captain is, or was, in an Italian jail, and it is unlikely that he, born in Britain, and now living in Egypt, by way of the Italian cruise industry, would be using an e-mail address originating in Japan. Who knows, unless you contact him I won't myself.

Who's Who Directory Scams

Another set of messages, which I prefer to call a scam, involves the myriad of 'Who's Who' books that all seem to come out this time of year, and want to include you in their latest edition. Now strictly speaking, these are not illegal scams; they are brazen attempts to get you to give them a lot of information, buy their book, and think you have done something important for yourself.

These books are 'knock-off' directories, modeled after the original *Who's Who* series of publications. Marquis Publications, and a few others have been creating these directories for many years, and they are a respected part of the reference book landscape. Over the past few years, the number of directories has multiplied, mostly because of second-rate publishers who want to make money off their more well-known predecessors. What better opportunity than to create your own directory, and then simply solicit information for it, like the message below.

> FROM: Worldwide Registry for Business Professionals
> TO:[e-mail deleted]
> RE: Worldwide Registry Publication
>
> Hello,
>
> You were recently chosen to represent your professional community, deeming you eligible for the inclusion in the new 2013 Edition of Worldwide Registry for Business Professionals.
> We are pleased to inform you that your candidacy was formally approved on February 1st, 2013. Congratulations!
> Click here to verify your profile and accept the candidacy <http://www.benchmarketer.com/link.php?M=xxxxxxxxxx(Part of validation script deleted)>
> The Publishing Committee selected you as a professional based not only upon your current standing, but focusing as well on criteria from executive and professional directories, associations, and trade journals. Given your background, the Director believes your profile makes a fitting addition to our publication.
> As we are working off of secondary sources, we must receive verification from you that your profile <xxxxxxxxx(Part of

validation script deleted)> is accurate. After receiving verification, we will validate your registry listing within seven business days.

Once finalized, your listing will share prominent registry space with thousands of fellow accomplished individuals across the globe, each representing accomplishment within their own geographical area.

To verify your profile and accept the candidacy, please click here <*http://www.benchmarketer.com/link.php?M=xxxxxxxxxxxx(Part of validation script deleted)*> .

Please kindly note that our registration deadline for this year's publication is June 1st, 2013. To ensure you are included, we must receive your verification on or before this date.

On behalf of our Committee I salute your achievement and welcome you to our association.

Sincerely yours,

James S. Richardson
Vice-President, Research Division
Worldwide Registry for Business Professionals
<*http://www.benchmarketer.com/link.php?M=xxxxxxxxxxxxx (Part of validation script deleted)*>

1332 Oakwood Avenue
New York, NY 10019

Now, doesn't this seem to be a wonderful opportunity for someone to get recognition for their work? Of course it does, and Mr. Richardson wants to help you do that, by providing a bunch of information to complete your 'profile', and also give them enough information to sell your name to other bidders, as well as try to sell you some books to impress your friends and associates.

Sounds too good to be true?

Well. Unfortunately it is. In addition to Mr. Richardson, these gentlemen also claim to be the Vice-President, Research Division:

- Robert F. Anderson
    Vice-President, Research Division
    Worldwide Registry for Business Professionals

<http://www.virtualbiller.com/link.php?M=1042619&N=152&L=9&F=H>

- William M. Kemp
  Vice-President, Research Division
  Worldwide Registry for Business Professionals
  <http://www.virtualbiller.com/link.php?M=1087951&N=155&L=9&F=H>

  JT Richards
  Vice president Research Division
  World-wide Registry for Business Professionals
  <http://www.aviabank.com/link.php?M=1026427&N=161&L=6&F=H>

Take your pick. There are others as well, although I have limited the examples to those which I received. You may have heard from others.

Several problems here. First, 'virtualbiller.com' is a domain currently for sale by a marketing URL registry firm, and information on the owner of the domain is private information; protected from disclosure through a firm in Queensland, Australia.

The Worldwide Registry for Business Professionals is basically nothing more than an attempt to get information, extract money for books, and provides no value to a businessman, or anyone else for that matter. Avoid getting sucked into scams such as this one.

There are a number of other, newer scams, coming on the market every day. Some are more egregious than others; some simply want information and money; and some are dangerous, in that they can leave software – actually malware – on your system, received when you reply.

Epilogue – Saving Yourself from Fraud

A few suggestions on how to avoid getting caught by e-mail scam artists.

SUGGESTION #1: Avoid sites you do not know, or who demand you visit them.
<http://blog.tmcnet.com/blog/rich-tehrani/uploads/new-microsoft-logo.png>

Dear Mail User,
As part of the security measures to secure all email users across the world,All email users are mandated to have their account details registered as requested by the Microsoft Cyber-Crime Dept (M C D) .You are here by required to validate your account within 24 hours so as not to have your email account suspended and deleted from the world email server.
To get started, please click the link below:

https://login.com/config/login_verify2?.intl=us&.src=ym
<http://megacom.mk/mcfmk/WebMail_Server/webmail.htm>
This instruction has been sent to all Webmail Users Worldwide and is obligatory to follow.

Thank you,
Copyright? 2013 Microsoft Inc. All rights reserved. .

Let's look briefly at this message. First, it is supposedly from Microsoft, one of the largest software and operating system makers in the world, and chief supporter of the Internet. Yet, in asking you to respond to them, or at least their 'Cyber-Crime Department', they make some odd requests. You are asked to respond to a 'login.com' URL, which belongs to a very large mega-center in Tucson, Arizona USA.

Of course, you are not really logging to that address. You are really being routed to a website in Macedonia (megacom.mk), which is supposed to be a film distribution company, and certainly is not the Microsoft Cyber-Crime Department. Your connection is to their e-mail server.

What is the bottom line here? Well, if Microsoft wanted to contact you, and expected a response, it would be to Microsoft.com, and not some third-world address. So many people know Microsoft, and know their e-mail and internet addresses, but there are always those will fall for such a scheme.

SUGGESTION #2 – Look carefully at e-mails you receive, decide which to keep, and which to delete. Always include in the 'deleted' group, any message which gives any appearance of being a scam. Err on the side of caution – if one message out of many is real, they will re-contact you if it is important to do so.

OK, so we better have a test. Here are three brief e-mail messages; which would you possibly keep, and which would you delete?

Message #1:

FROM: Vidal & Perez (<u>vidalandperrez@gmail.com</u>)
TO: Undisclosed Recipient
SUBJECT: FINAL NOTICE
ATTACHMENT: VIDAL PRIZE FUND.doc (40KB)

GOOD DAY

ENCLOSED WE SEND YOU THIS INVESTMENT.

Sincerely yours

Yours Sincerely
VIDAL AND PEREZ INCORPERATED.

Message #2:
FROM: Mark Lynch <u>celestin@mdp.edu.ar</u>
TO: Undisclosed-recipients
SUBJECT: =Business Proposal =NUE=

Hello,

I have a legitimate business proposal worth a huge sum. Get back to me for the full details.

Mark Lynch

Message #3:

Dear.
This is Barrister Mohammed from London, writing you on behalf of my client searching for a reliable person for his proposed Real Estate / property investment in your city.

Kindly contact me with project details / propsal via email if interested in this proposed investment ONLY .

thanks
Mr. A. Mohammed
Office: 0044-7010083188
Skype: associate.mohammed
ADVOCATE AND SOLICITOR

Hopefully, this short test did not give you much difficulty. Message #1 claimed you won something, and all you need to do is open the attachment to find out what you won. The lesson here is ***never open attachments from someone you do not know***, and especially when they promise the world. Trust me to say that the message was not about winning anything.

Message #2 also promises huge amounts, if only you will get back to 'Mr. Lynch'. ***These kinds of messages only want to validate your e-mail address,*** and will results in money FOR HIM, as he sells your name and e-mail, along with others, and will only get you bombarded with other spam and junk e-mail messages.

Message #3 might take a few second or two longer, especially if you happen to be a person involved in real estate yourself. Personally, ***I would delete this one quickly as well since***

I do not know him, but some of you might want to explore 'Barrister Mohammed', just to see if he is legitimate. What you will find, with a simple Google search is that there are a number of 'Barrister Ali Mohammed' references, although this particular e-mail message has not yet made the scam blogs. The e-mail return address, '222@telcom.net.et' is from Ethiopia, and has a wide user base. Best bet on message #3 is to delete it as well.

SUGGESTION #4 – Be especially careful of foreign or foreign-sounding messages. So many messages originating in foreign countries, particularly those in Africa and Asia, create their messages in their own tongue, and get them translated into English, and other languages, as they transmit them. What often results is a poorly constructed, badly grammatical, and almost nonsensical set of sentences, which are supposed to be from people, such as barristers and government officials whom you would expect to be well-educated and capable of ensuring a properly structured sentence.

It is one thing to have an occasional lapse of spelling or grammar, and yet another to see it throughout the message. If you do, deleting it is probably the best bet.

APPENDICES

Appendix A – United States Secret Service
PUBLIC AWARENESS ADVISORY REGARDING "4-1-9" OR "ADVANCE FEE FRAUD" SCHEMES

4-1-9 Schemes frequently use the following tactics:

- An individual or company receives a letter or fax from an alleged "official" representing a foreign government or agency;
- An offer is made to transfer millions of dollars in "over invoiced contract" funds into your personal bank account;
- You are encouraged to travel overseas to complete the transaction;
- You are requested to provide blank company letterhead forms, banking account information, telephone/fax numbers;
- You receive numerous documents with official looking stamps, seals and logo testifying to the authenticity of the proposal;
- Eventually you must provide up-front or advance fees for various taxes, attorney fees, transaction fees or bribes;
- Other forms of 4-1-9 schemes include: c.o.d. of goods or services, real estate ventures, purchases of crude oil at reduced prices, beneficiary of a will, and recipient of an award and paper currency conversion.

If you have already lost funds in pursuit of the above described scheme, please contact the U.S. Secret Service in Washington, D.C. at 202-406-5850 or by e-mail.

Nigerian Advance Fee Fraud Overview

The perpetrators of Advance Fee Fraud (AFF), known internationally as "4-1-9" fraud after the section of the Nigerian penal code which addresses fraud schemes, are often very creative and innovative.

Unfortunately, there is a perception that no one is prone to enter into such an obviously suspicious relationship. However, a large number of victims are enticed into believing they have been singled out from the masses to share in multi-million dollar windfall profits for doing absolutely nothing. It is also a misconception that the victim's bank account is requested so the culprit can plunder it -- this is not the primary reason for the account request -- merely a signal they have hooked another victim.

- In almost every case there is a sense of urgency;
- The victim is enticed to travel to Nigeria or a border country;
- There are many forged official looking documents;
- Most of the correspondence is handled by fax or through the mail;
- Blank letterheads and invoices are requested from the victim along with the banking particulars;
- Any number of Nigerian fees are requested for processing the transaction with each fee purported to be the last required;
- The confidential nature of the transaction is emphasized;
- There are usually claims of strong ties to Nigerian officials;
- A Nigerian residing in the U.S., London or other foreign venue may claim to be a clearing house bank for the Central Bank of Nigeria;
- Offices in legitimate government buildings appear to have been used by impostors posing as the real occupants or officials.

The most common forms of these fraudulent business proposals fall into seven main categories:

- Disbursement of money from wills
- Contract fraud (C.O.D. of goods or services)
- Purchase of real estate
- Conversion of hard currency
- Transfer of funds from over invoiced contracts
- Sale of crude oil at below market prices

The most prevalent and successful cases of Advance Fee Fraud is the fund transfer scam. In this scheme, a company or individual will typically receive an unsolicited letter by mail from a Nigerian claiming to be a senior civil servant. In the letter, the Nigerian will inform the recipient that he is seeking a reputable foreign company or individual into whose account he can deposit funds ranging from $10-$60 million that the Nigerian government overpaid on some procurement contract.

The criminals obtain the names of potential victims from a variety of sources including trade journals, professional directories, newspapers, and commercial libraries. They do not target a single company, but rather send out mailings en masse. The sender declares that he is a senior civil servant in one of the Nigerian Ministries, usually the Nigerian National Petroleum Corporation (NNPC). The letters refer to investigations of previous contracts awarded by prior regimes alleging that many contracts were over invoiced. Rather than return the money to the government, they desire to transfer the money to a foreign account. The sums to be transferred average between $10,000,000 to $60,000,000 and the recipient is usually offered a commission up to 30 percent for assisting in the transfer.

Initially, the intended victim is instructed to provide company letterheads and pro forma invoicing that will be used to show completion of the contract. One of the reasons is to use the victim's letterhead to forge letters of recommendation to other victim companies and to seek out a travel visa from the American Embassy in Lagos. The victim is told that the completed contracts will be submitted for approval to the Central Bank of Nigeria. Upon approval, the funds will be remitted to an account supplied by the intended victim.

The goal of the criminal is to delude the target into thinking that he is being drawn into a very lucrative, albeit questionable, arrangement. The intended victim must be reassured and confident of the potential success of the deal. He will become the primary supporter of the scheme and willingly contribute a large amount of money when the deal is threatened. The term "when" is used because the con-within-the-con is the scheme will be threatened in order to persuade the victim to provide a large sum of money to save the venture.

The letter, while appearing transparent and even ridiculous to most, unfortunately is growing in its effectiveness. It sets the stage and is the opening round of a two-layered scheme or scheme within a scheme. The fraudster will eventually reach someone who, while skeptical, desperately wants the deal to be genuine.

Victims are almost always requested to travel to Nigeria or a border country to complete a transaction. Individuals are often told that a visa will not be necessary to enter the country. The Nigerian con artists may then bribe airport officials to pass the victims through Immigration and Customs. Because it is a serious offense in Nigeria to enter without a valid visa, the victim's illegal entry may be used by the fraudsters as leverage to coerce the victims into releasing funds. Violence and threats of physical harm may be employed to further pressure victims. In June of 1995, an American was murdered in Lagos, Nigeria, while pursuing a 4-1-9 scam, and numerous other foreign nationals have been reported as missing.

Victims are often convinced of the authenticity of Advance Fee Fraud schemes by the forged or false documents bearing apparently official Nigerian government letterhead, seals, as well as false letters of credit, payment schedules and bank drafts. The fraudster may establish the credibility of his contacts, and thereby his influence, by arranging a meeting between the victim and "government officials" in real or fake government offices.

In the next stage some alleged problem concerning the "inside man" will suddenly arise. An official will demand an up-front bribe or an unforeseen tax or fee to the Nigerian government will have to be paid before the money can be transferred. These can include licensing fees, registration fees, and various forms of taxes and attorney fees. Normally each fee paid is described as the very last fee required. Invariably, oversights and errors in the deal are discovered by the Nigerians, necessitating additional payments and allowing the scheme to be stretched out over many months.

Several reasons have been submitted why Nigerian Advance Fee Fraud has undergone a dramatic increase in recent years. The explanations are as diverse as the types of schemes. The Nigerian Government blames the growing problem on mass unemployment, extended family systems, a get rich quick syndrome, and, especially, the greed of foreigners.

Indications are that Advance Fee Fraud grosses hundreds of millions of dollars annually and the losses are continuing to escalate. In all likelihood, there are victims who do not report their losses to authorities due to either fear or embarrassment.

In response to this growing epidemic, the United States Secret Service established "Operation 4-1-9" designed to target Nigerian Advance Fee Fraud on an international basis. The Financial Crimes Division of the Secret Service receives approximately 100 telephone calls from victims/potential victims and 300-500 pieces of related correspondence per day.

Secret Service agents have been assigned on a temporary basis to the American Embassy in Lagos to address the problem in that arena. Agents have established liaison with Nigerian officials, briefed other embassies on the widespread problem, and have assisted in the extrication of U.S. citizens in distress.

If you have been victimized by one of these schemes, please forward appropriate written documentation to the United States Secret Service, Financial Crimes Division, 950 H Street, NW, Washington, D.C. 20223, or telephone (202) 406-5850, or contact by e-mail.

If you have received a letter, but have not lost any monies to this scheme, please fax a copy of that letter to (202) 406-5031.

Appendix B – Internal Revenue Service

IRS Warns Taxpayers of New E-mail Scams

Updated April 9, 2008 — *A scheme in which a tax refund form is e-mailed, supposedly by the Taxpayer Advocate Service (a genuine and independent organization within the IRS which assists taxpayers with unresolved problems), is particularly blatant in the amount and type of information it requests. The top of the form tells the recipient that they are eligible for a tax refund for a specified amount. The form asks for name, address and phone number and a substantial amount of financial information, such as bank account number, credit card number and expiration date, ATM PIN number and more. It also asks for mother's maiden name (frequently used by many people as an account security password). At the bottom is a phony name and signature, claiming to be that of the Taxpayer Advocate. The implication is that the taxpayer must fill in and submit the form to receive a tax refund. In reality, taxpayers claim their tax refunds through the filing of an annual tax return, not a separate application form.*

Updated Jan. 14, 2008 — *A new variation of the refund scheme may be directed toward organizations that distribute funds to other organizations or individuals. In an attempt to seem legitimate, the scam e-mail claims to be sent by, and contains the name and supposed signature of, the Director of the IRS Exempt Organizations area of the IRS. The e-mail asks recipients to click on a link to access a form for a tax refund. In reality, taxpayers claim their tax refunds through the filing of an annual tax return, not a separate application form.*

Updated Nov. 7, 2007 — *In a variation, an e-mail scam claims to come from the IRS and the Taxpayer Advocate Service (a genuine and independent organization within the IRS which assists taxpayers with unresolved problems). The e-mail says that the recipient is eligible for a tax refund and directs the recipient to click on a link that leads to a fake IRS Web site. The IRS recommends that recipients do not click on* links in, or open any attachments to, e-mails they receive that are unsolicited or that come from unknown sources.

Updated Nov. 2, 2007 — A new scam e-mail that appears to be a solicitation from the IRS and the U.S. government for charitable contributions to victims of the recent Southern California wildfires has been making the rounds. A link in the e-mail, when clicked, sends the e-mail recipients to a Web site that looks like the IRS Web site, but isn't. They are then directed to click on a link that opens a donation form that asks for personal and financial information. The scammers can use that information to gain access to the e-mail recipients' financial accounts. The IRS does not send e-mails to taxpayers soliciting contributions to a charitable cause.

Updated Sept. 19, 2007 — Another recent e-mail scam tells taxpayers that the IRS has calculated their "fiscal activity" and that they are eligible to receive a tax refund of a certain amount. Taxpayers receive a page of, or are sent to, a Web site (titled "Get Your Tax Refund!") that copies the appearance of the genuine "Where's My Refund?" interactive page on the genuine IRS Web site. Like the real "Where's My Refund?" page, taxpayers are asked to enter their SSNs and filing status. However, the phony Web page asks taxpayers to enter their credit card account numbers instead of the exact amount of refund as shown on their tax return, as the real "Where's My Refund?" page does. Moreover, the IRS does not send e-mails to taxpayers to advise them of refunds or to request financial information.

Updated Aug. 24, 2007 — The Internal Revenue Service today warned taxpayers of a new phishing scam, in which an e-mail purporting to come from the IRS advises taxpayers they can receive $80 by filling out an online customer satisfaction survey. The IRS urges taxpayers to ignore this solicitation and not provide any requested information. The IRS does not initiate contact with taxpayers through e-mail.

Updated June 19, 2007 — In another recent scam, consumers have received a "Tax Avoidance Investigation" e-mail claiming to come from *the IRS' "Fraud Department" in which the recipient is asked to complete an "investigation form," for which there is a link contained in the e-mail, because of possible fraud that the recipient committed. It is believed that clicking on the link may activate a Trojan Horse.*

IR-2007-109, May 31, 2007

WASHINGTON — The Internal Revenue Service today alerted taxpayers to the latest versions of an e-mail scam intended to fool people into believing they are under investigation by the agency's Criminal Investigation division.

The e-mail purporting to be from IRS Criminal Investigation falsely states that the person is under a criminal probe for submitting a false tax return to the California Franchise Tax Board. The e-mail seeks to entice people to click on a link or open an attachment to learn more information about the complaint against them. The IRS warned people that the e-mail link and attachment is a Trojan horse that can take over the person's computer hard drive and allow someone to have remote access to the computer.

The IRS urged people not to click the link in the e-mail or open the attachment.

Similar e-mail variations suggest a customer has filed a complaint against a company and the IRS can act as an arbitrator. The latest versions appear aimed at business taxpayers as well as individual taxpayers.

The IRS does not send out unsolicited e-mails or ask for detailed personal and financial information. Additionally, the IRS never asks people for the PIN numbers, passwords or similar secret access information for their credit card, bank or other financial accounts.

"Everyone should beware of these scam artists," said Kevin M. Brown, Acting IRS Commissioner. "Always exercise caution when you receive unsolicited e-mails or e-mails from senders you don't know.

"Recipients of questionable e-mails claiming to come from the IRS should not open any attachments or click on any links contained in the e-mails. Instead, they should forward the e-mails to phishing@irs.gov (follow the instructions).

The IRS also sees other e-mail scams that involve tricking victims into revealing private personal and financial information over the Internet, a practice that is known as "phishing" for information.

The IRS and the Treasury Inspector General for Tax Administration work with the U.S. Computer Emergency Readiness Team (US-CERT) and various Internet service providers and international CERT teams to have the phishing sites taken offline as soon as they are reported.

Since the establishment of the mail box last year, the IRS has received more than 17,700 e-mails from taxpayers reporting more than 240 separate phishing incidents. To date, investigations by TIGTA have identified host sites in at least 27 different countries, as well as in the United States.

Other fraudulent e-mail scams try to entice taxpayers to click their way to a fake IRS Web site and ask for bank account numbers. Another widespread e-mail tells taxpayers the IRS is holding a refund (often $63.80) for them and seeks financial account information. Still another email claims the IRS's 'anti-fraud commission' is investigating their tax returns.

Appendix C – Disclaimer of the Central Bank of Nigeria

Reference: http://www.cenbank.org/419/Index.asp

Advance Fees Fraud (419)
Fraud Disclaimer | Litigations | Nig. Letter Scam | Contact

The CBN Disclaimer

We receive several emails and other correspondences bordering on Advance Fee Fraud also known as 419 on a daily basis. 419 is a menace to the CBN. Scams are carried out by fraudulent people who plan to defraud gullible respondents.

Typically scammers:-
- Often contact you by unsolicited bulk mail, spam email but will eventually start calling by phone as soon as you give them your details
- Claim to have a lot of money stashed away in a Nigerian (African) account but there are several other variants - Inheritance, Wills, Next of kin, Contract claims and recently, Lotteries
- Often need someone to help them transfer it out of the country with a view to sharing the said sum with them.
- Assure you it's a risk free deal and encourage you to send them your personal details.
- Often lead you on by sending falsified paper work to support what they claim. They often include id cards, passports, faxes, memos, approvals; funds release certificates, fake cheque, fake Nigeria National Petroleum Corporation (NNPC) letter of contract award, agreements, fake CBN letter head, fake NNPC and CBN official stamps, etc.

- Often use yahoo.com (and other free email providers) e-mail address as a medium of communication.
- Often mimic Central Bank of Nigeria domain email accounts and other Financial Institutions to mislead ATM users.
- Some organized scammers often have a fake Central Bank of Nigeria website where they post fake documents to support their claims.
- Their preferred means of transferring money is by Money Gram and Western Union Money Transfer. They will never transfer via secure means like – Swift Code.
- Almost every scam is done with the name of a fake CBN staff or post or position.

* Please confirm all business propositions mailed to you with the Nigerian Embassy in your country or the Director, Legal Services of the CBN.

Click here to see frequently asked questions on 419

Though the CBN maintains a fraud helpdesk in her Legal Services Division, which can be contacted by mailing info @ cenbank.org, (Please remember to remove the spaces from the emails below. Want to know why?) the CBN may not be obliged to respond to any e-mails in the above scenarios.

Signed.
Head Corporate Affairs

If you suspect you have been contacted by scammers please read this

Index

NOTE: *There is some duplication here, due to keeping the e-mail messages exactly as they came in, without my own editorial corrections to spelling or formatting.*

. IBRAHIM LAMORDE, 58
82nd Airborne Division, 83
Abdullah Senussi, 121
AFD Bank, 209
Afghanistan, 19, 24, 84, 85, 87
African Union, 49
Agent Mark A. Morgan, 151, 153
Ahmed Hossain, 298
Alh Idris Abdullahi, 207
Alhaji Hussain Ahmad, 105
Allied Irish Bank, 237, 238
Ana La Chu Chu, 268
anji.gov.cn, 198
Ann Hargreaves, 193
Apex Bank., 34
Arkansas Lottery Board, 306
ATM MASTER EXPRESS CARD, 281
ATM SWIFT CARDS, 249
AUSTINE MORRIS, 119
Australia, 80, 81, 270
Australian Financial Services, 80, 81
AUYYR456, 33
Baghdad, 84, 87

Ban Ki-moon, 229
Banco di Santo Spirito/Rome/Italy, 249
Bank by the United Nations, 271
Bank of Africa, 209
Bank of America, 156, 168, 169, 170, 302, 303
Bank of East Asia, 222
Bank of East Asia (USA), 153, 173
Bank of England, 221
Bank Of Ghana, 34
Bank of NewYork Mellon Corp, 249
Bar William Johnson, 114
Barclay's Bank (London), 220
Barr Stacy Russel, 66
Barr.Daniels Andrew, 258
Barr.Paul, 33
Barrister David Johnson, 143, 145
Barrister George Alex, 54, 55, 56
Barrister George Anderson, 259
Barrister Walter Robinson, 313

Barrister.Jack Les,, 286
Bayfords, 313
beige.ocn.ne.jp, 152
bello wisdom, 98
Benin, 107, 108, 186, 187, 188, 196, 197, 198, 215, 216, 217, 218, 281
Benin Republic, 186, 187, 188, 215, 216
Benny K Joseph. *See* Benny Kanarathil Joseph
Better Business Bureau, 174, 175
blumail.org, 259
BMW LOTTERY DEPARTMENT, 305, 306
BMW MOTOR AWARDS, 307
Bode Williams, 147
Brian Edmond, 127
Brian Miller, 240, 241
BRITISH FINANCE MONITORING UNIT, 190
BRITISH GOVERNMENT, 283
BRITISH HIGH COMMISSION, 230
British High Commission for Nigeria, Benin Republic, Ghana and Burkina Faso, 196
British Lottery Board, 306
British Ministry of Finance, 220
Bulgaria, 317
Burkina Faso, 121, 197
cabis-ngeblogtoz.blogspot.com, 32
cable.net.co, 182
Caja De Madrid/Madrid/Spain, 248
Capt Kenneth Hogan, 84
Captain Paul Benson, 87
careceo.com, 182
Carmen LaPointe, 280
Carmen Young,, 280
Cecelia M Lum, 167
CENTER BANK, 208, 209
CENTRAL BANK (CBN) INTERNATIONAL, 209
Central Bank of Nigeria, 37, 38, 51, 202, 210, *See* Central Bank of Nigeria, *See* Central Bank of Nigeria
CENTRAL BANK OF NIGERIA, 17, 18, 51, 52, 202, 278
Chechnya, 72
Cheltenham & Gloucester International Bank, 271
China, 130, 132, 151, 173, 198, 227

Christopher thomas joyner, 148
CITI BANK, 17
　Arizona, 17
CITI BANK NIGERIA LTD, 278
Col. Archer Reese, 85
Colonel Gaddafi, 80
Colonel Muammar Gaddafi., 121
COMPENSATION PAYMENT COORDINATOR FOR UNITED NATION, 273
Concordia, 324
Costa Concordia, 324
Cote D'Ivoire. See Ivory Coast
Counter-terrorism Division and Cyber Crime Division, 147
Czech Republic, 317
Czechoslovakia, 259
DaiwaBank/Osaka/Japan, 248
David Ebersman, 179
David Lawrence, 224, 225
Department of Homeland Security
　Cyber Crime Division, 146, 147, 161
Derrick McCourt, 181
DHL COURIER SERVICE, 216

Diary Milk Farm, 122
Diplomat Collins Baker, 288
Dixon Company, 89
Dofle Bernard, 107, 108
DR CHARLES WILLIAMS, 59
Dr D. Subbarao, 229
Dr Daniel Chigudu, 76
Dr David Anthony, 219
Dr Galadima Hassan, 43
DR GALADIMA HASSAN,, 43
Dr Heward Wilson, 32
DR ISA MUSA, 45
DR Sanusi Lamido Sanusi, 203
Dr. David G. Alder, 281, 282
DR. ENNIS CAMPBELL, 267
Dr. Henry Jonathan, 209
Dr. Ibrahim Bello, 205
Dr. Linda Williams, 156, 157
Dr. M. S. James Alexander, 232
Dr. Nasser Daneshvary, 232
DR. OFFONG AMBAH, 243
Dr. Offung Ombah, 241
Dr. Richard Daniels, 216
Dr. Robert Brown, 221
Dr. Smith Paggy, 93

Dr. Usman Shamsuddeen, 147
Dr. William S. Adam, 209
Dr.Albert Mcain, 273
Dr.Kingsley C. Moghalu, 206
DR.LARRY G JAMES, 252
Dubai, 234
Dubai, United Arab Emirates, 100, 234
ECO Bank, 243, 244, 246
ECO BANK. *See* Eco Bank (London)
ECO Bank PLC, 241
ECOBANK ATM VISA CARD, 243
Economic and Financial Crime Commission of Nigeria (EFCC), 278
economic community of West African states (ECOWAS), 57
Economic Financial Crime Commission (EFCC), 56
Edmond Brian. *See* Brian Edmond
Egypt, 24, 324
Egyptian airline 990, 98
email.ch, 79
Emirate Nations, 234
Engr. Frank Thabi, 104
EROL FIDUCIARY, 223
Euro Million Support, 310
Euro MillionOlympic Ceremony Draw, 311
Euromillions, 313
FACEBOOK, 176, 177, 178
Facebook Lottery Team, 179
Facebook online free e-mail lotto, 179
Facebook Online International Lottery, 176
Facebook Online International Lottery', 176
Facebook Online Splash promo, 179
Fatima Hassan, 317
Federal Bureau of Investigation, 36, 39, 138, 140, 144, 147, 150, 153, 157, 158, 161, 173, 265
   Anti-Terrorism and Monitory Crime Division, 139
   Fraud Monitory Unit, 147
   Intelligence Field Unit, DC, 149, 150, 151
   Intelligence Monitoring Network System, 154
   Public Affairs Division, 153
   Transaction Department, 156

Federal Bureau Of Investigation, 36, 140, 155
Federal Government of China, 150
Federal Government of Nigeria, 278
FEDERAL GOVERNMENT OF NIGERIA, 36, 49
federal republic of Nigeria, 214
ficozone.com, 150
Finance Department of the United Nations. See United Nations
Financial Bank PLC, 217
FRANKFURTER BANK, 267
Freddie Shadrick, 310
Garry Fedrick, 200, 201
Gen. Sani Abacha, 45
George Biffers Ishmael,, 324
George Osborn. See Honorable George Osborne
Ghana, 34, 44, 105, 106, 117, 189, 257, 258
Ghana Chambers Of Commerce, 34
Ghana National Petroleum Corporation, 34

Global Agency and Trust Services division of World Bank. See World Bank
GLOBAL COURIER SERVICE (GCS), 218, 219, 220
Global Express Courier Company, 203
GLOBAL EXPRESS DIPLOMATIC COMPANY LIMITED, 202
gmx.com, 94, 105
Godfrey Williams, 189
Good Luck Ebele Jonathan, 278
Good luck Jonathan, 212
Government of Nigeria Payment Committee, 49
Great Britain Royal House of Treasury, 194
grupodelaware.com, 94
Gulf International Bank, 239
Hafsia Haider, 71, 72
Haider Group of Company, 72
HENRY KOKOMA, 110
HENRY SHAWN, 155
Herbert Smith, 312
HFDC Bank, 226
Hikmet Ursek. *See* Western Union

Ho Chi Minh City, 106
Hon Mack John, 244
Honorable George Osborne, 194
HSBC (Japan), 233
HSBC BANK LONDON, 118
Human Rights/Scam Payment, Department of International Affairs. *See* United Nations
HUSSAIN FATIMAH, 245
Ibrahim Sule, 147
IMF, 3
India, 75, 76, 189, 226, 228, 229, 231, 232
Industrial and Commercial Bank of China (USA),. *See* Bank of East Asia (USA)
Inga-Britt Ahlenius, 280
inmail24.com, 4
Intercontinental Bank Payment Center, 281
Intercontinental Bank PLC, 215
Internal Audit Monitoring Consulting and Investigations Division. *See* United Nations Office of International Oversight Services

Internal Revenue Service, 26, 204, 306, 338, 339, 340
International Association of Gaming Regulators, 305, 306
INTERNATIONAL FUNDS TRANSFER / AUDIT, 289
International Monentary and Compensation Unit, 3
International Monetary Fund, 3, 6, 19, 287
Internet Fraud Complaint Center (IFCC), 147, 161
investigators.wdc@gmail.com, 150
Iraq, 19, 24, 83, 84, 85, 87
Ivory Coast, 107
JACOB M. MOLOTSI, 30
JANET WHITE, 17
Japan, 53, 233
Jeanie Adams Smith, 73
JFK Airport, 151
Jim Sturman, 79
Joe McDonald Esq, 97
John Bannerman, 106
John Campbell, 186, 187, 188
John Davies, 178
Johnson George, 53
Juan Ferero, 182

349

Julius Tomari, 51
Kabil Edris, 317
Kelvin Young, 147
KEVIN PETTY, 177
Khalifa Bin Rasheed, 100
Kimo.com, 241
konsolavto.ru, 109
Kulman Smith. See
Leona Helmsley, 90
Lesotho, 30
LESOTHO, 30
Libya, 24, 80, 104, 105, 121
Lloyds
   Bank/London/England, 248
lmilda Elkousy, 98, 99
M.J Ola, 35
Madrid, 315
mailbox.hu, 135
Malawi, 72
Malaysia, 33, 123, 124, 243
MALAYSIA, 245
Mallam Issa Abba Abacha, 48
MALLAM KABIL EDRIS, 318
Mariam Abacha, 42, 43, 45, 46
MARIAM ABACHA, 45, 46, 48
MARK ZUCKERBERG, 178
Mathew Ugwu, 280

Michael Dennison, 274, 275
Microsoft, 181
Microsoft Corporation, 180
Microsoft Cyber-Crime Dept, 329
mina a Sudannes, 93
MISS JANET BROWN, 204, 205
Miss.Angie Hernandez, 261
Mister Jacob Molotsi, 30
Mister John Martin, 64
Mister Pauldou, 52
mkc-net.ru, 135
Mohamar Gaddafi, 80
Mohammad al-Mojil Group, 72
Mohammed Abacha, 43, 47
MORGAN EXCHANGE COMPANY, 267
Morgan Solomon, 109
Morganhorse.org.nz, 171
Morooe Gamez, 111
Mr Alfred Michael, 311, 312
Mr Anand Jude, 229, 230
Mr John Simmons, 198
Mr Lucky Kadiri, 48, 50
Mr Naoto Matsumoto, 233
Mr Norbert, 119
MR PAUL JOHN, 188
Mr. Abdullah Bin Hamad Al-Attiyah, 129

Mr. Adrain A. March, 270
MR. ANDREW TWEEDIE, 291
Mr. Benny Kanarathil Joseph, 226
Mr. Cheong, 237, 238
Mr. Edward James, 316
MR. ERICKS DAVID, 251
Mr. Frank Walcot, 306
Mr. George Brumley, 234, 235
Mr. Ibrahim Lamorde, 56, 57
MR. JACOB, 30
Mr. JAMES POWELL, 142
Mr. James Whistler, 277
Mr. JEFFREY MEYER, 271
Mr. Jerry Brown, 316
MR. JIM OVIA, 272
Mr. John Anderson, 275
Mr. Jose Manuel Flavior, 64, 65
Mr. Kulman Smith, 63
Mr. Louis Finley, 181
Mr. Mark Yassin, 234
Mr. Morris Osborne, 313
Mr. Musa Mohamed, 316
Mr. Nicholas Story, 143, 146
MR. OBALA OBA, 218
Mr. Patrick Aziza, 147
Mr. Peter Marriot, 190
Mr. Richard Lankford, 306
Mr. Robert Joseph, 166

Mr. Ronald Owen, 124
Mr. Y. Y. Yeung, 222
Mr.Jesse Peterson, 301
MR.JOHN ABOH, 212
Mr.John Hall, 121
Mr.Kulman Smith, 62
Mr.Michael Kingston, 142
Mrs Edna Mary, 4
Mrs Glenda F Ward, 67
Mrs Grace Gabriel, 219
Mrs masha Lee, 73, 296
Mrs Robin Sanders, 67
Mrs. Abir Joyce, 122
Mrs. Beatrice Perkins, 97
Mrs. Catherine Jones, 217
Mrs. Christy Richard, 56
Mrs. Connie Dutton, 54
Mrs. Elizabeth Dixon, 89
Mrs. Howard Gregg, 180
Mrs. Iszam R. Yahya, 74
Mrs. Janet Napolitano, 161, 162
Mrs. Judith Williams, 90
Mrs. Lilian Bryan Armstrong, 247
Mrs. Lucy White, 117
Mrs. Maria Mark, 113, 114
Mrs. Marilynn Corson, 267
Mrs. Perkins, 97
Mrs. Rosella Johnson, 78
Mrs. Shade Peter, 247
Mrs. Victoria Konan, 134, 135

Mrs.Reacheal Lampard, 307
Ms Leam Salihu, 299
Ms. Anne-Brigitte Madsen, 270
Ms. C. L. Lapointe, 279
Ms. Cecil Lawton, 296
Ms. Lin Homer, 192, 193
Ms. Valerie Amos, 255
National Bank of Abu Dhabi, 234
National Central Bureau of Interpol, 140, 144
National Oil Company, 103
Natwest Bank, 224, 225
New Zealand, 171, 194, 289
NFIU, 197, 198
Nicholas Powell, 156
Nigeria, 16, 19, 21, 24, 36, 37, 38, 40, 41, 42, 43, 44, 45, 46, 47, 48, 49, 50, 51, 52, 53, 54, 55, 56, 62, 67, 129, 130, 139, 140, 141, 144, 145, 147, 154, 156, 158, 159, 161, 186, 196, 197, 198, 202, 203, 204, 206, 207, 208, 209, 210, 211, 213, 214, 241, 246, 247, 251, 265, 271, 334, 335
    Federal Executive Council (FEC), 206
    Federal Ministry of Petroleum, 53

NIGERIA, 18, 50, 51, 155, 156, 157, 212
Nigeria Bank Fraud, 16
Nigeria Financial Intelligent Unit (NFIU), 197
Nigerian 412 scams, 196
Nigerian 419, 67, 77
Nigerian National Petroleum Corporation (NNPC), 51, 335
Oceanic Bank International, 210
Oceanic Bank, PLC, 212
Omaha Group, 293
Patrick Dankwa Anin, 93, 94
PATRICK WIDEN, 178
PAUL MOGAN, 157
Peter Marroit, 191
Petroleum & Gas Company Dubai, 100
President Good luck Jonathan, 141, 144
Prof. Soludo/Mr.Lamido Sanusi, 147
punch.com, 214
Qatar Petroleum, 129, 131
qq.com, 97, 142
Queen Elizabeth, Queen of England, 220
Raul John, 321
realgems international, 315, 316

rediffmail.com', 122, 189
Republic, Ghana, 196, 197
Reserve Bank of India, 232
    Foreign Exchange Transfer Department, 228
Resolution Cabinet of Lawyers, 257
Rev. Robert Aboh, 254
Rev. Udeca smith, 278
Rev.Father urbanski Brown, 278
REV.JAMES KUTO, 204
Rev.Murray Richard, 266
Revenue and Customs Service, 192
Reverend Attmash Josan, 130
Reverend John Balfour, 280
Richard Martin, 258
Rita and Morooe Gamez, 110
Rita Gamez, 111
Robert B.Zoellick, 248
Robert Mueller, 36, 39, 155
Robert S. Mueller III, 156, 157, 158
ROBERT S. MUELLER,, 149
Robert Zoellick, 248
Robin Sanders, 67

rocketmail.com, 61, 186, 187, 188, 244
Roland, 93
Royal Bank of Scotland, 240
Rumania, 109
Russia, 52, 72
Ruth Kokoma, 110
Rwanda, 297
saintly.com, 130
Salman H. Usmani,, 239
Sanni Abacha, 46, 47
Sanusi Lamido, 209
SANUSI LAMIDO AMINU, 17, 18
Sarah Bin Rasheed, 99, 100
scam-mail, 190
SCARLET SECURITY COMPANY, 203
Scotland, 180, 181, 182
Scott Mido, 212
Second Quarter Euro Millions Lottery 2013, 314
Shanghai Bangpu Industrial Group Co. ltd, 294
Sheerah King, 95, 96
Shehu Shagari, 40
Simeon.K.Mahama, 132, 133
SIMS GROUP, 73, 74, 296, 297

SKYBIRD INTERNATIONAL, 287, 289
Smith Paggy, 111
Spain, 40, 41, 126, 127
Special Agent Henry Shawn, 150
STANBICIBTC BANK NIG.PLC, 280
Sun Trust Bank, 171, 172
superposta.com, 65, 153, 166, 167, 207, 301
Susan Mcoy, 293
THE COUNTING HOUSE, 119
The Department of Homeland Security, 161
THE RUSSIAN FOUNDATION FOR BASIC RESEARCH, 260
The United Nations Office for the Coordination of Humanitarian Affair(s), 281
Thelma Johnson, 79
Theresa Morgana, 10
THOMAS PHILIP, 124
TNT parcel Service, 141
Togo, 41, 62, 64, 65
Trade Center Chamber of Commerce, 83
Trade Center Chambers of Commerce directory, 84
Tunde Lemo, 38
U. S. Secret Service, 16
U.N diplomat Edward Ortiz, 111
uark.edu, 182
UK SECURITY SOLUTIONS, 314
Ukraine, 72, 74, 296, 297
UN Compensation Unit. *See* United Nations
UN Compensation, African Unit, 265
UN Inspection Unit, Washington DC, 275
UNION STATE BANK, 67
United Arab Emirate, 127
United Arab Emirates, 64, 99, 126, 234
United Bank for Africa, 248, 249, 250
United Bank of Africa (Nigeria), Directorate of International Payments, 247
United Kingdom, 34, 40, 41, 65, 75, 80, 84, 122, 126, 150, 192, 240, 274, 276
UNITED NATION, 273, 277, 290
United Nation Anti-crime commission, 57

United Nation Office of the President in Nigeria, 58
United Nations, 19, 23, 139, 140, 191, 229, 251, 265, 266, 268, 269, 270, 271, 273, 274, 276
United Nations Compensation Commission,, 269
United Nations Compensation Unit, 253
United Nations Directorate of International Payment and Transfers, 283
United Nations Liaison Office, London (United Kingdom);, 283
UNITED NATIONS OFFICE OF INTERNATIONAL OVERSIGHT SERVICES, 277
United Nations Office of the Diplomatic Delivery Agent, United States of America, 273
United Nations Organization, 144
United Nations Secretariat, 277
United Nations Secretary General for Humanitarian Affairs, 255
United Nations Secretary-General, 23
United Nations Treasury, 191
United Nations., 9
United States Fraud investigation Department, 3
United-Nation Appointed Approved Payment Disbursing High Commission Office, 285
United-Nations Appointed Commission Office (UK),, 285
US 3rd Infantry Division, 87
US Department of Homeland Security Fraud Monitory Unit, 161
US Department of the Treasury, 165
  Office of Foreign Assets Control (OFAC), 165
Victor Chigudu, 76
Victoria Konan, 135
Vietnam, 106
Washington Post, 20

Web-of-Trust (WOT) rating, 101
Wells Fargo Bank, 170
WEMA Bank, 246
WEMA Bank PLC, 246
West African Committee of Commerce, 257
Western Union, 25, 149, 154, 155, 186, 245, 320, 321
Wilfred Lemke, 280
Wire Transfer Audit Unit. *See* United Nations
World Bank, 3, 6, 19, 211, 216, 248, 253, 269, 270, 284, 287, 289
World Bank and Paris Club, 211
World Selected Immigration Data Award International, 314
wp.pl, 92
www.un.int/nigeria, 283
xtra.co.nz, 193
YAHOO INC, 241
YAHOO INTERNATIONAL LOTTERY DRAW, 317
yahoo.cn, 49, 55, 78, 132, 306, 307
yuvideo.net, 259
Zenith Bank International, 251
Zenith Bank Plc, 272
ZENITH BANK PLC, 254
Zimbabwe, 75, 76
Zurich, Switzerland., 314

Made in the USA
San Bernardino, CA
24 April 2014